To vivian & Binky,
with best wishes,

SEX, LIES, AND RABBIS:

BREAKING A SACRED TRUST

By

Charlotte Rolnick Schwab, Ph.D.

Charlotte Rolnick Schwab
12/2002

ISBN: 1-4033-3804-3 (e-book)
ISBN: 1-4033-3805-1 (Paperback)
ISBN: 1-4033-3806-X (Dustjacket)

Library of Congress Control Number: 2002106832

This book is printed on acid free paper.

Printed in the United States of America
Bloomington, IN

1st Books - rev. 08/28/02

To My Parents

My mother, Miriam Kobritz Rolnick

and

My father, Jacob Rolnick

both of blessed memory.

**For the gift of life, their love and nurturance,
and the values they taught me.**

ACKNOWLEDGMENTS

This book has been made possible by so many people, it is impossible to acknowledge them all. Please know that you are all in my heart and that I extend my gratitude to each and every person who has been supportive to me in my life and in the research for and the writing of this book.

My heartfelt thanks to all my clients and students who taught me/teach me so much.

Special thanks and gratitude to all the women and families who shared their experiences of rabbis' sexual abuse with me.

My gratitude to the women in my Connecticut support group, who supported me through the time after the assault by my rabbi/husband and the Order of Protection Hearing.

Thanks to Dr. Newt Schiller for his support.

Thank you to Betsy Hutman and Sandy Krasnow.

Very special thanks to Rabbi Arthur Gross-Schaefer for his support and for his pioneering work and writings about rabbis' sexual misconduct.

Many thanks to Rabbis Jonathan Feldman, Allan Kensky, Bruce Warshal, and Marcia Zimmerman for their belief in this project and their support.

Many thanks and appreciation to Marcia Cohn Spiegel for her pioneering work about violence against Jewish women in the home, her other works which aided my research, her friendship, suggestions, information, and support.

Very special thanks and gratitude to Rev. Dr. Nils Friberg who mentored me on e-mail for many months, and provided immeasurable support, guidance, and information.

My gratitude to Dr. Maj-Britt Rosenbaum, who encouraged me from the beginning to write this book.

Special thanks to Dr. Gary Richard Schoener, for his support and his extensive knowledge and publications about clergy sexual abuse which helped me in my research.

Thank you to my graduate student-assistants, especially Tracey Ann Williams for her excellent research.

Thank you to Rev. Dr. Marie Fortune for her work, for encouragement, and who gave me important information very early in my research, especially about the study of the per cent of clergy who sexually abuse women.

Thanks to the librarians at the American Jewish Committee in New York, Cyma Horowitz and Michele Anish, who provided me with important information.

Thanks to Lilith magazine for listing my research in their pages.

Thank you to those who published my research and information about my work on their web sites.

Thanks to all those who referred victims of rabbis' sexual abuse to me so that I might help them.

Thank you to Michelle Samit for her support and information.

Thanks to Debra Nussbaum Cohen for her many excellent articles on rabbis' sexual misconduct.

Thanks to Gary Rosenblatt, Editor of the New York Jewish Week, for his courageous work.

Thanks to all the newspaper reporters and editors whose news articles provided me with valuable information.

Thank you to all the writers whose articles and books paved the way for this book to be written.

Thank you to all those who provide invaluable information on their web sites.

Thank you to Rich Kellman and Carol Kaplan of WGRZ-TV Buffalo.

Appreciation to Marilyn Ferguson for her support, and who insisted to me that, "God wants you to do this book."

Thanks to my International Women's Writing Guild (IWWG) writers group.

Thanks to my friends in the BJ EASTSIDERS *Chavurah* in Manhattan for all their support, their spiritual presence, and everything they taught me.

Thanks to Monica Getz, founder, and Marilyn Kane, leader of the Manhattan Chapter of the Coalition for Family Justice.

Thanks to Linda Winer for her pro bono editorial services and support.

Thanks to my many feminist and spiritual friends, especially Barbara Ehrenreich who introduced me and my book to her publisher; Jacqui Ceballos for her encouragement; Dr. Ann M. Ruben for her support; Sue Caplan for watching the newspapers and supplying me with articles.

Thank you to Chaia Sperling who provided me with the quote from the late Rebbe Menachem Schneerson.

Thanks to Doris Lubell for permission to use her original art work for the cover.

Thank you to Richard Marek for his praise, and for his encouragement to write my memoir as the first part of the book.

Thank you to Dorothy Sandman for her support and friendship.

Thanks to Dan Heise at 1st Books Library for his support and belief in this book.

Thank you to the late Rabbi Julie Spitzer for her support.

Thanks to the late Bernice Friedes, President of the New York Chapter of National Council for Jewish Women, for all her support.

Thanks to the late Roger Schafer, who started me on the road to independence by giving me my first paid professional employment as a community consultant.

Thanks to the late Max Wolf, who encouraged me to go to graduate school.

Thanks to Eleanor Guggenheimer for her support of The Feminist Center for Human Growth and Development.

Thank you to the late Harry Kimmelman whose book titles (although his books are works of fiction) inspired the title for my true story, my memoir, PART ONE of this book.

TABLE OF CONTENTS

PREFACE

It is disturbing and uncomfortable to think of rabbis as sexual predators. Kudos to Charlotte Schwab for having the determination and courage to address it!

This book has had a long and painful gestation period. It was conceived when the author personally experienced the shattering of trust as sacred boundaries were violated. In the process of healing her own wounds Dr. Schwab has witnessed and helped to heal the pain of many others with similar experiences.

Rabbis, as all clergy, have special relationships with their congregants and students. Coupled with heavy responsibilities, they are granted considerable power. As religious leaders they are looked to for spiritual, ethical and moral advice. They are seen as arbiters of social justice. They are consulted in family matters. They are teachers, confidants, counselors and consolers. They officiate at holidays and celebrations; they take part in the rituals that mark important milestones in life. They are there in need, in illness and in grief. In return they are often revered, respected, admired as good, wise and caring people, and yes, loved.

It can be an awesome position of power! We don't even have to add personal charisma, nor brilliance to the mix. Handled with a modicum of competence, skill, emotional warmth and psychological maturity, a rabbi can become a very important person in someone's life, a role model, a source of support and inspiration. The foundation for this is trust - basic trust, sacred trust. Serious trouble starts when this sacred trust is broken.

We all need to be loved and to feel special in the eyes of an important other. When these needs are not fulfilled we reach out to fill them. Needing sex or affection to such a degree that a rabbi crosses ethical professional barriers speaks volumes about the rabbi's own vulnerabilities and/or psychopathology. Rabbis are human beings with the whole range of human inadequacies, periods of vulnerability, psychological problems, and even serious psychopathology. When a rabbi abuses his professional position to gratify his own needs for domination and sexual gratification, he is not only behaving totally unethically, he is also causing serious damage to his victims. No amount of rationalization can obscure the fact that his victims are

xi

always in a more vulnerable position than he is and that they turn to him during especially susceptible times in their lives. We have to keep firmly in mind that there is no such thing as informed consent when the balance of power is so unequal.

We need to become more aware of the sad reality that rabbis, like all clergy, can cross the boundaries of sacred trust. Let us hope that the awareness and information that this book provides will lead to sustained efforts at education, prevention, detection, and treatment of the perpetrators when appropriate, or appropriate disciplinary action.

Maj-Britt Rosenbaum, MD.
Associate Clinical Professor of Psychiatry,
Albert Einstein College of Medicine, New York.
Formerly: Director, Human Sexuality Center,
Long Island Hillside Medical Center, New Hyde
Park, New York.

FOREWORD

Places of worship - churches and synagogues - are sanctuaries. They are temples of safety for families and individuals - often when trouble swirls around them. In certain times and places they are the only safe places. For a people oppressed for their faith, they are also the symbol of the survival, not only of a faith, but of a culture and of one's own family.

Although the temple serves as a gathering place and as a place around which life can revolve, it also serves as a community. The members of the congregation are a large extended family. Overseeing this 'family' and guiding it is a spiritual leader such as a rabbi. The rabbi teaches and guides, supports and encourages. He or she helps supervise the lay leadership of the temple.

The rabbi is in a position of trust. Members of the congregation are in a fiduciary relationship with him or her. Rabbis are given power and are trusted at all times to act in good faith and in the best interest of the congregation and its individual members. They are presumed to be guided by the Torah and other teachings of the faith, and also to have the spiritual maturity and understanding to help the congregational members fully understand and embrace these teachings.

When the rabbi steps down from this position of trust and turns out to be untrustworthy, much is lost. While such transgressions by Christian clergy have been widely publicized by the secular news media and by lawsuits in recent years, little has become public about similar rabbinical misconduct.

That someone in a position of trust, who is a professional, might abuse that trust by sexually exploiting someone in their care is scarcely a new idea. Nor it is limited to spiritual leadership. The Library of Alexandria in Egypt, one of the great libraries of the ancient world, housed a collection of texts referred to today as the Corpus Hippocratum. It contained a treatise entitled "The Physician", authored about 23 centuries ago that warned about physician sexual misconduct. An even more famous writing from that collection of writings, also more than two millenniums old, dating from the 2nd or 3rd centuries BC, was simply called "The Oath". Referred to today as the "Hippocratic Oath," it included the lines:

".... in holiness and purity I will practice my art.... and will abstain

from every voluntary act of Mischief and Corruption and further

from the seduction of females or males, of freemen and slaves...."

More than 2,000 years ago the issue was the same as it is today - trust. Trust in someone called to a professional role and duty - sacred or secular.

Despite this early recognition of the problem, for more than two thousand years the secular professions have struggled with the problem of professional sexual misconduct. Lawsuits and criminal charges have been brought against psychotherapists and health care professionals on all continents. In the field of psychology, in the United States, such cases have accounted for about 50% of the cost of all lawsuits for many years. Sexual misconduct is also a leading cause of licensing and ethics complaints against those in the counseling professions.

The failure of ethics codes and committees, and licensing boards and other regulatory bodies to alter this situation significantly has led nineteen American states to pass special criminal statutes relating to sexual abuse by therapists. When clergy are providing psychotherapy - counseling for emotional problems, they are included as 'psychotherapists' covered by these laws. In Canada special task forces have studied the problem and brought about regulatory changes. The German government commissioned a major study and report on the situation. Conferences in North America, Europe and the United Kingdom, Australia, and New Zealand testify to the worldwide concern about this problem. These conferences have examined sexual exploitation by all types of professionals - secular and religious - as examples of the same set of problems.

Awareness of clergy sexual misconduct has been slower in coming, even though reports of sexual misconduct by Roman Catholic priests date back to the Middle Ages and the Vatican archives contain many such cases. The rift which eventually led to the creation of the Church of England and its split with the Roman Catholic Church began with the arrest of a priest for debauchery.

The issue of sexual misconduct by clergy was articulated in what many believe was America's first 'psychological novel,' The Scarlet

Letter, written by Nathaniel Hawthorne and published in 1850. It depicted a clergyman, Arthur Dimmesdale, who was tortured by guilt as he watched a parishioner whom he had impregnated be abused publicly and have to wear the scarlet letter 'A' for adulteress. While the treatment of the female victim had much more historical precedent and reflected attitudes we still often find today, at least the pastor was depicted as troubled and as a culprit in his own eyes.

A quarter of a century after the publication of Hawthorne's novel, a similar case made it into the media coverage of the time. Charges and counter charges were filed in a libel suit in New York, in 1874. Famed clergyman Henry Ward Beecher was accused by Theodore Tilton, a friend and parishioner, of sexually exploiting his wife, Elizabeth Tilton, whom Beecher was counseling through a depression brought about by the death of her baby. Beecher was not only prominent in his own right, but the son of Lyman Beecher, an even more famous pastor, and brother of leading feminist Harriet Beecher Stowe, who subsequently became famous for the book Uncle Tom's Cabin, which exposed mistreatment of slaves. As a result, one group of feminists took Beecher's side. Journalist Victoria Woodhull, who wrote about the case, was jailed, and the Tiltons were excommunicated, while Beecher kept not only his job but his reputation. Encyclopedias and other sources do not mention this aspect of his career.

Most cases, however, were not public, and few people brought them. As result, until recently, there has not been a public perception that this is a major problem. Furthermore, there is a question as to what the problem is. Books such as A Circuit Rider's Wife by Corra Harris, published in 1910, and serialized in "The Saturday Evening Post," took the position that the only problem was seductive female parishioners who were characterized as a 'special class of criminal.' In fact, the book even referenced the Beecher case and presented it as a case of a good man brought down off his pedestal. It said that sexual misconduct in the church was a result of "the problem of women." Lest you think this is an attitude of only the early part of the last century, the book was reprinted in 1988 and 1990 as The Circuit Rider's Wife, apparently able to find a readership despite the fact that probably few even know what the term 'circuit rider' means.

Although sexual misconduct and exploitation by secular professionals was not treated much differently, by the early 1970's professional debate over <u>The Love Treatment</u> by psychiatrist Martin Shepard, and the highly publicized lawsuit, Roy vs. Hartogs (depicted in the book, <u>Betrayal</u>, by Lucy Roy and Julie Freeman) thrust this issue into the public arena. Masters and Johnson, holding center stage as the world's best known experts on human sexuality, declared that it was "rape" and that it was a serious professional problem.

Studies were done of incidence/prevalence of sexual misconduct by physicians, and to the shock of the profession, as many as 10% of physicians actually admitted that they had sex with clients. Subsequent surveys of psychologists and psychiatrists found similar results. The various counseling and health care professions spent the next two decades revising codes of ethics - mostly making them more specific. The solutions were not clear but the field knew it had a problem, and to some degree the public did too.

In the public arena, in 1984 Wisconsin made it a crime for a therapist to have sexual contact with a client. The rationale was that the professions and licensing bodies had not been able to control the problem, and that having tried the solution of relying on codes of ethics for 22 centuries, it was probably high time to try some alternative solution. The advent of TV interview shows such as "Donahue" played a role in not only public awareness but legislative action. Senator James Rutkowski, the author of the Wisconsin law became outraged when he happened to see some victims of therapists on the show and decided that something needed to be done. During the 1980's many other interview shows educated the public about this problem.

In 1985 Minnesota made it a felony and among those listed as "psychotherapists" covered by the law were clergy. If a clergy person such as a rabbi was counseling someone about emotional problems and had sex with that person, the sentence was a term of 2 years in state prison. A year later Wisconsin amended its law to include clergy. During the next 17 years an additional 18 states criminalized sexual misconduct by therapists. By the year 2002 there were 20. Most of these statutes allow for the prosecution of a clergy person if they are providing "psychotherapy" as it is defined in that state's statutes. Most such definitions are quite broad.

As a byproduct of the acquittal of a pastor who had sexually exploited a counselee and parishioner due to his defense that he was actually doing "spiritual" or "pastoral counseling," the Minnesota legislature expanded its law to include clergy doing spiritual or pastoral counseling. Texas, which passed a criminal statute in the mid-1990's and copied much of Minnesota's, also has this provision in its law which was signed by then-governor George Bush. A rabbi in Minnesota or Texas who is providing counseling to a member of the congregation and who then has sex with that person can be charged with sexual assault.

In 1984 the exposure of a case of serial sexual abuse of children by Roman Catholic priest Gilbert Gauthe in Lafayette, Louisiana, brought about national attention to sexual abuse of children by clergy. This case was chronicled by Jason Berry in <u>Lead Us Not Into Temptation</u>. Periodically, in the USA or elsewhere in the world, other cases surfaced in the news media about sexual abuse of children by clergy.

But, attention to the problem of the sexual betrayal of adults has still remained behind the scenes in many places. Again, TV interview shows and some high visibility lawsuits and criminal trials have provided for greater public awareness, but it appears all too easy to pass this off as an 'aberration,' or as a problem for somebody else's faith group or denomination. The focus has often been on the 'bad apple' theory - the idea that there are a few bad apples rather than a more systemic problem. In the United States some major denominations now have written policies for dealing with cases of pastoral sexual misconduct, but it is still not easy to bring charges. Furthermore, standards for resolution of cases - how to compensate or assist the victim, how to explain things to the congregation, and questions of rehabilitation and restoration are often unresolved. Books like Rev. Marie Fortune's <u>Is Nothing Sacred?</u> and many which have followed it such as Pamela Cooper-White's <u>The Cry of Tamar</u> have provided guidance, but most groups have a long way to go.

Consumer activism and awareness has been growing for some years. In the 1990's Clergy Abuse LINKUP and a victim of the infamous Father Porter, Frank Fitzpatrick, established newsletters and eventually web sites devoted to abuse by Roman Catholic priests. Eventually LINKUP expanded to include other types of clergy. In 1987, Advocateweb (www.advocateweb.org) was created. It is a web site for those who are on the Internet which can provide both information and support to victims of sexual abuse by professionals and their advocates. But, not everyone is on the Internet.

Some victims have attended one of the four international conferences held in North America (Minneapolis, 1986 & 1992; Toronto, 1994; Boston, 1998). Conferences have also been held in the United Kingdom (1996, 1998, 1999) and Switzerland (2002 & 2001), and there have been two Australia/New Zealand conferences (Sydney, 1994; Melbourne, 1996). There have also been local conferences held in the US and Canada. Others have gained from reading books such as Peter Rutter's <u>Sex in the Forbidden Zone</u>, or John Gonsiorek's <u>Breach of Trust</u>, or other books which discuss this issue.

But, none of this is sufficient, and none of these programs or books discussed problems in Judaism although these professionals, including myself have consulted in cases involving rabbis. The problem of abuse by rabbis has not been 'on the radar screen' in terms of either publicly visible lawsuits or mainstream media articles and books. There has been no book as yet about the problem of rabbis' sexual misconduct. This book by Dr. Schwab is the first. Until this book by Dr. Schwab, the victim of a rabbi felt quite alone. Those who have consulted us are sure that they are 'the only one.' As such, the obstacles to their coming forward are very high indeed.

For those who cross those hurdles and do come forward, there is considerable personal risk via exposure of one's personal life and of events about which one is not proud. There is fear and vulnerability. This risk is usually taken out of desperation - in hopes of resolving the feelings of guilt or remorse, in hopes of protecting others, in hopes of gaining closure on a painful chapter in one's life.

The victim looks to the church, synagogue, or national faith organization or rabbinical association for justice and for resolution. It is difficult to have resolution without having justice. Faith groups need to be concerned about this problem. As one religious leader once said to me, the religious institution "is in the morality business and there is no middle road; either (they) take the high road or one day (they) will no longer be trusted with spiritually guiding people."

As more and more victims come out of the closet, the pressure will increase for religious institutions to do a better job of handling these complaints and resolving them. Books like Dr. Schwab's remind us that people victimized in this manner do not intend to go quietly into the night. Her challenge to us is that we can do better and that we need to do better.

Gary Richard Schoener 4 February 2002

Gary Richard Schoener, Licensed Psychologist and Executive Director, Walk-In Counseling Center, Minneapolis, Minnesota, USA, has been a consultant in more than 3,000 cases of professional misconduct, including clergy. He is an internationally known speaker and is senior author of <u>Psychotherapists' Sexual Involvement With Clients: Intervention and Prevention</u> as well as numerous professional articles. He has consulted to many religious groups in North America, Europe, Australia, and New Zealand, including evaluation of rabbis and consultation to rabbinical associations. He has served as an expert witness in a number of legal matters concerning sexual misconduct by clergy and religious figures.

INTRODUCTION

This book covers the story of what has been called a breach of "sacred trust," a book about the betrayal of women and teen aged girls by male rabbis, and, thereby, of these rabbis' wives, families, congregations, communities, denominations, and all Judaism. This is a book about rabbinic power, sacred power, and how having this power can lead to its abuse, to the victimization and abuse of those less powerful, vulnerable, particularly, to their sexual victimization, and even to violence and murder.

This book delineates the crisis in the rabbinate, in congregational Judaism, the alarming extent of this problem, and what we need to do to bring about healing and change for the betrayed women, teen aged girls, synagogues, congregations, communities, movements, all Judaism. Most important, this book is about the victims/survivors of rabbinic sexual abuse. Being able to read about this problem, obtaining information about it, especially the extent of it, and knowing that they are not alone is healing for the women who have been abused, including the rabbis' wives who have suffered through their husbands' abuse of other women. This book provides a healing program for victims/survivors.

This first part of this book is a memoir about my own experience as the wife of a rabbi-perpetrator of sexual abuse of other women, and his violence toward me, especially when I found out about his nefarious activities. Part One tells my own story of survival of a marriage to a rabbi who, by his own admission in a court of law before the public, is a sex addict, a frequenter of S & M prostitutes, a sexual abuser of many women, including congregants, former congregants, and students. The court awarded me an Order of Protection from him as a result of his assaulting me and threatening to kill me when I found out about his "secret double life." Part One also tells the story of why and how I married this rabbi, including who I was when I married my first husband, and why and how my first marriage led to my marrying this rabbi-perpetrator, why I thought marriage to this rabbi would be entirely different: safe and happy. Part One tells the story of my suspicions about my rabbi/husband before I married him, leading me to hesitate for three and a half years before marrying him, but also tells of a storybook courtship and romance which finally won me over to consent to marrying him.

The memoir describes the horrors of his increasing abuse, which in hindsight, seems to have resulted from the pressure on him of keeping his dirty secrets from me (and from the world), and of my finding out the truth, which he wanted me to know, told me, disclosed to me in a brutal manner, and which he said with this disclosure, if I did "not rock the boat," not "tell **anyone**," that we would continue as we had been, except that I would "know and **accept** the truth" (of his nefarious sexual double life) so that he would "finally have some peace." The memoir tells about the abuse by my rabbi/husband which he escalated because I would not "accept" and would not agree to "not rock the boat." Rock it I did. I still am. Rocking with great strength! I believe the truth about sex, lies, and rabbis must be told for the benefit of all Judaism. This book tells the story of my survival of this abuse, and documents other women's stories which have been told to me as well as cases of other rabbi-perpetrators which have been documented in the media.

One of my hopes in writing this book is that I may be a role model for other women victims/survivors because, in spite of all the abuse I endured from my rabbi/husband, I have accomplished a great deal in the years since I was married to him and since he *sued me*! for alimony and dragged me through the courts for almost two years trying to bankrupt me, ruin me, when I found out. It is important for other victims/survivors of rabbis' abuse to see how/that I have not only survived abuse by this rabbi-perpetrator but also that I have grown and changed from the experience, achieved a self-defined identity and self-esteem, and helped others to do so.

My (now ex) rabbi/husband-perpetrator has not made *Teshuvah*[1]; has not admitted his abuse to me, has not apologized, has not made amends; nor has he shown that he has repented. The current policy of his denomination's rabbinical organization (the CCAR) requires that when an offending rabbi has been suspended from the rabbinic organization for a breach of their ethical policy, "to be eligible for reinstatement, the offending rabbi must have fulfilled the following requirements:

---

[1] Yiddish and Hebrew words and terms which appear in italics are defined in the Glossary.

A. Unequivocal acknowledgment of responsibility for harm done to victim(s), the congregation or institution and the honor of the rabbinate, with specific violations and actions acknowledged;

B. An acceptable expression of remorse to those who have been harmed;

C. A resolve never to repeat any offense of this nature;

D. The making of restitution which may include expenses incurred by the victim(s) and/or other appropriate actions as mandated by the CCAR;

E. Mentoring by at least two rabbinic colleagues appointed by the CCAR."

Since, at the time of my complaint outlining the details of my rabbi/husband's sexual misconduct and his violence toward me, the rabbinic organization told me through its then spokesperson that, it "did not concern them;"[2] since he is still in the same rabbinic pulpit; since the psychiatrist who treated him as an inpatient in a mental hospital for two months after he assaulted me and threatened to kill me told me that he would likely never stop his nefarious sexual misconduct, was dangerous to me, is a sociopath, sex addict, and manic depressive, it is likely that he is still perpetrating his abuse on others.

My additional hope in writing this book is that he and others who are exposed here will be properly dealt with, victims/survivors will be acknowledged and made amends to, and that other victims/survivors, families, congregations will come forward to expose other rabbi-perpetrators so they can be properly dealt with, and when necessary removed from the rabbinate. Rabbis, synagogues must be safe for teen aged girls and women. When they are not, they and rabbis' wives must be safe to tell the truth, be heard, be protected, be helped, and be made amends to when required.

---

[2] When I appealed to representatives of the CCAR (the Central Conference of American Rabbis, the Reform rabbinic governing organization) to help me, I felt like, "a voice crying in the wilderness" (Isaiah 40:3. Hebrew text and English translation with an Introduction and commentary by the Rev. Dr. I.W. Slaatki, M.A., Litt. D. Revised by Rabbi A. J. Rosenberg, New York: The Soncino Press, LTC. 1987. Page 185).

The victims/survivors of rabbinic sexual abuse I learned about and include in my composite cases include other ex-wives of rabbis who are or have been guilty of sexual abuse of some kind, whether of women or of teen aged girls. I count myself as a survivor. Acquiring the knowledge that I was not alone as a wife and then an ex-wife of a rabbi-predator, learning of the alarming extent of the problem, reading the newspaper reports of rabbi-predators, lecturing about it, appearing on television about it, becoming a pro bono counselor for victims/survivors, interviewing rabbis and others in some way connected with this problem, conducting the years of research leading up to this book, and writing this book have all been healing for me. I am grateful for the experience, and for the support of the many people, including some rabbis, I have had on this journey. Being able to read about this problem, obtaining information about it, especially the extent of it, and knowing that they are not alone, is healing for the women who have been abused, including rabbis' wives and ex-wives who have suffered through their husbands' predation and abuse.

This book tells other women's stories, other documented cases of rabbis' sexual abuse of teen aged girls and women, cases I have documented from all over the country as a result of my years of research, my being listed in Lilith magazine, and on several web sites. I have counseled many of these women, pro bono, and where needed, have tried to find them therapists in their locations. I have created composites of the women's stories and changed their names and other information to protect their identities. Also included are cases documented in both Jewish and secular newspapers all over the country, and on the World Wide Web. I interviewed or consulted to the affected parties in too many cases to list here, including survivors of rabbis' sexual abuse, parents of survivors (in these cases the survivors were teenagers at the time of the abuse), ex-wives of rabbis who endured their husbands' sexual abuse of other women and often endured their husbands' violence toward them, rabbis of other congregations in the same denominations as the rabbi-perpetrators, and affected congregants and members of the Boards of Directors of affected synagogues. I stopped counting when I accumulated two hundred cases in my files from across the spectrum of Jewish denominations, including Orthodox, Reform, Conservative, Reconstructionist, and the Jewish Renewal movement. Experts estimate that between 18 and 39% of all rabbis are guilty of sexual misconduct of one kind or another, the same as for clergy of other faiths who are not required to be celibate.[3] The large number of cases I have investigated myself would corroborate this estimate. This makes it imperative that the truth about rabbis and sexual abuse of teen aged girls and women be told.

It is my hope that my book, along with the proliferation of media coverage of this problem, will work to bring about change: change in how rabbis are recruited to seminaries; change in how they are trained; change in the decisions about those who are ordained; change in how rabbis are monitored; change in how they may be removed from pulpits when necessary, and from the rabbinate when necessary; change in the hearing of complaints by those whom rabbis have abused, in acknowledging these complaints, helping these survivors, and requiring that the rabbi-perpetrators make amends. Since my beginning to work on this book, my lecturing about this problem, my inquiries about policies to the various denominations' rabbinic organizations, I believe the policy making bodies of these denominations regarding rabbinic sexual and ethical conduct are taking some notice. The Reform movement, the movement to which my rabbi/husband belonged, belongs, has issued an amended policy. It does not go at all far enough, but it is a start. (Policies or the lack of them and what needs to be done are discussed in PART III).

In PART IV, I identify and discuss definitions of sexual abuse, cautioning that, as Gary Schoener, a clinical psychologist in Minneapolis who specializes in treating clergy who have engaged in sexual boundary violations a well as their victims, points out, sometimes, what seems like a "mild" sexual verbal harassment by a rabbi can be as difficult to overcome as physical sexual abuse. I also briefly identify and discuss the six types of clergy who violate sexual boundaries, as identified by Schoener, although I leave the scholarly in-depth analysis regarding personalities of rabbi sexual predators to scholars of this aspect of the problem, like Schoener and others. This book is written for readership at large, not specifically for scholars, but while it is not a scholarly tome, it is my hope to inspire other scholars to thought and additional work; nor is it directed solely to clergy, although it is my intention to reach them as well, for it is they, in the end, who must do the most to bring about positive change.

---

[3] Telephone conversation with the Rev. Marie Fortune. (See Bibliography).

Rachel Adler, Rabbis Nina Carlin, Arthur Gross-Schaefer, and others have been writing about and working on bringing about change, including the need for those rabbis found guilty of sexual predation to make *Teshuvah*. I make some suggestions in this book for rabbis ready to take this step. I leave development and expansion of these ideas to Adler, Carlin, Gross-Schaefer, and others. I hope this book will aid them and inspire them further to continue their efforts. At this writing, an amended policy statement regarding rabbis' sexual behavior and misconduct has been adopted by the Reform rabbinic organization, the CCAR, the Central Conference of American Rabbis. (See PART III). The CCAR has also taken a step forward by suspending for two years the President of their seminary, whom they investigated for sexual misconduct. He resigned as President of the seminary, Hebrew Union College. I lament the necessity for these actions. This rabbi was a friend of mine when I was a member of a synagogue where he was rabbi, and I am very saddened by this news, for him, his family, Reform Judaism and all Judaism. However, I applaud the CCAR for taking this major step. They need to go much further. I write about this in this book.

I have lectured and conducted seminars on the problem of rabbis' sexual misconduct to the Conservative Jewish Theological Seminary and the Reform Union of American Hebrew Congregations. Much more than one lecture/seminar needs to be given to rabbinic students, faculties, rabbis, and congregants. First, prospective rabbinic students need to be better screened. Perhaps scholars and practitioners in this field can help concerned rabbis and enlightened congregants to develop these screening policies. (The day of my lecture/seminar at the Jewish Theological Seminary, several women students approached me to ask if they could talk to me and enlist my help about the sexual harassment they had suffered *from faculty and rabbinic students.*) An in-depth course needs to be *required* of *both faculty and students every year.* Perhaps other scholars in this field like Adler, Carlin, Gross-Schaefer, and Dr. Gary Schoener can help to develop these screening policies. Other religions are working on this problem.[4] Some of their denominations have made much more progress than Jewish denominations have to date.

---

[4]See the ISTI (Interfaith Sexual Trauma Institute) web site www.csbsju.edu/isti for information about sexual abuse by clergy and about

A few have questioned my writing this book, saying, "We shouldn't hang dirty laundry out for all to see." "There's enough anti-Semitism, enough criticism of Jews." "This is not a good time to reveal this problem; Jews have enough troubles." Or, "How can you persevere in light of the hostility of many, if not most of the rabbinic establishment?" My answer is that, to paraphrase Sigmund Freud, as quoted in Rabbi Joseph Telushkin's book, [5] "I am a Jew, in my case, a committed Jew. I am prepared to do without agreement from the 'compact majority' to effect much needed, healing change within the rabbinate, within the Jewish community. I am free from the many prejudices which restrict others, even other Jews, in the use of their intellect to perform acts of courage to effect change even when there is a crisis." Yes, just as many of Freud's writings, much of his work was "good for" medicine,[6] this book will be "good for the Jews."

Telling the truth is always good. Hopefully, this book will bring about a new era in rabbinic Judaism, an era in which, as Rabbi Arthur Gross-Schaefer has written, "The goal of responding to rabbis' sexual misconduct is not to punish or brand, rather to protect and help insure healthy relationships between rabbis, congregants (and others). We should keep in mind that the issue of boundary violations is not about

---

their extensive work in this field. The Pope recently apologized for abuse by Roman Catholic clergy, saying it has caused the victims "great suffering" and "spiritual harm and has damaged the Church." It is time for the rabbinic heads of denominations to apologize, to stop denying the extent of this problem, to stop covering up for their rabbi-members' transgressions, to stop protecting these rabbi- perpetrators, to stop getting them other positions when they have to leave because of sexual misconduct, and to take the steps needed to rid the rabbinate of these rabbi/perpetrators of sexual misconduct. Also see the web site of the Center for the Prevention of Sexual and Domestic Violence, www.cpsw.org, Rev. Marie Fortune, Executive Director. This Center provides extensive materials for dealing with clergy sexual misconduct. They produced a video about Jewish clergy sexual misconduct called, "Not in My Congregation," a "dramatic video of the story of one congregation faced with a betrayal of trust by its religious leader.... a story that could happen in any congregation...."

[5] Rabbi Joseph Telushkin. Jewish Literacy. New York. William Morrow & Co. 1991. pp. 251, 252.

[6] Of course, some of Freud's work was not good for women. I, and others, have written about this elsewhere.

sex, but about abusing a trusted relationship. When a rabbi abuses the power given to him.... then we are all diminished. When we help create safe and Jewishly nourishing leaders and environments, then we are all enriched."[7]

According to Barbara Marx Hubbard, "evolutionary change is crisis driven." The large numbers of rabbis sexually abusing women is creating a crisis for all the denominations in Judaism. But, we cannot expect radical change overnight. Marcia Cohn Spiegel, who has written much about and has worked for many years to alleviate the problem of Jewish domestic violence, told me that there is rampant denial of Jewish domestic violence by denominations, by rabbis, by congregations and by Jewish organizations, and that it "took fifteen years" before it was possible to get *any* acknowledgment that the problem of domestic violence even exists in the Jewish community. And that *"much* still needs to be done in most locations around the country."

We must all work hard to bring about change in the problem of rabbis' sexual misconduct and abuse. Let us pray that this book will help to bring about significant change and help for healing of victims/survivors, that it will not take another 15 years.

I have researched and written this book because, to paraphrase author Michele Samit in, No Sanctuary: The True Story of a Rabbi's Deadly Affair, *"If I guarded this secret and kept silent, then I, too, would become one of Anita's (and Carol Neulander's) killers. I believe with all my heart that it was the silence, as well as the (killers' weapons) that killed (these women)."* This is the same silence that I and other women found/find when we reported/report our experiences to rabbinic authorities.

Silence, secrecy, and protection of these men, of rabbi-perpetrators of sexual abuse must cease. Women and teen aged girls[8]

---

[7]Rabbi Arthur Gross-Schaefer, "Rabbi Sexual Misconduct: Crying out for a Communal Response." Working Together Winter 1997. pp. 3-5.

[8]I only had one male person contact me who was abused by a (male) rabbi when he was a teenager. In the case of Rabbi Lanner, which I discuss in PART TWO, he allegedly abused teen aged boys as well as girls, although, according to reports, he abused the boys physically, not sexually. I know of one other case of a rabbi who, as of this writing has pleaded guilty and has been sentenced to prison for abusing teen aged boys. This book is about

must feel safe. *They* must be protected, not the perpetrators. Synagogues, rabbis' studies must be safe places for them. *Rabbis* must be safe for them; they must be safe anywhere in the presence of rabbis. The "old boy" network which has hidden, lied about, and protected these rabbis must be changed to a new network of men *and* women: clergy, lay people, communities knowledgeable about the truth of this problem and prepared and strong enough to stop it and prevent it from continuing. The investigations by rabbinic organizations of those rabbis found "guilty" and suspended from the rabbinate as a result must be open to concerned parties.

I applaud the amended policy statement regarding rabbis' sexual behavior which has been adopted by the Reform rabbinic organization, the CCAR.[9] I applaud the fact that they included women on the committee which produced it. According to one of the members of this committee, this is the reason for the progress they have made. However, they need to go much further.

The Reconstructionist Rabbinical Association provided me with their policy statement adopted June, 1996, entitled "Breach of Professional Trust: Sexual and Financial Ethics." While I was told they have taken some actions against some offending rabbis, from what victims told me, and my review of this policy statement, I believe that they, too, must go much further, including, in the words of the late Rabbi Julie R. Spitzer, "In order for justice to be served, we must end the secrecy that surrounds such abuse, acknowledge the violation, and hear the victim. We must act with compassion,

---

male rabbis and their abuse of teen aged girls and women because these cases overwhelmingly predominate. In a conversation with Gary Schoener, he told me about the two cases of women rabbis and abuse he has in his files. However, abuse is a result of those with power abusing those less powerful. I predict that, even as the numbers of women rabbis increase (and it will take many, many years before there is even an equal number of women rabbis as there are male rabbis in those denominations which allow women rabbis), their abuse will not be of the magnitude of male rabbis in my opinion because of the difference in male/ female socialization, because of the differences in biological nature between men and women, and because of sexism in society.

[9]"Code of Ethics for Rabbis: Adopted in convention assembled, June, 1991, and as amended in 1993, 1998, and 2000." Central Conference of American Rabbis.

protecting the vulnerable by preventing further abuse. The abuser must be held accountable and consequences must be imposed. Restitution should be made to the victim, and help provided to free all involved from the suffering so that healing can begin. At one retreat held by the Center (for the Prevention of Sexual and Domestic Violence) for victims of clergy sexual abuse, a question was informally posed to the group: What was the cost of the abuse to you, in measurable terms? The eleven victims wrote their answers down, and they were added up. The total? Fifty-five years, and $278,000. Denominations around the country are becoming increasingly embroiled in lawsuits relating to such misconduct. There are many moral arguments that are certainly compelling us to take a long hard look at this issue and how it is handled. But if those aren't enough, the dollars are a most compelling argument, too. If not now, when? "[10]

At this writing, there is as yet no policy, let alone an effective policy, in existence for the other denominations I contacted: Conservative, Orthodox, or for the Jewish Renewal movement. I discuss this in PART III. The lack of policies is not for the lack of rabbis in their denominations who are guilty of sexual misconduct. The cases in my files (and in the news media) are of rabbis from all these denominations.

The problem of dealing with rabbi-perpetrators of sexual abuse is compounded by the fact that individual synagogues have sole power over hiring and firing of their rabbis. The rabbinic organizations can suspend them from membership, can recommend that they resign. They can also recommend that the synagogues fire them for cause. It is shocking that many of these synagogues, even in the face of several women accusing the rabbi, vote to keep him on. I discuss reasons for this and what needs to be done to rectify this problem in this book.

The large number of cases of sexual harassment, sexual exploitation, and sexual violence toward girls and women by rabbis makes this a subject and this book of great concern to the community at large, and to the Jewish community in particular, and most

---

[10]Rabbi Julie R. Spitzer. "Response." CCAR Journal: A Reform Jewish Quarterly. Spring 1993. P. 54. The late Rabbi Julie R. Spitzer was the Regional Director of the UAHC Mid-Atlantic Council. She represented the CCAR on the Advisory Board of the Center for the Prevention of Sexual and Domestic Violence beginning in 1985.

especially to women. Women victimized by rabbis include congregants, non-congregants, employees, students, women clergy (rabbis and others), and includes non-Jewish women who may consult them for counseling in Jewish matters - they may be married to a Jewish man, for example - or they may be their students. The rabbi-perpetrator senses which woman is vulnerable (this is true of most women in our society,[11]) and then abuses her by pursuing, allowing, or causing, even forcing sexual contact with her.

A few of the rabbis I have interviewed around the country have been supportive of my work, and of my writing this book, and do believe this problem has to be exposed and dealt with in a "much more open, direct" and official manner than it has heretofore by any of the denominations. They have told me they are "appalled by the attitude" of those of their colleagues who say, "Boys will be boys" and "look the other way." They have also told me that "there needs to be clear policy and guidelines for dealing with those rabbis who take advantage of women's vulnerabilities, who violate the Ten Commandments, who do not practice what they preach from their pulpits, who breach a "sacred trust," and who cause grave harm."

This book concludes with a "Seven Step Healing Program" - for women who have been sexually abused by rabbis who abuse their sacred power, for ex-wives of these rabbis, for congregants and other synagogue personnel who have themselves been victims because a rabbi of theirs was exposed as a perpetrator, for anyone wishing to heal from such an experience. I developed this seven step healing program as a result of surviving my own experience with my (now ex-) rabbi/perpetrator-husband, and by talking with and helping other ex-wives of rabbis who perpetrate sexual abuse of other women, as well as women victims/survivors of rabbis' sexual abuse. In developing this healing program, I drew on my more than 25 years as a practicing psychotherapist, my training as a "healer," considerable related literature, interviews with colleagues who are therapists, and with rabbis and Jewish educators, especially women rabbis and educators who have been developing healing prayers and rituals for women.

---

[11]See paper presented to the <u>American Psychological Association</u> by Dr. Charlotte Schwab, "External Causes of Depression in Women." New Orleans. 1989.

The years I have spent researching and writing this book have been a healing experience for me. Helping women survivors has helped me. Helping families of survivors, synagogues, communities has helped me. I have come through writing this book blessing life, cherishing life, mine and others. The experience I went through with my rabbi/husband-perpetrator and researching and writing this book has reinforced my desire to contribute to *Tikkun Olam*, repair of the world. I pray this book serves that purpose.

Deeper questions are raised by this book, such as: What does the betrayal of women and teen aged girls by rabbis mean for male/female relationships in general? If icons of Judaism - deified rabbis - can perpetrate such betrayals, how is there a future for honest, non-exploitative relationships between men and women? How is there a future for marriage, for monogamous, committed, 'holy' marriage?

I do believe that my work, and the proliferation of legal cases and media coverage of rabbis' sexual abuse of women and teen aged girls is working to bring about change, as evidenced by the improved policy of the CCAR, and by more women feeling safe to come forward with the truth.

Only if rabbis who have transgressed take an active role in healing themselves, in making radical changes in their lives, in making *Teshuvah*, can we trust them again.

One of my hopes in writing this book is that I may be a role model for other women victims/survivors, because, in spite of all the abuse I suffered from my rabbi/husband, I have accomplished a great deal in the years since I was married to him, since he assaulted me, sued me for alimony, and in the years since I got away from his abuse (just as I had before I married him). It is important for other victims/ survivors to see how/that I have not only survived abuse by two husbands, one a rabbi-perpetrator of sexual abuse of other women and emotional, verbal, financial and physical abuse of me; but also that I have grown and changed from this experience, achieved a clear and strong self-defined identity and self-esteem, and helped others to do so.

Being able to read about this problem, obtaining information about it, especially the extent of it, and what can be done about it, helps to bring about change.

My (now ex-) rabbi/husband still, as of this writing, has not made *Teshuva*h: not admitted his abuse to me, his physical assault, dragging me through the court to pay *him* alimony, nor has he apologized, made amends, shown that he has repented, nor has he asked for my forgiveness. As of this writing, the CCAR has never responded to my report of his sexual misconduct, of his abuse, let alone investigated it.

Researching and writing this book has brought me solace. I pray this book will bring you, the reader, especially victims/survivors of rabbis' or other clergy abuse, some solace, and will bring you hope that we are embarking on a promising new road of healing and change in the rabbinate and for the Jewish community.

PART ONE

Memoir

Charlotte Schwab

SUNDAY,
THE RABBI ASSAULTED HIS WIFE

"RABBI NEULANDER SUSPECT IN WIFE'S SLAYING"
Philadelphia Inquirer[12]

"THOU SHALT NOT KILL OR COMMIT ADULTERY
CHEATING NEW JERSEY RABBI
CHARGED IN WIFE'S SLAY"
New York Post[13]

That murdered woman could have been me! As I stood in the hallway between the kitchen and dining room of our home, my rabbi/husband threatened, "If you tell anyone about my secret sex life, I'll kill you, and I will be exonerated because I am a rabbi"! Then he repeatedly slammed me against the wall!

Hours before this frightening, murderous scene, my rabbi/husband[14] finally gave me his appointment book. During the three and a half years of our marriage, we always checked our calendars together in order to plan time to spend with each other. Yet, for several weeks, he refused to show me his calendar. That day, he finally slammed his calendar down on the kitchen table. Then he slammed a box on the kitchen table and told me to look through it. As he did so, he shouted, "Good! Now you will know the truth, and we can have some peace." He constantly talked about, preached about, "Peace." Then he left to perform a 'baby naming' ceremony at the home of the new parents.

---

[12]Photo caption of story in <u>Philadelphia Inquirer</u> by Nancy Phillips, 9/4/96. As of this writing, this rabbi is in prison awaiting trial for the capital murder of his wife.

[13]Headline of two page story in the <u>New York Post</u> by Peter Fearon, 8/22/00.

[14]I use either rabbi/husband, Rabbi H, or Jon to refer to my (now ex) rabbi/husband.

I looked at the calendar first. I saw many dates and times painted with "Whiteout." I became suspicious. I looked at the box. It was a large, square box. The box was covered in red velvet. I didn't think this odd at the time, because my husband was very romantic. I opened the box. There were pornographic magazines, novels, pictures of naked women, and audio tapes. I started shaking. The worst was yet to come.

A photograph of him with a naked woman using her fingers to open her vagina to the camera sent me reeling. She was completely naked. He was fully clothed. He had his hand on one of her naked breasts. The expression on his face was of complete pride and satisfaction. I stared at the picture in utter shock, crying out, "No! No"! I could not believe what I was seeing. Also in the box was a list of what seemed to be about 500 names of women, and many slips of paper with women's first names and telephone numbers. I felt that I could not breathe. I was shocked and afraid at the sight of the scandalous picture and contents of the now, not romantic, but alarming red box. I looked around the beautiful kitchen of our brand new, exquisite home. The home for which we had such wonderful dreams.

I was sitting in our tranquil, light, bright, spotlessly clean, brand new, cozy kitchen. I looked at the maple colonial chairs; the almond flooring, appliances and cabinets; the beautiful, round light oak table where we shared many delicious meals that we both joyously cooked together; the table where we discussed and planned his spiritual sermons, shared our calendars to plan our shared time, and the disgusting, pornographic contents of his secret red velvet 'hot box' shockingly sitting on this beloved, beautiful table in what I had thought was my safe, happy, homey kitchen. The contrast was too much. I put my head down on the now sullied table and shed tears of anxious grief and fear.

Several hours later, when my rabbi/husband returned from the 'baby naming' ceremony, he told me that the woman in the photograph was one of the many prostitutes he frequented. Because she had a "specialty," called "Golden Showers," he said, her last name was "Sprinkle," a name in keeping with her "service," for which she charged him $100! He explained to me that this "service" was a form of "S&M," and that she would sit above a toilet seat placed over his face and urinate onto his face and in his mouth. He told me he frequented many such prostitutes, some at a place called "The Dungeon" in New York. He also made appointments with them at their apartments. The names and telephone numbers on the slips of paper that were in the box were prostitutes whom he currently called. Some of them were the same names and numbers I had seen before because he frequently left them around the house, perhaps for me to find. Some of the telephone numbers were in Manhattan and some in Connecticut.

He boasted that the list of women's names were women he had sex with, not just prostitutes. They were also women congregants from when he was a student-cantor, a cantor, and a student-rabbi; students at Hebrew Union College when he was Dean of the School of Sacred Music; women he met at religious organization functions; women he met anywhere.

Some of them were single, some married, some divorced, some widowed. He especially bragged about a "joint conquest" of a "wealthy married woman who lived on Park Avenue," with whom both he and a friend of his, also a rabbi, had "threesomes."

He affirmed that I was "special," and that for this reason my name was not on the list. He made his mind up about that, he told me, after he took me to a 'swingers' place early in our relationship and I was horrified when he told me what kind of place it was, and insisted we leave immediately, which we did. As he put it, "I married *you*, didn't I?"

He cockily told me about the many single and divorced women on the list who tried to get him to marry them, and how he resisted. He bragged that he became engaged to one of them to "keep her quiet" so he could continue "screwing" her, before he finally broke it off. He proudly told me of an ongoing affair that he carried on for years with a married woman high up in the echelons of the denomination's national organization. He was especially proud that she "risked" her husband finding out, and so did he. He thrived on "living on the edge," "taking risks," he bragged. He insisted that I was "different," and that he knew it from the start. "Nothing has changed. Just accept this. Don't rock the boat" he ordered, wildly, "and *you'll have a marriage, the same marriage you've had"*!

"Now you know why I didn't want to show you my calendar," he shouted. "Yes, I go to prostitutes. I told you I had gone to some prostitutes before we got married. I know I promised you and my

5

mother (who died in September of 1986) that that was only because I was lonely when I was single for nine years after my first divorce, and before I met you, and that I certainly would not do it again. But I **never** stopped going to prostitutes. **I like it.** I'll **never** stop. I've been doing it for 16 years. I went to prostitutes when I went to Las Vegas and left you in Laguna Niguel. I went to prostitutes in Paris when I left you at the Hilton. I'll **never stop!** I go to prostitutes in Connecticut, in New York, wherever I am and can find them! I go to S & M prostitutes. I'll never stop! And I'll never stop having sex with other women. I need and want variety, and the stimulation. I love women. All shapes, sizes, ages. I like being with women, women I have never met, new ones, and ones I have. Yes, I 'swing' with the two couples in Westchester you suspected. **I won't stop that either! Don't rock the boat and you'll have a marriage; the same marriage you've had**"!

I could not believe what I was hearing. I told him that to me this was not a marriage. This was not the marriage he had promised me. I reminded him that this was the main reason - that he had told me he went to 'some prostitutes' before we were married - that I had not agreed to marry him for more than three years.

Why/how did I come to marry this "sociopathic," "sex addicted," "character disordered" rabbi?[15]

I married my first husband when I was in my early twenties. What led me to marry him, and then down the primrose path[16]

---

[15]These are the words used to describe my rabbi/husband by the chief psychiatrist at the hospital to which he admitted himself voluntarily to get out of being arraigned for assaulting me and threatening to kill me. They kept him hospitalized for two months. My rabbi/husband chose this hospital because it was near his synagogue and he knew some staff workers because they were members of his congregation. He was able to convince these staff workers and others in his synagogue that he "did not really belong in the hospital."

[16]Carol Matas. The Primrose Path. Winnipeg. Bain & Cox, Publishers. 1995. This is a novel written for young adults about a rabbi's sexual abuse of teenage girls.

to marry this rabbi? Who was I when I married them? Who were *they*? *Would that I had known*!

The following background is important in order to understand.

Charlotte Schwab

GROWING UP INNOCENT, NAIVE, AND JEWISH IN BANGOR, MAINE

I was brought up by observant Orthodox Jewish, immigrant parents in a small town in Maine. My life in Bangor revolved around:

THE JEWISH COMMUNITY CENTER. I went to *Cheder*[17] (Hebrew School) every day after public school and on Sunday. There was no *Bat Mitzvah* for girls there at that time, but we did have confirmation. At the Jewish Community Center, we also had activities such as ping pong and formal dances. I won a ping pong tournament in seventh grade.

PUBLIC SCHOOL. I was determined to excel, and did, especially in English. I still have my Senior Essay, "What Meaning Has Life", in which I quoted Henry Wadsworth Longfellow's poem, "A Psalm of Life." My senior essay reflected my interest in spirituality. I have always been a spiritual person. I have been grateful all my life for the education I received at Bangor High School.

THE BANGOR PUBLIC LIBRARY. I spent much of my time reading in the public library. I remember when I was a very young child, walking to the library, which was a considerable distance away, and, in winter, climbing over what seemed to be mountains of snow to get there, to sit on the small chairs and read the children's books. I was so proud when I 'graduated' to the adult department. Before backpacks were invented, after I was too "grown up" to wear a snow suit, I trekked to the library in winter (Maine winters, remember), with bare legs, bobby sox. I used to carry piles of books home in my arms, as many as they would allow and I could carry. The library opened up the world beyond the cocoon of my small hometown, and I knew from a young age that I would leave Bangor as soon as I graduated high school to discover the world.

---

[17]Yiddish and Hebrew words and phrases that appear in italics are defined in the glossary.

PIANO LESSONS. I learned to love classical music from my piano teacher, whom I will always remember, Harold Annas. Mr. Annas studied at the Eastman School of Music, and, to my ear, was the best pianist ever! Sometimes at my request, he played some of Rachmaninoff's Second Piano Concerto (my favorite for many years) and other music for me after my lesson. A favorite pastime of mine was wearing out my recording of Rachmaninoff's Second Piano Concerto, and records of Chopin's music, and other classical music which I grew to love thanks to my piano teacher. Playing in piano recitals was a goal I looked forward to at the end of the school year. For my last recital, I played the Rachmaninoff Prelude in G. My picture, in which I was wearing a gorgeous tulle sea green strapless gown appeared in the Bangor Daily News. All the senior girls wore formal gowns for the recital. I was thrilled to be able to play in such a setting. {Playing the piano was to provide a very important escape for me years later from the painful reality of being married to an abusive husband who was far from the romantic man I dreamed about when I listened to Rachmaninoff.}

PLAYING THE PIANO. We had an old upright, which I loved and played as often as possible. I never 'practiced,' I just played. Years later, whenever I hear Mel Brooks say on the recording he made with Carl Reiner, "The 2000 Year Old Man," that he "never practices," he is "very good at it," (although he is speaking about being a non credentialed psychiatrist), I laugh, because that was what I thought about my piano playing. I never practiced, I just played. At least, I was good enough for my own ear.

LISTENING TO MY (FIRST 78'S, AND THEN 33₁/₃'S) COLLECTION OF RECORDINGS OF BOTH CLASSICAL AND 1940'S 'BIG BAND' MUSIC. I am grateful to Viner's Music Store, where I spent hours in the private, glass enclosed listening rooms, enjoying my much loved music. I was one of Viner's best customers, and accumulated a collection of hundreds of recordings. My father had a cabinet especially built by a carpenter for my collection. The cabinet covered one whole wall in my upstairs den. By the time I was nine years of age, my four much older sisters had all gone off to be married, to college, or to live elsewhere, and there were enough bedrooms so that my younger sister Nina and I could each

9

have our own, and I could have 'a room of my own' to listen to music, sing, write, dream. I listened to Glen Miller, Tommy Dorsey, Frank Sinatra, and others. Jo Stafford's "It Could Happen to You" became a special favorite. I dreamed 'it' would happen to me: I would fall in love with a wonderful man who would adore me, the way my father adored my mother. Other favorite songs included "Long Ago and Far Away" and "I Can Dream Can't I." I used to sing them, along with others like "Pistol Packin' Mama," my father's favorite, to my father when he would take me on rides in his truck to purchase cows and calves from farmers in the surrounding countryside.

My father was what I always called a "cowboy." He bought cattle 'on the hoof' for his meat market, which offered prime meats to residents all over Eastern Maine. My father could look at a cow or calf across a pasture and know what it was worth, offer the farmer the price, and load it onto his truck. I was very proud of how highly respected my father was for his gentleness, kindness, and honesty.

I remember one trip vividly when I was four years of age. We rode out into the country. My father stopped the truck to go out and look at the calves in the pasture. He chose one calf, talked with the farmer, and put it in his truck. Then, he counted off twenty one dollar bills into the farmer's hand. I stood there watching incredulously. Finally, I could stand it no longer. I blurted out, "Papa, don't give all that money for that scrawny, little calf! You better take back your money and let's go home"! My father and the farmer had a good laugh. Then my father explained money to me, showing me a $1, $5, $10, and $20 bills. I still thought it was too much to pay for the little calf.

Once, when I was ten, I decided to ride out on my bicycle to see a friend who was a daughter of a farmer from whom my father bought cows. I did not realize that it was over eleven miles to their farm. They were very glad to see me, and marveled that I had ridden so far on my bike. They called my mother and told her where I was and asked her if I could stay a few days, since my father was coming out there anyway then, and he could drive me and my bicycle home in his truck. We had a great time together. One of the things my friend Rita and I did was ride back and forth in front of a boy's house we thought was handsome (he must have been about 15), and sing, "Put Your Arms Around Me Honey" at the top of our lungs. We had such fun. We laughed and laughed. He never found us out.

10

Sometimes I would ride in the back of my father's truck, before the animals were loaded on, and sing at the top of my lungs, with the wind in my hair, riding through the gorgeous Maine countryside. I sang all my favorites, including Jo Stafford's "It Could Happen to You."

I dreamed of one day going to New York and falling in love with a wonderful, romantic, handsome man, that it 'would happen' to me.

In high school, I sang in operettas - "A Waltz Dream" was one of them - and I acted in plays - one was "Nine Girls" - the latter at the Jewish Community Center. I dreamed of becoming an actress, like the ones I saw every week at the movie theaters in Bangor: the Bijou, the Opera House, and the Park. I especially loved Vivien Leigh, and, in later years, Doris Day.

JUDAISM. My life in Bangor revolved around Judaism, which was very important to my parents, and became so to me. My faith in God was very strong, although tested severely very often in my life because of events shaking all of humanity. I lost most of my family to Russian pogroms and most of the rest to the Holocaust. I recall many, many times, as a young child, my mother sobbing uncontrollably and wringing her hands in despair when learning of yet another death, and especially when learning about the Nazi concentration camps. I was a young girl during World War II.

After the war, my mother and father were able to respond to a notice by one of my mother's nieces in the *Yiddish* newspaper which my father read every *SHABBAT* after lunch. My cousin Bella wrote that she had survived the war, was, in fact, the only one of her family to do so, by escaping into the woods and joining the underground when the Nazis came one day and shot all her family and *shtetl* residents into a trench they had dug for the bodies. She was looking for family. My father and mother, and my mother's brother, my Uncle Moishe, brought Bella and her husband, Boris, and their young daughter, Sonia, to the United States.

The synagogues in Bangor, there were three on the same block, were around the corner from our house. My parents would not drive on *SHABBAT* or certain holidays, so, my father, when I was born, bought a very large house to accommodate his growing family. I was the fifth of what were to be six daughters. My father proudly told everyone that he "did better than Eddie Cantor," a famous comedian who had five daughters. He bought a house around the corner from the synagogue so we could all walk to *shul* because we were *frum*. The Jewish community was quite close knit in those days. All my friends were Jewish. We all went to *cheder* at the JCC. There was very little, if any, mixing socially between Jews and gentiles, or non-Jews, in Bangor[18] and, certainly, not between Orthodox Jews and gentiles.

My parents invited students who were far from home and attending the University of Maine in Orono, which was a few miles away, or servicemen serving in World War II at Dow Air Force Base in Bangor to *SHABBAT* dinners on Friday nights, and for Chanukah and Passover Seders, and to eat in our *Succah*. I remember how joyous these dinners and celebrations were, and how much they meant to the students and servicemen. My belief in doing *Mitzvot* (commandments and good deeds), and *Tzedakah*, (giving charity), in *Tikkun Olam*, healing the world, and my belief in family and community, all of which I learned from my parents and their observance of Judaism, have sustained me all my life.

I was accepted to the University of Michigan in Ann Arbor. It was the only college I wanted to attend. My guidance counselor had recommended it to me. My parents did not want me to go. Not only was it 1300 miles away, but also, they worried that I would not be able to observe my Judaism, have Jewish friends, and most importantly, that it was a risk that I might meet and fall in love with a non-Jewish man. They did everything they could to dissuade me. I said that if I could not go to the University of Michigan, I would go to New York and get a job. And go to New York, I did. I had a cousin twice my age, Sally, living in Manhattan. She was my mother's niece. Although she was a beautiful, brilliant young woman, she had not married, and was considered an 'old maid', a sexist term of the time. I left Bangor after I graduated from high school in June, took the train to New York, and I moved in with Sally. I got a job selling hats in

---

18 Judith S. Goldstein. Crossing Lines. New York. William Morrow. 1992. Goldstein writes about this in her history of Jews and Gentiles in three communities in Maine, although many of her other 'facts' are not accurate, according to my experience.

Bloomingdales, and was accepted at a famous acting school. I was happy.

One day in August, Sally and I were doing dinner dishes and the doorbell rang. It was my mother. I was delighted, though shocked. I could not believe that she had traveled alone to New York, and found the apartment, without even telling me that she was coming. She had never been to New York before, and, to travel alone was not something she liked to do. After we welcomed her and got her settled, she told me that she had persuaded my father to let me go to the University of Michigan. I was in heaven. I will be eternally grateful to my mother for bringing this about and to my father for sending me there.

I loved Michigan. A whole new world opened up to me. I met and made friends with people from all over the world, of all races and religious backgrounds. I was excited by my classes, especially English composition and literature, and Psychology. I was was very proud that I was given an exemption from English Composition II and told I had excellent writing skills. I was frequently asked to write a poem for my friends for their birthdays or other special occasions. I developed my leadership skills at the Women's League. I organized and led dance classes, which would attract as many as 70 students, and I took care to equalize the number of female and male students. The League hired a teacher from Arthur Murray in Detroit. I learned to dance so well, that I appeared on the stage of the famous Hill Auditorium, dancing with a chosen group of dancers from the classes in an Exhibition. I had a regular dance partner, and we danced the tango and the waltz for Fraternity and other formal dances. At one of these balls, my partner and I danced to the music of Harry James, a special thrill. These dances were the smooth, graceful, lovely dances of the '50's, not the staccato, abrupt dances performed as 'ballroom' today. By request of the students in the dance classes, I organized a dating bureau, and arranged for many of my classmates to find boyfriends and girlfriends. I loved making others happy, facilitating relationships, a skill which I utilized successfully as a psychotherapist many years later.

While at the University of Michigan, I taught Sunday School for children of faculty and Ann Arbor residents, and I learned about other denominations besides Orthodoxy. But, at that time, I did not yet feel drawn away from Orthodox Judaism. It had been a special treat to be

13

taken to *shul* with my father and stand with him at his special place to *daven* before I was 13 years of age. After I was thirteen, my father considered me a "young lady," and I could no longer stand with him to *daven*, but had to go upstairs to sit with the women. I was so proud when I learned to *daven* the *Shmoneh Esrai* by heart and saw how proud and happy that made my father. I am very grateful to this day for the education my parents provided me at the Jewish Community Center in Bangor - that I can read Hebrew, *daven*, that I learned Torah. I benefit from this education and knowledge in so many ways today.

For example, for several years, recently, I led a *Chavurah* in Manhattan which I founded - a spiritual group which met once a month to hold a Friday night *SHABBAT* service and *SHABBAT* dinner at a member's home. We sang almost the entire service, accompanied on the piano by our members, Barry and Richard. I gave a short talk about the passage from the Torah and led the discussion (a *Dvar Torah*: a teaching on the portion of the Torah read at the next morning's *SHABBAT* service in the synagogue). Some members of the *Chavurah* (still) refer to me as 'rabbi-Charlotte' or 'rav-Charlotte,' which is one of the greatest compliments anyone can give to me.

The synagogue, Congregation B'nai Jeshurun, which supported my founding and leading the *Chavurah*, is Conservative. In my adult life, I have been a member of synagogues of the Reform and Conservative denominations, and a member of The Jewish Renewal movement. All movements of Judaism are important to me. I want to see Judaism thrive, and thrive in vibrant communities. Community is/has always been important to me,[19] as is combining Judaism and community.

I am gratified to see the resurgence of spirituality we are experiencing in society today, and especially the proliferation of groups of all kinds holding *SHABBAT* services, the proliferation of 'Jewish meditation' groups, Jewish healing centers, etc. It has been a source of puzzlement to me that so many people of Jewish descent and background have been drawn to Buddhism - the so-called 'Jew-

---

[19] I wrote my doctoral dissertation on, "A Study of Political Behavior in Community Building." New York University, New York. 1973.

Buds,'[20] when we have such an important mystical and meditative history and resource in Judaism. I particularly enjoyed studying *Kabballah* (as well as Torah) with Rabbi Jonathan Feldman both in a private group in a group member's home, and at Aish Hatorah, an Orthodox learning center in Manhattan, and learning about the marvelous spiritual resources emanating from Judaism.

I cherish continuing to learn about Judaism, and teaching about it and sharing it with others in a communal setting. Of course, it is important to me that women have an equal role to play in these communities - in communal prayer, and the leading of communal prayers,[21] and as leaders in the denominations. While there are now women rabbis in Reform Judaism and Conservative Judaism, for example, there has still never been a woman head of the UAHC (Union of American Hebrew Congregations, the North American Reform synagogue organization), the CCAR (Central Conference of American Rabbis, the Reform rabbinic organization), the Rabbinical Assembly, the Conservative rabbinic organization, or the JTS, the Jewish Theological Seminary. In fact, there have been few women members of the CCAR's board, and these only recently. At this writing, a woman has been elected for the first time to head the United Synagogue for Conservative Judaism.

Women are still rarely senior rabbis of large synagogues (there are a few exceptions). They are most often assistant rabbis, or rabbis of very small synagogues, or serve in other roles, such as in education, fund raising, administration and the like, where they have little decision making power. Judaism is a communal religion. Yes, it is a "civilization," as Mordecai Kaplan wrote in his book,[22] a "people," a "culture;" but, most important, Judaism is a religion: a belief in One

---

[20] Rodger Kamenetz. The Jew in the Lotus. New York. Harper Collins. 1994

[21] At this writing, I am teaching classes at the Conservative synagogue in Florida where I am currently a member, including: "Celebrating Women's Wisdom: A Woman's View of Torah, Liturgy, and Ritual," "Women in the Torah," and "The Rise of Egalitarianism in Conservative Judaism: What the Future May Hold."

[22] Mordecai M. Kaplan. Judaism As A Civilization: Toward A Reconstruction of American-Jewish Life. New York. The Reconstructionist Press. 1957.

God. The core of Judaism is the *Sh'ma*, the prayer which asserts, affirms that our God, the God of Israel is one: there is one God.

It is a sad fact to me that synagogues, and, especially synagogue *SHABBAT* services, have become so out of touch with what people actually want and need from them that most Jews, even those who are members of a synagogue only attend on the High Holy Days. Perhaps one of the reasons is because, in my opinion, it is very hard to be spiritual at a *SHABBAT* service with a great magnitude of people present. I think that encouraging the formation of *Chavurah* groups such as the successful one I founded, the BJ EASTSIDERS, at Congregation B'nai Jeshurun, is an important step for offering people an intimate communal setting for *SHABBAT* services where they can make connections to fulfill their needs for spirituality, expression of belief in and praise of God, observance, study of Judaism, and community. On the *SHABBAT* when the *Chavurah* does not meet, the members can sit together to pray at the synagogue and feel like a more intimate community within a larger community. Unfortunately, of the over five million estimated Jews who live in the U.S., a majority are not members of a synagogue. There is a new movement toward a spiritual awareness, which seems to be finding its way to the denominations, into synagogues. Hopefully, this will attract more and involved members.

After graduating from the University of Michigan, I took a position as an assistant to a professor of psychology because I wanted to earn a graduate degree in psychology. Because Professor Wagman was blind I learned and did a great deal more as his assistant than I otherwise would have. However, I was not able to earn enough money as his assistant to support myself financially and attend graduate school. I took a position as a high school teacher, but it was in a town 70 miles away from Ann Arbor, was a long commute in severe winter weather, and, for many other reasons as well, was not a good decision. A friend told me that a friend of hers who lived in Manhattan was getting married and that her roommate needed a new roommate. I loved Manhattan when I lived there briefly before college. It was 'The Big Apple.' It was the place to 'make it.' The myriad cultural attractions strongly beckoned me. I decided to move to Manhattan. Marilyn[23] had an apartment to share in a beautiful brownstone - the parlor floor - on 75th Street just off Central Park West. I was excited to be living in Manhattan.

Within two days, I found work as a motivational researcher at a Madison Avenue advertising agency, and met the man who was to become my first husband. He came to a party my roommate Marilyn gave for her friends to meet me. He came with one of her friends. He asked me to go to dinner with him after the party. I knew my first husband under seven months when we married. I was very young and naive, and thought that what I knew about him was enough. My first husband was from an Orthodox Jewish background. It was very important to me that my parents approve of and like my husband. They did approve of him and were happy for us to marry. He seemed to be very moral. For example, he did not pressure me to have sex with him before marriage. I liked that. I was to find out after we married that his not pressuring me for sex before marriage had nothing to do with morality.

I also met another man at the party, and I dated him for three months at the same time that I was dating my first husband. I went out with him on Friday and with my first husband, whom I will call Mort, on Saturdays. Mort asked me to see him both Fridays and Saturdays. I told him I was not ready to do that. One Friday, because I had a cold, the other man, whom I will call Matt, and I decided to stay in. We were playing chess when my doorbell rang. It was Mort. He said he wanted to see me. I told him I had a guest and I would see him the next evening. He left, but called me from the corner pay telephone to say he really wanted to see me and take me for a drive. He had borrowed his brother's white convertible. I told him it would have to be Saturday. He insisted that I make a decision to stop dating Matt and to see him both Friday and Saturday evening. I told him I would think it over.

I decided to choose Mort. I thought that his insisting we see so much of each other and that I see only him meant that he was serious about our relationship, and I wanted to explore this possibility. Matt was not of Orthodox background. His parents were German Jewish immigrants. I was afraid that his background would not be compatible with mine. So, although we, too, had many shared interests, and

---

23I have changed her name.

enjoyed our time together, I broke up with him and began seeing Mort more frequently. My parents were of Russian Jewish and Ukrainian Jewish background, and Mort's, although deceased, were from Poland. I thought our families would have more in common. He invited me to a dance where I would meet several of his siblings and their wives. As it turned out, none of his siblings or their families except for one sister were ever close to me or treated me like 'family.'

Before we were married, Mort behaved toward me with the utmost respect and affection, even admiration, and behaved as if he were in love with me, although he never verbalized that. He was not at all verbally expressive. But, he was very attentive and thoughtful. In August, when we had known each other and been dating for five months, he invited me out to his co-ed shared house on Fire Island for two weeks. I decided to quit my position as a motivational researcher at Young & Rubicam, the advertising agency, as I was not challenged at all by the position, and, because I thought it had no chance of advancement. I decided to go out to Fire Island, and look for another position when I returned. I believed that Mort was going to propose to me, and I planned to adjust my job hunting to the prospective marriage, something, unfortunately, women did, and I believe still do for the most part. Mort was only able to come out to Fire Island on weekends. I spent the time getting to know his other four house mates and their friends.

When Mort did come out to Fire Island, although we had to share a double bed, he told me in advance that we would not have sex, as he wanted to "wait 'til marriage." This was the late nineteen fifties, when 'nice girls didn't,' and I thought this indicated he had the utmost respect for me and was planning to ask me to marry him. I was naive and thought it was not strange that a young man 28 years of age could sleep in the same bed with an attractive young woman, his girl friend, and not want sex. I was relieved. I knew about 'bundling,' a practice in which a boy and girl were allowed to share a bed, although, usually, with parental supervision, prior to marriage, and reasoned that we were 'bundling.'

When I returned to New York, I talked this over with my roommate. Marilyn's dating behavior was quite different from mine. I knew Marilyn to be sexually experienced. The friend through whom I met her told me she was probably even promiscuous. She was much older than I, I suspected by ten years. On the one hand, I did not respect her sexual behavior. On the other hand, I wanted her opinion, as she was, after all, 'experienced.' Marilyn thought Mort's behavior 'strange' and she did not think I should continue seeing him. However, Marilyn had never married. Women of her age in those days were looked at as beyond marriage ability, referred to by the sexist term, 'old maids.' I did not think hers was good advice. I thought Mort would be a loving, attentive, and faithful husband. We seemed to have similar values and goals in life. We both wanted children; we both wanted to raise them in a Jewish home; and we both wanted to live in a 'good community,' which to me meant one where people knew each other, were good neighbors, and most important, where there were Jewish people. I once observed Mort being attentive to children, and I thought this indicated that he would be a good father. He was an attorney in a private practice, and, although it was in a store front in Brownsville, a poverty stricken area of Brooklyn where he grew up, he told me that he was planning to obtain a position with a law firm in Manhattan, and that he would be a 'good provider' for me and our children. In the 1950's, this was something that was important to most young women. There was virtually no opportunity for women to advance in careers, and women were financially dependent on husbands to support them.

Although Mort was not interested in Judaism, and had never been a member of a synagogue, he had been a *Bar Mitzvah*. He said he wanted to raise his children as Jews. We seemed to have shared interests: civic consciousness and participation; the same classical music; ballet; 1940's 'big band' music; ballroom dancing. We made good dancing partners. Once, after we were married, we won a prize in a ballroom dancing contest at a resort. We were best at the Lindy hop, waltz, fox trot, and rhumba.

Mort revealed to me that his parents were deceased, his father since he was seven, his mother since he was sixteen. I was sad about that, and disappointed not to to have the prospect of parents-in-law; but he had five older brothers and three older sisters, and I thought I would have a family with them. My parents still lived in Maine, and my only cousins in the New York area were Sally, who had never married, and Bella and Boris and their children. Family is, and always has been, an important value of mine, and I wanted the pleasure of celebrating Jewish holidays, as well as Thanksgiving and other secular holidays with family. I also wanted the mutual support of a

19

family nearby. He took me to Brooklyn to get to know his two sisters who lived there. One was married with no children. I liked her very much, and we had an instant bond. The other was married with two children. I looked forward to sharing many happy family times with them.

Mort asked me to marry him at the end of August, five months after we met. My parents and my sister Ronnie, who is 14 years older than I and whom I was especially close to and with whom I talked about most things, suggested that we be married in New York. Since my parents were not well, and were advanced in years, they felt it would not be a good idea for us to hold the wedding in Maine. Also, it would have meant asking my husband's five brothers, three sisters and their families to travel to Maine. My siblings were scattered around the country anyway, and would have to travel to come to the wedding wherever it was.

My parents expressed the hope that, in November, they would be well enough to be able to travel to Florida for the winter, and they would stop in New York to visit with us for a few days. My sister Ronnie lived in Florida and had two young children. She and her husband would not be able to come to the wedding, but she advanced the idea that perhaps we could travel there in the near future to see them. She encouraged me to set the date for the wedding in New York, and asked her elderly mother-in-law, whom I loved, and who lived in Manhattan, to attend. I had known her since I was ten, when my sister married, and always called her "Aunt Hattie." One of my sisters and her husband were able to come down from Massachusetts, where they lived at the time. My cousin Sally, and my cousins, Bella and Boris, who had survived World War II in the resistance, and whom my parents had brought to this country, came. I was very close to my cousin Bella. She was 13 years older than I, and she was like an older sister to me, closer to me than any of my siblings. She was my only real 'family' in New York. When she died, 22 years later, it was a tremendous loss to me. She and her husband Boris arranged for their Orthodox rabbi to officiate at our wedding.

Mort's brother offered his home in Brooklyn as a site for our nuptials. We had a small wedding. I must have had some premonition about the marriage, because, although I know it is common to get cold feet before a wedding, I felt a sense of panic. My sister and her husband were late in arriving, and I said I would not go through with it until they got there. When they arrived, they walked me the short distance to the *chupah* in the living room. My knees were knocking. I could hardly put one foot in front of the other. I felt like a lamb to the slaughter. I wanted to run away. My sister said it was just wedding jitters. I felt so 'blue' about the wedding that I did not even buy a white wedding dress. I bought a blue one. The choice was not a conscious one. I did not realize this until many years later. Perhaps, if anyone had asked me if I loved my husband - to - be, I would have been shocked, and, if they did, perhaps I would not have married him. I married him because he seemed to be what I was 'supposed' to marry: brought up Orthodox Jewish, a potentially good husband and father, a potentially good 'provider.' He acted as if he loved me. I thought I would grow to love him. None of those 'potentials' came true.

After the ceremony, one of my first husband's brothers, who was single, generously offered to pay for a wedding trip to Miami Beach. We had made a reservation at a resort in the Catskills, which we canceled. My husband had no savings. My parents gave us money to start our marriage. We felt all we could afford was the Catskills. We were pleased to be able to go to Florida.

MARRIAGE TO MORT: MY FIRST
EXPERIENCE WITH ABUSE

On our honeymoon, I got an introduction to what our 'sex life' would be. Namely, none. My new husband contrived to get a severe sunburn, which he admitted he had never done in his life, and which he never did again. It wasn't easy, as he is quite dark skinned, had very dark, almost black hair and dark brown eyes, and doesn't burn easily. I later learned that he contrived to get the sunburn so he could get out of making love. He sat in a tub of ice for an entire night and day. I always thought the movie, "The Heartbreak Kid," with Cybill Shepherd and Charles Grodin, was about my marriage, although it was the newlywed wife (played by May's daughter), in the tub of ice in the movie. Even after the sunburn was better, my new husband had no interest in making love. We spent our honeymoon with my sister and her family visiting us, their children enjoying swimming in the hotel pool, and going to tourist spots like The Parrot Jungle.

I maintained my optimism about the marriage. Because I am by nature a very positive person, and, as I have said, was very naive, I thought that once we were at home, we would settle into a positive love life. This was not to be. On our first day home, I shopped for groceries and cooked a delicious meal, cleaned and shined our small apartment 'til it sparkled, put candles on the table, and was giving the dining area one last sweep when my new husband walked in.

He grabbed the broom out of my hand, and started berating me that I did not know the proper way to sweep a floor, shouting in such a hostile, hateful tone of voice that I ran crying into our bedroom. He had never yelled at me before, had never spoken to me in a hostile tone, and I was shocked. I learned that this was to be his pattern: being verbally, emotionally, and much later, physically abusive. In the beginning, the opinion of many therapists we were to consult over the course of our marriage was that he became abusive to get out of "performing sex," as they termed it. As time went on, being verbally, emotionally, and physically abusive was his habit. He was abusive often, when he was stressed in any way. And much stressed him: finances, getting work, my becoming pregnant, my studies and work, almost anything.

Our first night at home, he apologized, which also became a pattern; but he said that any possible romantic mood was destroyed, which was his objective. When he apologized after being abusive, he would do extra things around the house, such as clearing the table, doing dishes, and sweeping the kitchen floor. In later years, when we had dinner guests, everyone thought I had a 'model husband' and many women expressed envy because their husbands did not clear tables, do dishes, or sweep the floor. Hopefully for them, their husbands were also not abusive. I would quickly have chosen the absence of abuse over help with dishes.

I learned very early in this marriage how to 'cover up,' to deny what was really going on, how to feign happiness. I became quite an expert at it. People told me they believed I had a wonderful husband and that we had a wonderful marriage. This belief was fostered because my husband took care not to be abusive in front of others, but only in private. I learned much later that this is common for "battering men." I, too, fostered their beliefs. I was practiced at the Pollyanna smile, looking externally as if I were the happiest of wives, while in truth I was becoming more and more unhappy and afraid. I did not dare let people know the truth about my husband, my marriage to him. I was afraid I would not be believed, or that I would be blamed for his behavior toward me, since he didn't behave that way in front of anyone else or toward anyone else as far as I knew, and he took care not to be abusive to me in public. In the '50's and beyond, women were held responsible for making marriages happy, for making their husbands happy. It was their 'fault' if the marriage was unhappy, or, perish the thought, if the marriage 'failed.'

(My life with my first husband sowed the seeds for my becoming a feminist, more about which, later.)

I soon realized that, not only was I not to have any sex life with this husband, or even affection for that matter, but that I was not to be financially provided for either. He kept telling me to ask my parents for money. I did not want to ask my parents for any more money, but he said we did not have enough to pay our 'expenses,' so I was forced to ask for their help. My husband kept promising me that this would change, and I believed him. He did leave his store- front office in Brownsville, and took a position with a law firm on Wall Street, so I thought I had good reason to believe him. In the meantime, although I had hoped to go to graduate school, I realized that I had to help with our income. I took a six week speedwriting and typing course, and got work typing legal papers on an old Royal manual typewriter for other lawyers, being paid by the page.

My husband left his new position on Wall Street, complaining that the lawyers for whom he worked were impossible to get along with. This, too, was to become a pattern. I once calculated that in 24 years of marriage my husband had obtained approximately 24 positions as an attorney, and later, as an insurance salesman. Every position he obtained he complained that the people for whom he worked were "impossible to get along with."

Before he took his first position as an attorney for a law firm in Manhattan, we took a trip to Maine. I wanted him to visit with my family, to see where I had grown up, and to meet my friends who still lived there. I believed that a trip would help him to be relaxed and to make love. We had not yet consummated our marriage, and we had, by now, been married for nine months. On the trip to Maine, we planned to stop in Massachusetts and stay for a couple of days with my sister and brother - in - law who came to our wedding, and then drive to Bangor to stay with my parents for a week. We also made reservations for a week at a resort. At the resort, we did attempt to make love. What happened, I was later to learn, constituted what Masters and Johnson called "premature ejaculation." (Therapists at Masters and Johnson and other therapists we consulted in later years at my initiation said that this pattern was called "withholding", and was due to unresolved anger and hostility that my husband carried into our marriage and took out on me. My husband withheld making love, withheld earning a living, withheld affection, withheld communication, and "withheld" in other ways. "Withholding" is a form of abuse. This pattern persisted throughout our marriage, and in spite of all the therapy that we tried.)

Although we did not have intercourse, miraculously, I conceived on this trip. I knew nothing about birth control at the time. I wanted to become pregnant, to have a child. I wanted a child very much, wanted a family, and I also thought that, somehow, if I became pregnant had a child, my husband would become the husband I was led to believe by him he would be. My becoming pregnant without penetration reinforced for me how easy it is for some women to become pregnant, and I caution women who consult me in therapy about this to this day, caution them that even without penetration, if a man ejaculates near their vagina, or if they are not careful to withdraw the penis and condom 'intact' if he does achieve penetration and he ejaculates while his penis is inside their vagina, that they can become pregnant.

I was ecstatic to be expecting a baby. I did not think that the lack of a normal sex life would be important. I did not even know at that time what a 'normal' sex life was. I was unhappy about my husband withdrawing affection and communication, but I thought having children to give my love to would be all I needed to be happy. I also thought that having a family would cause my husband to want to earn a living, and that it might make him be affectionate and to communicate.

What followed were signs that this man would never be a good husband. However, my denial was in full force by then. I denied to myself and others that my husband was not only not affectionate, would not make love, did not keep a job and make a living, but, worse, was hostile and abusive emotionally and verbally. I did not learn until many years later that, as Lenore Walker states, <u>most men who abuse women do not do it until after the marriage when they have control.</u> And, that <u>one out of two women will be battered by a man who loves them.</u>

As the years went on, Mort became more and more abusive. Yet, I continued to put on a false front to the world, acting as if my husband were the best husband in the world, loving, communicative, romantic, helping with the children and housework. I believed then, as many, if not most people do today, that Jewish men do not abuse their wives. That it was my fault if he did this, and that it was up to me to get him to stop doing it. Again, I did not learn until many years later that I was far from alone, that the numbers and percentage of Jewish men who verbally, emotionally, and physically (batter) abuse their wives is similar to the percentage of all men who are batterers and abusers.[24] I

---

[24]Marcia Cohn Spiegel (See her Bibliography about Jewish "domestic violence" and Jewish clergy sexual abuse listed in the Bibliography of this book) told me that it took 15 years to get the Jewish community anywhere to accept this fact. It is still not accepted by many, if not most, Jewish communities that Jewish men can be batterers, and those who are working to change this still have an uphill battle.

lived a lie, and he continued not being a responsible, loving, giving husband. I acted to others as if he were the best husband in the world. I needed to believe he was a good husband. At that time, women were made to believe that they were solely responsible for a marriage 'working,' for a husband's being a 'good' husband. Women were blamed when a husband was abusive. "What did you do to cause him to....?" was the prevailing attitude. And, of course, battering men say, "She caused me to hit her, beat her; she asked for it." Even today, we put the focus on women by calling them "battered" - "battered women," not by calling the men "battering men," and calling the women victims or survivors of "battering men." [25]

I chose to have natural childbirth. I went to classes regularly, learned the breathing, and was determined not to have any drugs or intervention for the birth of my baby. My husband did not choose to participate in any preparation for the birth. In fact, he was unhappy and hostile at the prospect of having a child. His hostility came to full fruition at the time I was in labor in the hospital, and when I was giving birth. The doctor told him to "coach" me and "support" me in the "pushing" for the birth. My husband's idea of coaching and support was to snarl, "Push, damn you!" into my ear when I was giving birth. The shock of this was so great it echoed in my ear for years. As I write this, I can still hear his hostile snarl.

Despite his hostility and anger about the pregnancy and birth, I did deliver a beautiful, healthy, happy baby girl who became the light of my life. I remember her entrance into the world as the happiest moment of my life.

The presence of a baby daughter brought no change to my husband's behavior. He was still unwilling to give any affection, let alone make love. He still was not able or was unwilling to hold a job for any length of time. Somehow, I began to believe that if we had a son, he would change. Remember, this was the late 50's and early 60's. Betty Friedan had not yet given us The Feminine Mystique, her

---

[25]The brochure of the Kolot of Broward County, Florida, Voices - A Coalition for Ending Domestic Abuse in the Jewish Community states that "'Domestic abuse' occurs as frequently in Jewish homes as in the general community. Jewish women stay longer than others in an abusive relationship. Every day, Jewish children witness violence in their homes."

book about "the problem that had no name." There was not yet a National Organization for Women, The Third Wave of Feminism had not yet begun. I had been brought up in a sexist society, in a home of all daughters.

Although I was fortunate that my parents sent me to the University of Michigan, and I graduated hoping to go on to graduate school, my parents did not encourage this. I wanted to major in psychology, but they wanted me to obtain a teacher's certificate, "just in case." The "just in case" was in case I did not marry. The joke going around campuses in those days was that girls went to college to get their Mrs. 'degree.' The real goal of going to college was to find a husband. In my case, not just any husband. He had to be Jewish, preferably from an Orthodox family, be observant, and be a good financial provider. I honored my parents' wish by majoring in English, minoring in psychology, and obtaining a Secondary Teacher's Certificate in English and Social Studies. I taught high school before my marriage, and junior high briefly after my marriage. I am grateful to my parents for urging me to obtain the teacher training, which proved valuable later on: when I substitute taught to earn money while I was a graduate student; when I became a professor at CUNY after obtaining my Ph.D.; when I was Executive Director of The Feminist Center for Human Growth and Development and trained psychotherapists, taught seminars and workshops; and, much later, when I became a human resources development trainer for non profit organizations and companies - all about which more later.

I was trained well in the sexist stereotypes to which women were subjected: to put marriage before career. Career was not even a word I knew or used. I knew of no career women, or even any women who worked outside the home who were married. Two of my married sisters did 'help out' part time in their husband's stores. I was trained to please a husband, to be a dutiful wife, to put him and family first - to do whatever it took to keep marriage and family intact; to 'get my husband to' be the loving, attentive, husband I was led to believe he would be, even if it meant giving up my own dreams. I was trained by society to believe that it was the woman's job to create a good marriage. That it was the woman's fault if the husband was not loving, attentive, a good financial provider.

My parents' marriage served as a role model for me. My father adored my mother. He was loving and attentive to her. He always

27

backed her up in everything, took her position, not us kids'. They shared values, goals, interests. I wanted a marriage like my parents had. My parents talked with each other often, shared much. I remember very much about their 'sharing' times. One of the reasons I became a psychotherapist was that every *SHABBAT*, after coming home from synagogue and having lunch, my father would read the *Yiddish* newspaper to my mother, including a column by a 'Dr. Klorman.' People would write to Dr. Klorman asking advice for a wide range of problems. My father would read the letter asking for the advice to my mother, and then they would discuss what they thought the answer would be. Then he would read Dr. Klorman's answer and they would discuss that. I remember sitting and listening from the time I was a young girl. The way they admired Dr. Klorman, respected his answers led me to believe that a 'doctor' who helped people with their problems was the most wonderful job to have in life. I wanted to become such a doctor. Another reason why I eventually became a psychotherapist, which I believe was a 'calling' in my life, was that in eighth grade, we had a class called General Living. One of the assignments was to choose a job from the list the teacher provided us that we thought we would like to have when we grew up, research it, interview someone who held such a job, and write a report which we delivered orally in class. I chose "psychiatrist." I even managed to get an interview with the chief psychiatrist at the local hospital, learned about how he helped people, and resolved that one day, I would be a doctor who helped people.

I always wanted a marriage like the one I observed my parents had. Though my parents never had a son, and my father was a wonderful husband and father to daughters, I believed that if I had a son, my husband would change and be the attentive, affectionate, loving, responsible, providing husband and father my own father was, and that I was led to believe by my husband before the marriage that he would be. Before I ever heard the word 'feminism,' I knew that males were considered to be the 'important' people in society. I was determined, in spite of the fact that my husband and I had no sex life, to have a son. I reasoned that I managed to have a daughter, and now I would have a son.

We were living in a one bedroom apartment in Greenwich Village. We needed a larger place to live, especially if I achieved my desire for a second child. I began learning about the housing situation, the lack of housing for middle income people in New York. I learned about the possibility of creating, building a 'middle income cooperative.' In April of 1960, about the time of my daughter's first birthday, I put an ad in the Village Voice, a newspaper in Greenwich Village, asking others interested in this prospect to contact me. I got 5,000 replies from people who became members of an organization I created which I called MI-COVE, an acronym for Middle Income Cooperators of the Village, but also a name which meant to me creating my own "cove," my own community in the vicinity of Greenwich Village.

MI-COVE blossomed into an effort to create and build an innovative "New Town in Town," a planned community to house 5,000 families of varying incomes, with socio- economic services. My work was written about in The New York Times, The New York Herald Tribune (which published almost a full page article with a large picture of me), The New York Post (which wrote about me and my work in their "Close-Up" column and also published a picture of me), the Village Voice, which wrote an article and published a picture of me with my baby daughter. I was filmed for and appeared on educational television, both WNET and ETV Canada. I was speaking publicly at events drawing up to 1200 people.

With the help of many volunteers, a few of whom baby-sat for me when I had to make speeches or appear at meetings and other events, I created committees, produced and published a Newsletter for the 5,000 member families of MI-COVE, and sponsored community events. I obtained the pro bono services of the prestigious architectural firm of Victor Gruen Associates and the pro bono services of the prestigious legal firm Szold, Brandwen, Meyers and Blumberg. I obtained the support of organizations, churches and synagogues in Greenwich Village and throughout the city for MI-COVE. I established liaisons with the state and city agencies which would be involved in developing this project, spoke at public hearings, met with government officials, including Mayor Robert Wagner about the project, and obtained a promise of $38,000,000 in funds from the New York State Division of Housing and Community Renewal to build MI-COVE. The site we chose was called "Hell's Hundred Acres" because it contained cast iron front buildings which had been the cause of terrible fires including the infamous Triangle

Shirtwaist Fire in which many women lost their lives. The Fire Commissioner and others believed the area desperately needed to be redeveloped.

My work received wide media coverage. As a result of this volunteer work, I was offered paid part time consulting work by the housing and urban renewal consultant Roger Schafer, among others, and was able to stop my Herculean typing work. I enjoyed working in the housing and urban renewal field. My work on MI-COVE and the consulting work gave me a sense of identity outside of my abusive marriage, a sense of self esteem, validated my belief in my abilities, gave me a community, which, if not yet a physical entity, was at least a community socially and civically, brought me friends, a sense of family. The paid work also brought in much needed funds. Because of this work, I thought we would be able to afford another child. Also, although we were living in a one bedroom, one bath apartment in Greenwich Village, I had every expectation that the community I was working on would be built and that we would have a comfortable home at a price we could afford. I grew up in a very large, old rambling house in Maine, and when I talked to Victor Gruen about wanting more space, he said not to worry. He would make sure I had a spacious, lovely apartment in MI-COVE which we could easily afford.

In March, 1961, my husband caught a bad cold. He complained of "freezing." I got into bed with him, offering to keep him warm. I initiated making love. He never did. I never did, either, because when I had in the past, he would become angry, and find something about which to become abusive. This time, I risked it. Although, as before, the lovemaking was not 'successful', meaning there was no penetration, I became pregnant.

I was sure that I was pregnant with the son I was praying for. My husband was extremely angry about the pregnancy. This time, he found a doctor who would perform an abortion and say that it was medically necessary, since there was no legal abortion in this country at that time. I was in shock and extremely afraid. There was no way I would have an abortion, legal or otherwise. I don't think that in 1961, prior to my husband's telling me I must have an abortion, I had ever heard the word abortion. There was no way that I was not going to have my child, whether it was to be another girl or a boy. In those days we did not have the methods we do today to find out in advance the sex of the child. I knew I would love either.

I put on my best 'acting' face. Even without the acting classes I had wanted to take, I was a good actor. I told everyone we were both ecstatic about the pregnancy. The pregnancy was very difficult, perhaps caused, or at least compounded by my husband's increasing anger and hostility. I sustained myself with loving my daughter, and anticipating my new baby. I love babies and children very much. I baby-sat frequently during my junior high and high school years, and spent school holidays and vacations at my sister Ronnie's, taking care of her babies and children. If I had a happy marriage, I have no doubt that I would have wanted several more children.

Just as Leah, the first wife of Jacob, the Biblical patriarch, hoped that each time she gave birth, Jacob's attitude toward her would change[26] I, too, hoped that my husband would give up his hostile ways with the birth of each child. But, just like Leah's, my hope was not fulfilled. I did not, though, like Leah, go on to have more children. I was not a glutton for punishment. I did not want, seek, or crave abuse. I wanted it to end, to get away from it. In fact, sometimes, when my husband came home in his hostile, abusive mood, after the children were asleep, I got in the car and drove around, finding myself in front of the home of the rabbi of our Temple, the very rabbi to whom I was to appeal in person many years later for help about my second husband, the abusive rabbi. I never told the rabbi of our Temple about my first husband, never told anyone outside of psychiatrists and psychotherapists we consulted, and my sister Ronnie. None of them helped.

My work on MI-COVE, my many friends, and loving my children sustained me. My friends admired my work, and were very supportive to me. One friend was a registered nurse name Claire who was in her fifties. She loved my daughter, had never had children of her own, and loved to baby-sit my daughter, who loved her, as I did. I did not lack for sitters whenever I had to fulfill a public speaking engagement or appear at government officials' offices for meetings or fulfill other obligations for MI-COVE or my paid work. I will always be grateful to all of these friends.

---

[26]Rabbi Joseph Telushkin. Jewish Literacy. NY. William Morrow & Co. 1991. p. 33.

I think that because of the stress of my husband's anger and hostility, my obstetrician said my physical condition was such that I could not have natural childbirth this time and would have to have the baby "by induced labor, by appointment." I was somewhat relieved as it meant that I would not have to suffer my husband in the labor and delivery room snarling hostile commands in my ear.

It was a big price to pay. I knew nothing about what "induced labor" involved. The doctor merely told me "not to worry," and as was the practice of the time, I trusted him, did not think I was entitled to more information and did not ask for it. Also, I was so relieved my husband had not succeeded in getting my child aborted, was under such stress with his hostility, that I just went along with what this doctor planned. I didn't want to do anything to jeopardize having my baby. I would have done anything to have my baby.

The drugs given to me to induce labor produced violent contractions. The pain was more than I thought I could bear. I did manage to survive, and was blessed with a beautiful baby boy. Because the doctor "put me out" when the baby was actually born, I did not get to know anything until I woke up sometime later in the recovery room. There, I learned I had given birth to a fine son. In spite of all the pain, not only the physical pain of the induced labor, but the emotional pain and resultant stress of my husband's abuse, this was the second happiest time of my life.

Because of my work and connections in the housing and urban renewal field, we were able to move to a two bedroom apartment in the ILGWU (International Ladies Garment Workers Union) housing development called Penn South in the Chelsea area of Manhattan. I was able to obtain this apartment through my consulting work. My father gave us the money for the down payment. It was a middle income cooperative, the same as I wanted to create with MI-COVE. I continued to work on bringing about the creation of the 'New Town in Town,' MI-COVE.

When Betty Friedan's book, The Feminine Mystique was published, a friend I'll call Flo (she later became one of the friends who helped me by loaning me money to pay the court when my husband declared bankruptcy and perpetrated yet another abuse on me and his children) called me to tell me about it: that I "must read it." The book changed my life. (I was able to thank Betty Friedan publicly for this at a banquet the Veteran Feminists of America gave to honor her a few years ago.)

I decided to go back to school to earn a doctorate. I believed that I would always have to work to support myself and my children, since my husband, after six years of marriage, two children, and a great deal of financial help from my father, and my heroic efforts to earn funds to sustain us was still unwilling to do so. I believed that with a doctorate I would be more sure of being able to support us financially.

One of my part time consulting jobs was to sociologist Max Wolf. He urged me to go back to school for my doctorate. He knew the Dean at the Graduate School of Public Administration (now the School of Public Affairs) at New York University and arranged an interview for me. Dean Rae Harvey was so impressed by my accomplishments that he said he did not have to wait for the results of my Graduate Record Exam for me to be accepted into the graduate program. I designed a course of study for an interdisciplinary degree which would satisfy my interest in psychology, sociology (especially creation of community), political science, public law, urban affairs, organization, and management, all fields with which I was involved at the time.

My first experience with overt sexual discrimination and sexual harassment, although the term was not yet known or yet a legal concept, was with a professor at NYU. He called me into his office to tell me my paper on public law was so good that he wanted to know how I was able to write it. He said that I was a "just a housewife," and housewives did not write such excellent papers, especially in a field like public law. I felt put-down by the term and how he spoke it. He went on to declare, "Your husband is a lawyer. Did he help you write it or write it for you?" I was outraged. Not only had my husband not written it, he knew nothing about the field. Further, he sabotaged my efforts to do well in graduate school, and even to go to school. I did not tell this professor anything about this. I believed that his harassment came about because this professor had asked me to have dinner with him before class one night, and 'made advances' to me and I rebuffed him. He had invited me to dinner, and I thought he was so impressed by my work in his class that he wanted to discuss the course with me. This sort of naiveté, fortunately or not, has never left me. I always tend to believe the best about people. I handled his 'come-on' (he was a married man) by telling him all about my husband and children, as usual making up how happily married I was, what a wonderful husband I had, that he was a "successful lawyer." Now, facing his put-down and accusation, I took special care to point out that my husband was a negligence lawyer, and that he knew nothing about public law.

After this meeting with this professor, whom I'll call Professor Como, I was able to persuade my husband to come to class with me. I was sure he did not come to help me out, but for whatever grandiosity of his own he was pursuing. We were able to find a baby-sitter, (my children were 6 and 4 1/2 at the time), and off we went to my class. After class, I introduced Professor Como to my husband, and he invited the two of us to dinner at The Cookery, a favorite haunt in Greenwich Village of faculty at NYU, and the former scene of what would these days be considered to be sexual harassment committed by Professor Como. At this dinner, Professor Como learned that my husband knew nothing about public law, that I had 'done my homework' and could discuss the course and my paper intelligently and with knowledge. Professor Como later became one of my greatest allies at the school, and I earned high marks in his class!

There were no other children for my children to play with at the ILGWU Penn South housing project where we lived. My daughter had attended public school for Kindergarten, but the few children who lived in Penn South attended private schools and she/we did not know them. When she entered first grade, we tried bussing both children to a private school (my son to nursery school) in Greenwich Village, but this was a logistical nightmare. A good education for my children was very important to me, and I wanted my children to attend good schools. I also wanted them to have friends where we lived and with whom they attended school. We moved to Scarsdale, in Westchester County, where they could attend the Edgemont schools which were considered in the top ten in the country. We sold the middle income co-op and my father gave us the additional money for a down payment on a modest house, and enough money to move and buy a used car. I found a four year old Mercedes Benz in mint condition for $2500. My husband, who was handling our finances, assured me that the mortgage payments and cost of commuting came to less than the cost of private school for the children and our costs in Penn South and that we could "easily swing it."

I completed two years of graduate school and was awarded a Masters Degree. I continued to work for my Ph.D. I was substitute teaching in the Scarsdale Junior High and High School and continued some part time consulting to help pay our expenses. I earned a scholarship, but I needed funds to pay baby sitters for the hours when I had to be working and at school and my children were not at school, and for my commute to New York University, as well as the cost of my books and supplies. I enrolled in the Graduate School of Arts and Science, and pursued the interdisciplinary course of study I had designed. I loved my classes, my professors, and had many friends at school. When our school needed a new Dean, I was elected to be the student to sit on the search committee.

During this period, my husband's emotional and verbal abuse continued. When my husband came home evenings, I thought he had been at work during the day. He always managed to start his tirades when he knew I had a test or a paper was due. Somehow, I managed to get A's and continued to be awarded scholarships. I was awarded my Ph.D., and I earned the Founder's Day Certificate from New York University for "....having achieved a place in the highest bracket of scholastic preferment recognized by the University.... a mark of special honor...."

When my father died, suddenly, my husband's abuse escalated. He disclosed to me when my father died, and after we had been married 13 years, that he expected to be "financially set" when he married me. He thought he had a "free ride." My father left me a five figure inheritance, which the IRS promptly seized because my husband, who I thought had been preparing our tax returns and paying our taxes, had, in fact, not done this. Again, he had been lying to me. He revealed to me that much of the time when I thought he was commuting to Manhattan to work, he was, in fact, unemployed. He said that he went into the city anyway. My husband had accumulated unpaid bills with stores where we bought such things as clothing for the children. He was supposed to be paying the bills. From the beginning of our marriage, he told me because he was a lawyer he would "handle our finances." I had no idea he was not paying our taxes and our bills. I did not know he was unemployed so much of the time.

After the IRS seized my inheritance to pay taxes that my husband, who was a lawyer, and whom I trusted to be handling our tax returns, had evaded, and I learned the truth, he declared bankruptcy. This triggered a court hearing about the court seizing his half ownership of our home and car and proposing to sell them to pay the outstanding bills. My husband had convinced me to put our home in our joint names "for tax purposes." The judge at the hearing allowed that, if I could come up with some $1500 for his share of the house and $750 for his share of the car, I could buy him out.

I was shocked at the proceedings. People appeared at the hearing to examine the car and to bid on his share of the house. I was aghast. Could someone actually buy his share and move in with us?! My husband had created a horrible nightmare, but I was fully awake, and testifying on a stand in court to save the now ten year old car I needed to buy groceries for my family, etc. Although the car was a Mercedes Benz, (which I purchased with misgivings because of where it was manufactured, and because my father did not approve) I had purchased it for $2500 six years before, when it was four years old, and had only 1500 miles on it, from an elderly lady who happened to be the sister of General Omar Bradley. It now had only 50,000 miles on it, and that many only because of our summer trips to Maine to see my parents. The car was considered a 'find' by people who valued Mercedes Benz motor cars, and there were many vultures ready to pounce on it. They came to the court hearing and looked the car over before entering the courtroom. The experience was a humiliating nightmare for me, a crowning one in the by-now 15 years of nightmares my husband had created. I had never been a party to a court case, had never had to appear in court. I had to sit on the stand and beg the judge not to put strangers in my home with me, not to take away the car, which was necessary for me to get to the A& P to buy groceries for my family, milk for my children, to do other errands, and for me to get to work.

The judge gave me a short time to come up with the funds. He wanted me to pay $1500 to buy my husband's share of the house. We had purchased the house for $48,500 with a $15,000 down payment my father gave us as a gift. With the 5 ¼ % mortgage, the payments and cost of commutation to Manhattan on the train for my husband came out to less than it cost us to live in Manhattan and send our children to private school. The judge wanted me to pay $750 to 'buy' my car. I was able to borrow the amount from friends, and was able to keep our home and car, which were then, thankfully, both legally put in my sole name. I also signed a written agreement with my friends to pay them back in a reasonable time. I managed to pay it all back back in full in the agreed on time. I had been brought up never to owe anyone money, to pay all bills on time in full. I was incredulous that my husband had done what he did. He also revealed to me that he had borrowed money from other people, which he still owed. I stopped short of believing that I had to pay back people from whom he had borrowed without my knowledge. I know that he declared bankruptcy again in the future. I do not know how many times he did this. He told me one "could do it every seven years." I now believe this man is an abuser in many ways: of his family, of his 'friends,' of his creditors, of the government.

My husband took all this out on me. He became even more abusive than he had been. One morning when I came down to breakfast, I had a glass of water in my hand. He was on one of his tirades and ran at me, smashing the glass into my hand. I had to have several stitches in my hand, as he did.

I realized that I had to get out of this marriage. I called my sister Ronnie, who now lived in Massachusetts, to talk it over with her, as I had done many times before. Once again, my sister deterred me from this goal. She urged me to stay with Mort because my children were still young (they were 13 and 11 when this particular nightmare occurred). She told me that she did not see any way I could make it financially with two children on my own - my father was gone and not able to help me now - and that my children certainly would not be able to continue in their schools and graduate if I broke up the marriage. She pressured me to finish my dissertation as soon as possible, and to earn my doctoral degree as soon as possible, so I could get a better job and ensure my children's education. I wanted to be sure they would be able to stay in their schools and graduate from high school where we lived. I thought this would give them the best chance of going to a good college, of having a good start in life. My sister convinced me that I should stay with my husband until both my children were off to college. Somehow, I managed to do it.

MY INTRODUCTION TO FEMINISM and GROWING INDEPENDENCE

What gave me enormous help was the Feminist movement, of which I had become a part very early in its activities. I got into a National Organization for Women "consciousness raising group" and the women in it were very supportive of one another. I also became the first co-chair of the Manhattan Chapter of the National Organization for Women Psychology Committee, where I began lecturing and appearing on panels with police officers and others about such things as 'domestic violence.' I learned enough about domestic violence to be able to tell my husband that I would report him to the police if he ever attacked me again. I coined the term "battering men," and still refuse to talk about "battered women," a term which puts the focus on women, as if they are the cause of battering and not the battering men. My new knowledge and resultant strength, and probably, more important, my vow to report him if he ever hit me again seemed to put the brakes on Mort's physical abuse.

A year after my husband's declaration of bankruptcy, I was awarded my doctorate and obtained a position as Adjunct Assistant Professor at Hunter College, City University of New York, in Manhattan. I took training in Rogerian and other psychotherapy modalities, and I opened a private practice. I began lecturing at the Association for Humanistic Psychology conferences and other venues. The Hunter Junior High School Guidance Department hired me to do a training for their faculty and staff because the school was going co-ed, and they wanted me to prepare them for this change. They were so impressed with my ideas and my work, that they started referring families of students to me for counseling, and my practice was off to a running start. I was able to make enough money to keep us in our home by taking another temporary adjunct position at Mercy College, a temporary Research Associate position at Columbia University, along with my position at Hunter College, my private practice, and working summer sessions at Hunter College. For awhile, I was working four jobs, going off in several different directions to work, by train and subway and by car.

In order for me to work in the summer, my children attended summer camps. I also sent them to several different camps, including specialty camps to pursue their interests: my son to science camp, and my daughter to a ballet camp, and to one where she could act in plays and learn to play the guitar, which were two of her favorite interests. I was able to obtain a scholarship for my daughter to one such camp, a camp operated by the Federation of Jewish Philanthropies, Surprise Lake. There, she had a role in a production of "Fiddler of the Roof."

Surprise Lake Camp reminded me of Camp Lown, a Jewish camp in Oakland, Maine, which I attended when I was 13 years of age and of which I have the fondest memories. We made up our camp song, called "Our Camp Lown" to the melody from George Gershwin's "Rhapsody in Blue," and I can sing the words to this day. One not-so-fond memory I have of Camp Lown is coming home to our cabin one night with my bunk mates, and walking in to find all our cots pushed into the center of the room. When we tried to get into our beds, we found that, not only had they been "pied," the sheets arranged so that you could not put your legs into them, but also that snakes had been put into them. We all screamed and ran out. We found out that the senior boys (we were the senior girls) had done this prank. A "memento" I have from this prank is a tiny scar, now practically invisible, on my left knee. When I walked into the cabin in the dark (the boys had removed the light bulb), I walked smack into the cot in the middle of the floor, and cut my knee on the metal.

. My daughter attended Mountain Lakes camp where she lived in a tent as I did at ten years of age, when I went to Girl Scout camp, Camp Natarswi, in Millinocket, Maine. I have fond memories of Camp Natarswi. We lived in tents on a lake, hiked, climbed Mt. Katahdin, walked across Knife's Edge, went on overnight canoe trips, slept in sleeping bags, and went skinny dipping in clear, freezing cold, pristine lakes. To this day, one of my fondest past times is to go hiking. One of my favorite hiking places is at Mohonk Mountain House, a beautiful castle designated as a historic landmark on ten thousand acres at the top of the Shawangunk foothills of the Catskill Mountains. I credit Camp Natarswi with giving me much of my adventurous spirit, my love of travel, exploring new landscapes, countries. My daughter loved Mountain Lakes Camp. She made friends there with children of other races, ethnic backgrounds, and religions, something I was not able to do until I went to college.

Charlotte Schwab

By the time I was married to Mort for 17 years, I had learned a great deal about sexism and male violence toward women. I also learned a lot about feminism and the importance of equal rights for women. I was a member of the committee to create a Women's Studies Program at Hunter College, helped fight it through to establish the first Women's Studies program in any college in the City University of New York. I designed and taught the first courses there in feminist psychology. I called my course "Woman: Self and Identity." This title was the only way the Social Science curriculum committee would pass it. The male member who was chair of the Psychology Department refused to acknowledge that "feminist psychology" was any different from psychology as it was already being taught, and he refused to agree that I could call the course "Female Psychology." I thought of the title at a curriculum committee meeting, and asked him if he would approve the course with that title. After he chewed on his cigar a while, he, reluctantly, agreed. I also created and taught "Women and Social Change" and other feminist courses. In addition, I taught a course in "Marriage and the Family," and a course in "Sociology of Sex Roles." I was asked to teach graduate social work courses, including, "Deviant Behavior and Social Control." I titled the syllabus of the course, "Socially Stigmatized Behavior." The knowledge I gained from this study and teaching convinced me that not just women, but men, too, needed "consciousness raising;" that we all needed re-education, re-socialization. I learned that the social psychology term "socialization" meant, "the process by which, in the interaction with significant others, we learn a sense of self and self identity." I was convinced that women and men were learning a sense of self that was sexist, and was damaging to both women and men, that sexist conditioning led to violence toward women, and that there were many forms of violence toward women in our society that were damaging to both men and women. I wanted to create a center where women and men could be educated, supported, re-socialized, re-nurtured to learn a nonsexist sense of self and self identity and where both could learn to be both tender and strong, to oneself and to each other, and, where men, especially, could learn that "Tenderness is Strength."[27]

---

[27]Harold C. Lyon, Jr. Tenderness is Strength: From Machismo to Manhood. New York. Harper & Row. 1977.

I attempted to bring all of my new knowledge and awareness to my husband. I asked him to go to a men's consciousness raising group, to join NOW, in which there were men members as well as women. He refused. I asked him to read the books I was reading. I presented at a "Conference on Men and the Male Sex Role" at a college in New Jersey, and I asked him to attend. He refused to do anything I asked. He adopted a stance that he was "already a feminist" and was "above" any man who wasn't. I continued on a path of denial, and professed to others that, indeed, my husband was a feminist, was very supportive of my work, that we were egalitarian partners. People seemed to believe me. This was far from the truth. Although we had settled into a sort of peace with regard to physical abuse, my husband was still verbally and emotionally abusive. He was unable, or unwilling, to be loving, affectionate. He still did not earn anywhere near his share financially, especially considering that he was a lawyer. All of this was very difficult for me. Ironically, I was by then considered to be an expert on "How to Effect an Egalitarian Marriage," a seminar I created and presented and which helped many women and men to marry, make their marriages 'work.' Yet, my own private life was a nightmare.

I did what Freud would probably have called "sublimate" my desire for a loving, affectionate, communicative, sharing husband, and my sexual desires. I threw myself into my work. I founded The Feminist Center for Human Growth and Development, a feminist therapy training center. By doing the research and training to found The Feminist Center for Human Growth and Development, and, particularly by leading it as Executive Director, I learned a great deal more about how egalitarian relationships should function. I brought my knowledge about overcoming sex role stereotyping and raising one's self esteem to become a "whole" woman or man, which I had first developed by studying and teaching at Hunter College, to trainees who wanted to become nonsexist and/or feminist therapists, and to a clientele in private individual, couples, family, or group therapy who wanted to establish active loving, egalitarian relationships. I developed and taught a workshop called, "Love is and Active Verb." One of my most successful workshops was "How to Effect an Egalitarian Marriage." I helped many couples to create happy, successful, egalitarian marriages. I also helped many women

41

to find suitable, loving husbands and then helped them both to make the marriage 'work.' I helped many women who came to me for help with "miserable" marriages to improve their marriages (when their husbands also agreed to come for help) to both their satisfaction. I went to many wedding ceremonies as an honored guest, and many of my couples have credited me with the children they have had, either biologically or by adoption, and the happy family life they enjoy. All of this was extremely gratifying to me. I felt very privileged to be able to help so many people. This work sustained me.

I developed and led the training program for the trainees at The Feminist Center, managing a part time staff which sometimes grew to 34 people. I developed many seminars and workshops for our clientele. I brought in many guest seminar leaders. I led the center to a point where we conducted 22 seminars or workshops in one semester, and served a large clientele, pro bono, or paying a small fee, and some who paid a reasonable fee for the services. We wanted to open our services to women (and men, couples, and families) who were not able to afford the price of traditional therapy, as well as to those who did not want traditional therapies. One of the seminars I developed identified some 180 different theories and therapy methodologies, none of them nonsexist or feminist. We were the first psychotherapy center in New York offering nonsexist and feminist psychotherapy and training for those who wanted to become nonsexist and/or feminist psychotherapists. We were also pioneers of the "holistic" and alternative health movements, and offered services and workshops in many innovative modalities. We called ourselves a nonsexist, feminist, holistic center, another first. We had alternative healers (to traditional medicine) on our staff, including a chiropractor, a nutritionist, and others.

We attracted a prestigious Board of Directors to the Center, and volunteers to staff the offices. We endeavored to raise enough funds to continue to offer pro bono or low cost nonsexist and feminist counseling to those in financial need, as well as to those who could afford to pay. We wanted no difference in service between the two populations, and we wanted them all to be able to come to pleasant, well furnished, comfortable offices in a beautiful, safe neighborhood. We opened an office near Hunter College on the Upper East Side of New York to be near my own separate psychotherapy office and because I was an Assistant Professor at Hunter College. Then, because we needed much larger space, we relocated to a prestigious hotel in the Murray Hill section of Manhattan, an old, quiet, residential neighborhood in the East 30's, taking a suite on the first floor which contained 2,000 square feet of space, divided into a large group and seminar room; a large office, which served as my private office and another group room when we needed two, and the training room; several smaller consultation rooms; a storage room, with room for staff mailboxes; two lavatories; and a large reception/waiting area.

I learned about "direct mail," and built the Center by sending brochures to subscribers of such publications as Ms. Magazine who lived in areas convenient to the Center. Our peak mailing consisted of 10,000 brochures. During this time, I also kept my private practice. I gave up the adjunct positions to focus on the Center. I was doing a great deal of public speaking on feminist therapy and related topics, and I wrote a column for a feminist journal called Majority Report. The column was called, "Feminism and Therapy." This work was quite courageous for its time. We were pioneers in the field of feminist therapy. All this work was giving me enough knowledge and strength to begin moving toward separating from my husband. In addition to all this work, I was, of course, raising my children (who were then teenagers), keeping a large home, and commuting from the suburbs. I accomplished all this while feeling like I was single, a single mother, although I was married, by now, twenty years.

During this time, I studied assertiveness, and communication and negotiation skills. I developed a process which I called "Positive Self Identity and Assertiveness," and models and processes for communication skills, which I called "VECAM tm."[28] I also developed a process for negotiation skills for male/female relationships which I called "Gender Negotiations tm" (also known as GN tm.) I trademarked both these processes. I taught assertiveness, communication skills and "Gender Negotiations tm" to individuals, couples, in groups, and in seminars and workshops. There is a proverb that, "We teach the things we have to learn." It certainly seemed that

---

[28]VECAM tm is an acronym standing for "Validate, Express, Communicate, Assert, Motivate." It is the foundation of a communication and negotiation process (GN tm) I created, wrote articles about, and have taught for many years to individuals, couples, in groups, and at workshops and seminars. Two of these articles appeared in Contract magazine.

way to me. I learned and taught the skills I needed in my own life, but which I could not effect in my marriage, because my husband refused. I was considered an expert in these areas and sought out by people and companies to teach them, to train them in assertiveness, communication and negotiation skills.

For a brochure I published about some of my work, Richard H. Raboy, Executive Vice President of Epstein, Raboy Advertising, Inc. wrote that, "The communication techniques Charlotte Schwab taught me have affected - in a very positive way - both my social and business relationships....Dr. Schwab has made people in my company more successful communicators.... She teaches effective, positive communication." Hillary Gal, a vice president of a financial corporation wrote, "I learned to empower myself professionally and personally." Connie Cohrt, CLU, PCP, at Penn Mutual Insurance Company wrote, ".... Amazed!.... Qualified, sales production club.... reached my other goals...."

I had become assertive with my husband in our private life, brought my communication skills to my marriage. But, communication takes two. He was still *not a husband* in the important ways: no affection, no communication, not carrying any reasonable share of the financial burden of raising two children and maintaining a home. He was still "withholding," including sexually. We had no sex life.

Mort was still emotionally and verbally abusive to me in private. He took care never to behave this way in front of others, and people still thought we had an ideal marriage. I did not leave what was in reality an abusive marriage because I wanted to keep the family intact until my children had gone off to college and I accomplished that.

Amazingly, for the last years of my marriage (as well as all through my second marriage to my rabbi/husband), suffering all the abuse I did, I was able to achieve all my accomplishments, including seeing clients in therapy and helping them enormously. I was determined to help other women not to make bad marriages, or to help those already in unhappy marriages to help their husbands participate in making their marriages happy. I helped many single women to marry, couples to make their marriages work, families with teenage children to learn communication and negotiation skills, and positive, active loving. I taught them that, "Love is an active verb." I taught men that "tenderness is strength," and women that it is OK to be strong; that strong and gentle are important characteristics for both men and women; helped men to be verbally expressive, affectionate, tender, and both women and men to be strong emotionally. I taught these concepts and skills long before the Mars / Venus books appeared about the differences between men and women. I taught them to acknowledge those differences, speak about them, honor them, celebrate them. In my seminars on gender differences, I taught communication and negotiation skills, utilized my trademarked processes of VECAM tm and GENDER NEGOTIATIONS tm. taught men and women to understand each other, how to act in a positive manner, to *be* positive, active, loving partners.

I saw, realized that I could teach and support others *who wanted to* to create healthy, loving, happy relationships, marriages, families. I was very strong with these clients, especially strong with the men. I was the opposite of naive and was able to tell it like it was with them, not taking any guff. I told men who disclosed to me that they were unfaithful to their wives that unless they were willing to stop it, I would not, could not help them. I told them telling the truth in marriage was one of the most important requisites if not the basic requisite. I believe as a result of this work helping others, I became able to stand up to my husband, although he was not willing to do his part to create a loving, happy, healthy marriage. He was not a loving, happy, healthy man. At last count, it takes two. I was gratified by helping these women and men, and by the number of women and men I helped to make good marriages. This work, somehow, made up for the abuse by my husband, bad marriage to a husband who did not want to change. I was focused on helping others.

Most of my clients have remained my friends to this day. Recently, before I moved from New York to Florida, a couple whom I helped to marry, make their marriage work, and adopt a beautiful baby son, invited me to lunch with their now 9 year old son. They are a loving, close, beautiful, happy family. They thank me to this day, and express love to me to this day. I gave them and many, many clients unconditional love, caring, support, and education. I feel very privileged and grateful for having helped them and all the people I have helped. I am extremely proud of the work I have done with people to help them make their lives positive, loving, honest, happy. This work and the results I saw with the people I helped, seeing that I could teach and support others who wanted to, to create healthy, loving, happy relationships, marriages, experiencing my strength with male clients, teaching women clients to be strong, being the opposite of naive, telling it like it was with male clients, not being taken in by any cons from them, and some of them did try to con me, reinforced for me that if I had a loving, willing, honest partner, I could do the same in my own marriage.

One of the other things in my private life that helped me to deal with my husband's abuse and become strong was that I changed our sleeping arrangements, replacing our double bed with two beds. One of his favorite abuses had become to twist my arms until I cried when we were in bed. Now, perhaps because we were sleeping separately, he stopped doing this. This change in sleeping arrangements also made the symbolic statement that we did not, would not make love, which took a lot of pressure off both of us. I settled into a life of conscious celibacy. I do not know what he did. I suspected, as I do to this day that he is gay (a term I never liked; my husband was hardly a gay human being). Once, after we were divorced and I had occasion to be in his presence where no one could overhear, I quietly intimated this to him. He became hostile, angry, almost to the point of violence, controlling himself because others could see him, snarling that I was "maligning" him. The sheer force of his reaction reinforced my belief. If this is true, and he never acknowledged this to himself, I am sad for him. In any case, I am sorry for him for what I see as the waste he made of his life. He revealed to me after we separated that he was very unhappy alone, and hoped to get back together with me, and that because of this hope, he went to a therapist who provided him with a young woman in her twenties hired as a "surrogate lover" to teach him to function sexually. It was unsuccessful. He was 52 years of age at the time.

At about this time, I began to feel that my husband was an albatross around my neck, that he was a burden on my back. I told him to "get off my back." Shortly after that statement, I wound up in the hospital in traction for herniated discs. Several orthopedic surgeons whom I consulted all told me that if I did not have a double laminectomy (back surgery), I "would be paralyzed." I continued to seek other help. I found a celebrated surgeon who, in his '70's, no longer performed surgery. He followed the protocol of traction, which he said was more effective and did not leave one with the possibility of damage from surgery. I spent one month in the hospital flat on my back with 14 pounds of traction. All during the month, I saw my therapy clients while flat on my back. I was fortunate to have a private room. The nurse would put a sign on the door which a client had made, "DOCTOR IN SESSION: DO NOT DISTURB." I spent 50 minutes helping my clients. I also held supervision and training groups for students of The Feminist Center, and functioned as Executive director of the Center from my hospital bed. The month, while difficult physically, proved to be a rest from my husband.

I left the hospital to go to a rental apartment in Manhattan for three months. My niece Joni, who was 26 years of age, came from California to live with me. She wanted to pursue a career in New York. We had a wonderful time together. I took a one bedroom apartment where I continued seeing my clients, functioning as Executive Director of the Center, supervising and training students, and began going for physical therapy treatment at New York Hospital. Also, at this time, I pursued study of alternative and holistic medicine and nutrition. One of the members of my staff at the Center was a chiropractor. I began treatment with him.

All this served to keep me apart from my husband most of the time, which, I believe was the best 'therapy' I had. He was living in Scarsdale in our home. I don't know how he spent his time. My daughter was a freshman at college. My son had completed all his high school requirements and, at 16 years of age had taken early admission to college. I was learning a great deal about alternative and holistic medicine, and I suspected that my belief that my husband was "on my back" was a strong component to my back problems. I recently read a book[29] which confirmed this belief.

After both my children were in college, I asked Mort for a separation. I now had no reason to remain in this abusive marriage. My children were no longer at home. I had remained in the marriage long enough to see them both through high school. Both my parents were now dead so I no longer had to fear upsetting them by the prospect of my getting a divorce; my sister Ronnie had moved to California, so I had no one pressuring me to remain in the marriage. I

---

[29]Barbara Hoberman Levine. Your Body Believes Every Word You Say. Fairfield, CT. Wordswork Press. 2000.

realized that, were I to continue to put up with my husband's abuse, the "body" that my sister kept urging me it was important to have in the house, might be my dead one instead of my husband's unhelpful, abusive one. I chose life.[30]

My daughter was very supportive of the separation. She had become a feminist herself, founding a feminist club when she was 13 years of age at her junior high school which she called SHE (Students for Human Equality.) I had taken her with me to Association for Humanistic Psychology conferences and to the International Women's Year conference in Albany, NY in 1977 where I was Co-commissioner for Mental Health and gave a speech. She was/is very proud of me, as I was, and am of her. She went on to write her college senior thesis on a feminist critique of Fritz Perls and Gestalt therapy. She quoted my work in her thesis, which made me very proud. Before leaving for her senior year in college, she spent two weeks with me in Easthampton, Long Island, urging me to take the steps necessary to split from my husband, her father.

---

[30]Deuteronomy 30:15 "I have set before thee life and death, the blessing and the curse; therefore choose life, that thou mayest live, thou and thy seed." I was afraid that my children would become negative, like Mort, and learn to accept abuse or be abusive from the example set by their father, because men are more powerful in society, and were especially so when my children were growing up in the '60's and early '70's, and especially because they were well aware of his abuse of me. Only once did my husband hit my son (to my knowledge.) When I found out about it, I told him that if he ever touched my son again I would report him to the police. I regretted that I had not been able to leave my husband before my children had the experience of growing up in an abusive home. I had been convinced by my sister that they would never "make it" if I divorced while they were still at home.

FREEDOM

Mort came out to Easthampton, uninvited. I reminded him I had gone there for a month to get away from him and his abusiveness. I told him I wanted a separation. I asked him if he would be moved out of our Manhattan apartment when I returned after Labor Day, or if he wanted me to move. The previous year, I decided to sell my home and move to a "convertible" three bedroom apartment in Manhattan so I would no longer have to commute to work, but so my children could come home if they wished on school holidays. He tried convincing me to change my mind about the separation. He promised that he would go to a therapist, and that, this time, he would stick with it. I was resolute. I said that if he would not be moved out, that I would find another place to live. I did not know how I could carry the rent on the large apartment, anyway, for too long. Finally, he said he would move out before I returned. He also said that he would prove to me that he could, would be a good husband. He would go to a therapist, and work towards our getting back together. He promised to pay the rent on the apartment so that I would not have to move, and because he was hoping to return. In fact, when I later insisted we get a legal separation, he signed an agreement to pay alimony to me for the rest of my life of $450 a week or 40% of his income, whichever was greater. He does not honor that legal agreement.

I was married almost 24 years. I had put up with his abuse for almost a quarter of a century. My children were out of the house and on their way to their own lives. I had had the courage to sell my house and take an apartment in New York. I no longer had to commute. I no longer had children at home to look after. I was now on my own physically. I felt I was on my own emotionally and financially and in other ways during my marriage. Mort had not only not been a financial "provider," which he had promised he would be, which women of my generation were led to expect by marriage, he did not pull anywhere near his weight financially in the marriage, relying on my father, and then on me to support us. At the time we separated, he was still not earning a 'living.'

I felt an enormous relief not to keep up the 'front' of having a loving marriage while living with a man who was distant, withholding, and uncontributing at best and abusive at worst. I knew I

49

had lived a lie for many years. I felt free, strong, happy, and looked forward with joyous anticipation to an independent life of meaningful productivity and pleasure not marred by constantly dealing with abuse from my husband. I felt very optimistic about my life. I was 48 years of age. I also looked forward to returning to Judaism, to my Jewish spiritual roots.

I regret that I married my first husband, that my children had, have the biological, abusive father they had, have, and that they suffered the effects of his abuse of me and, of course, of them. I regret that I stayed with him for as long as I did, did not see any way out for so many years. But, "coulda, shoulda, woulda, what if, if only," does not count. I now do everything I can with the knowledge I have gained, to live my life so that I will not have any more "couldas, shouldas, wouldas, what ifs, if onlys." However, I believe that because I went through what I did, I was able to help others, and to write this book.

In Judaism there is a concept called, "*gam zu la tova*," Hebrew for "this, too is good." What it means is that we may not be able to see at the time of suffering, of the perpetration of evil, that there may be a good purpose for our suffering. That the pain and suffering may be an impetus for a contribution we may make to *tikkun olam*. While this doesn't justify what Mort did, I believe this about what I went through with Mort.

Many years later, after we had been separated and divorced for fifteen years, and after I had married and divorced my rabbi/husband, Mort turned to me for my help when he was in a hospital he considered inadequate in Brooklyn, New York. He was taken there by ambulance after having a heart attack on the subway on his way to a court appearance for one of his clients. He conceded that I probably saved his life then, and, again, when he had two subsequent heart problems over a three year period. I arranged for him to be taken from the Brooklyn hospital by ambulance to Mt. Sinai Hospital in Manhattan, considered a top hospital for cardiac care, and found him one of the best cardiologists in Manhattan.

I saw him through three angioplasties over three years, visiting him every day in the hospital and tending him in the recovery room after these procedures. For a period of time afterwards, I told him to call me every night to be sure he was OK, and if I were not at home, to leave a message on my answering machine. Mort requested that I spend each Sunday I was not out of town or did not have other plans, walking around Manhattan or driving to the country to walk with him He said he would curb his abusiveness if I would do this. I agreed. But, he gradually returned to his abusive self, and I ended the arrangement.

Before I stopped seeing him on Sundays, Mort gave me a signed a legal agreement to pay the money he owed me from the divorce settlement and for my inheritance from my father taken by the IRS, as well as for money he borrowed from me after our legal separation. He boasted to me repeatedly that after our divorce, he started making "barrels" of money as a negligence attorney, and that he would pay me weekly toward what he owed me, because I needed this money after what my rabbi/husband had put me through. He said he would not pay me because I stopped seeing him on Sundays. I stopped because he had returned full time to his hostile, abusive self.

When I called and I asked him for the money he owed me, or, at least to go back to the payments he sent me for awhile, that I really needed it, he was his old, true self. He snarled, "Get a lawyer." It was the same tone of voice, the same hateful, hostile, menacing snarl he had used when I was giving birth to our daughter, the same snarl he had hissed at me for years and years. It echoed in my ear until I finally did "get a lawyer." The judge, after a court hearing, awarded me a large sum of money. Ironically, after our divorce, it was true that Mort had established a law practice and earned a great deal of money. To this day, he has not paid me what the judge ordered him to pay. At the last hearing, the judge, who happened to be a female judge, said he was "looking at jail time" if he did not pay. He arrogantly thumbed his nose at me on the street after the hearing.

THE SEEDS ARE SOWN FOR MY SECOND MARRIAGE

The day after my daughter left Easthampton, where we had had a wonderful 'alone' mother/daughter time, to return to her senior year at college, I met the rabbi who was to become my second husband. Jon walked into my life when the last thing I wanted was to enter another relationship.

I wanted to be truly on my own. I wanted a peaceful home. I wanted to do what I wanted at home and away from home, when I wanted to, without fear of abuse. One of the first things I did was to go to a Friday night service at the Easthampton Jewish Center to say *Kaddish* for my mother. She had been dead for one year. My father had died ten years earlier. My father had not lived to see my children become a *Bat* and *Bar Mitzvah*. It was a special joy to me that my daughter asked the rabbi of the synagogue for permission to have me pass the *Torah* to her, not her father. Since this had never been done before the rabbi said he had to take it before the board. The board agreed, and I had the special joy of passing the *Torah* to my daughter, and the distinction of being the first mother to do this at the Westchester Reform Temple.

After my son's *Bar Mitzvah* I had not kept any connection with organized Judaism. My husband had no interest in Judaism. I could have gone to synagogue alone, but I worked so many and such late hours, and had so much commuting to do in so many different directions, that to go to synagogue seemed an impossibility. I also believe that I was not able to attend *SHABBAT* services because I was afraid of not being able to keep the secret about my husband's abusiveness if I were to go.[31]

I now had one month of vacation, one month of freedom. My husband was in Manhattan. I felt totally removed from him for the first time in 24 years. I knew I would never go back to living with him and his abusiveness.

---

[31]Marcia Cohn Spiegel. "No More Secrets," in Rachel Josefowitz Siegel, Ellen Cole, & Susan Steinberg, eds. <u>Jewish Mothers Tell Their Stories: Acts of Love and Courage</u>. New York. The Haworth Press. 2000.

Friday, a friend, who was also renting a house in the Hamptons, invited me to go out to hear a new singer. I had seen a listing in the local paper for *SHABBAT* services at the Easthampton Jewish Center. I asked her if I could meet her after I attended services there, as she had no interest in going. We made plans to meet at a restaurant called The Palm after the service.

I found the service very enjoyable. Jon H_____ was the guest rabbi. He was also an invested cantor, and had a beautiful tenor voice. He gave a sermon about liturgy. He illustrated his points with recordings of famous cantors singing the liturgy, or sang himself. He played guitar to accompany himself. I went up to him at the *Oneg SHABBAT* after the service and complimented him on his knowledge and presentation. He told me he was the Dean of the School of Sacred Music at Hebrew Union College in Manhattan, the seminary that trains Reform rabbis and cantors. I asked him if he knew a particular *Yiddish* song, a melody which my mother sang to me as a child, called, *"Maidele, maidele zing mir a lidele"* (little girl, little girl, sing me a song). He did, and sang it for me. I was delighted. I had sung the melody to my daughter when she was a small child, but I had not heard the song sung by anyone else since my mother sang it to me.

Rabbi H asked me to go to a party with him. I declined and apologized, saying I had to leave to meet my friend. I was surprised at the invitation. First of all he was/is a rabbi, and I had never thought of rabbis dating. All the rabbis I ever knew were married. Also, he was clearly much younger than I, and at that time, it was very uncommon for older women to date younger men. It is still not very common, although it occurs somewhat more frequently. I left, and thought nothing further about it or him. The next day, I returned from spending a rainy day at a spa in Montauk. I was carrying my groceries of fresh fish, and freshly picked corn on the cob and vegetables into the house. I planned to cook and enjoy my dinner before leaving to meet my friend to hear Dave Brubeck at an outdoor concert on the lawn next to The Jewish Center. The telephone was ringing 'off the hook.' I put down my groceries and picked up the phone to hear a man's voice saying, "I have been calling you every hour all day. My friends want to know what the emergency is, as I am spending the day with them at their country club." "Who is this?" I asked, not recognizing his voice. "Jon," he said. "Jon who?" still not recognizing him. "Jon H, the rabbi you met last night." "Oh, rabbi. What can I do for you, rabbi?" I asked. "You can have dinner with me tonight." Surprised, I responded, "Oh, thank you, but I can't. I am just about to fix my dinner and then rush off to meet my friend to go to a concert." "Please, would you cancel it?" he begged. "I only have tonight out here, and I so much want to have dinner with you. Please." He kept insisting that he just had to have dinner with me; that this would be his only opportunity. He exhorted me to come to the synagogue for the *Havdalah* service because he had planned something "special" for me.

He was so persistent that I told him that I would call my friend and ask her if she would come to the service with me. When I called Roz, she told me to "go alone to the synagogue and with the rabbi for dinner. It would be a nice thing to do." She would go to the concert with other friends who were to join us. So, fatefully, I went. Little did I know that it would again ultimately prove to be that I was a 'lamb to the slaughter.'

I thought I was doing a *mitzvah*, a good deed, for this rabbi. At the service, Jon sang the entire *Yiddish* melody I had asked him about that my mother used to sing to me when I was a child. He was charming, outgoing. He offered to take me anywhere I wanted for dinner. I wondered how he would accomplish that since Easthampton restaurants were booked solid far in advance for Saturday nights. He charmed his way into a lovely restaurant on the water. We had a delicious dinner. Jon was quite flirtatious. It was a long time since I had been with a man who was attentive, complimentary, interested in me as a woman. He said he wanted to date me.

I informed him I was just getting out of an abusive 24 year marriage and was not ready for any relationship. He was totally understanding and asked if we could be just be "friends." I agreed. Since I had driven my car to the synagogue, and we took both cars to the restaurant, Jon left from there to drive back to the city so he could officiate at a wedding the next morning.

As soon as he could after the wedding ceremony, Jon called me. He repeated that he wanted to date me when I got back to New York. I reiterated that I was not ready for any relationship and that I needed to be legally free of my marriage before I would date. Again, he agreed to be "friends."

After Jon agreed to be "friends," we saw each other once a week for a Dutch treat dinner. He also called me several times a week and mailed me articles and other things about Judaism, feminism, psychology, and music which he knew would interest me. I had known him several months when Jon proposed that I be the Keynote Speaker at the Senior Colloquium at Hebrew Union College. The idea was accepted, and I gave the Keynote Address, "Sexist Language in the Liturgy and Its Psychologically Damaging Effects." My lecture was well received, even by the most senior rabbi on the faculty, a man in his eighties. He spoke up during the question period to say that, "There is no gender in the Five Books of Moses regarding God." When the Reform prayer books were changed to be unbiased with regard to gender, people at HUC told me that my Keynote Address had sown the seeds for this to happen. I was immensely gratified and grateful that I had played whatever part I had in the change.

As a result of my giving the Keynote Address at the Senior Colloquium, Cantor Norman Bellink asked me to teach a senior seminar at Hebrew Union College on "Self Identity, Self Esteem, Communication and Negotiation." He said this training was badly needed. As a result of my teaching this class, several cantorial and rabbinic students asked me to help them negotiate the salary and perks for their new positions. I was credited with helping to raise what were considered inadequate salaries and increase perks in many instances. I was happy to be of service to them.

One week, Jon suggested that I meet him at Central Synagogue for the Friday night *SHABBAT* service and to go to dinner afterward. At the restaurant, which had a pianist, he got up, tipped the pianist, and sang to me. It was a love song, called "Cuando Caliente El Sol." He sang it to me in Spanish and English. The English version was called, "Love Me With All Your Heart." It was to become one of the songs he sang often to me, and he sang often to me, in public places, and at home. I loved his voice, and, whenever he sang to me, I always smiled radiantly at him. He loved the reception I gave him when he sang, and couldn't sing to me often enough. Other songs that became our favorites included "One Alone" from The Desert Song, a musical we saw performed by a light opera company in Manhattan, and "My One and Only" from the Broadway show we enjoyed. All the songs he chose to sing just to me were love songs, most expressing that I was his "one alone," his "one and only."

By this time, we had been friends for almost four months. He called me on the telephone almost every day, and we shared a Dutch treat dinner once a week. That night, it was freezing in New York. We could not find a taxi, and had to walk the twenty city blocks to my home. When we got there, both shivering, I invited him up for hot tea. He told me he wanted to warm me/us up in a different way: that he loved me and he wanted to make love to/with me.

I reminded him that although I was in the process of obtaining a divorce, was legally separated, and that I had not lived with my husband since he moved out, before I would take our relationship to that level, I wanted to know that he would be monogamous, and that then we could see where we decided to take our love for one another. I asked him to agree that if either one of us decided not to continue the relationship, or to be with someone else, we would let the other know. He assured me that he agreed with me. We embarked on an exciting, loving, growing relationship.

ROCKY ROAD TO MARRIAGE TO JON

The first time Jon asked me to marry him, I had two reasons for hesitating. The first was that he had never had any children of his own. I thought that one day he might want to have children. I had two grown children from my first marriage, and did not want to raise any more. The second reason was that he was more than eleven years younger than I. I actually looked the same age as he when we met; some people even thought he was older than I. This was true all through our marriage. I remained looking young, and people were very surprised to find out I was older than he, and especially how much older. I think the combination of nutrition, exercise, attitude, and my genes afforded me looking so young.

Jon proposed to me after we had known each other for one year. He called and asked me to fly to California where he had gone for the cantorial convention. He wanted me to spend the rest of his month's vacation traveling with him up the coast. I told him I could not take the time off from my practice, that this was July, and that I always planned a month off in August. He called me every day from California wherever he was on his drive up the coast, and continued to ask me to join him. He imparted to me that the trip was proving so wonderful, the scenery was so gorgeous, he wanted to share it with me, that he missed me very much. I maintained I could not join him.

He called again to advise me he would cut his trip short, that he would fly to Chicago to stay at his mother's, and that he had asked his mother to invite me to come there. He declared that this was halfway across the country, not all the way across, as California was, and "would I meet him half way." I wanted a few days to think it over.

I talked it over with friends. They thought that he probably wanted to propose to me and wanted me to meet his family for this reason. I was not sure I would accept his proposal if this were true. However, I decided to be open to the possibility, to meet his family and see how I felt. I flew to Chicago. It was my first trip there. His mother, while polite and hospitable, was not overjoyed to meet me. He explained to me it was because of our age difference, to give her a chance, and she would grow to love me as he did. He showed me "his kind of town," Chicago. He loved Chicago. He took me to the museum, to concerts, to the top of the Sears tower, to all the sights. He wanted to take me to an especially romantic place, away from Chicago, for a few days. It was a lake resort in Wisconsin. There, he asked me to marry him. While I did not consent, we continued to see each other when we returned to New York. The love we shared was so strong that neither of us was ever able to stick very long to the decision to break it off. And we did break up, each year for the three years we were together before our marriage.

Jon proposed marriage again when we were on another trip to Chicago. In our room in the Drake Hotel, with his mother on her way to meet us for lunch, he disclosed to me that he had "gone to some prostitutes." I was shocked, horrified. I announced that I would not marry him unless we went to a psychiatrist whom I would be able to check out and trust, and that I got assurance from this therapist that this was not a serious problem, and that he would never do it again. He agreed to do this upon our return to New York. His mother, by this time, had grown to love me. The next day, she asked me after breakfast at her home why I was not marrying her son. I had been very good to her, very close to her, even though we lived so far apart. I asked him to tell his mother that it was because he had gone to some prostitutes, and that I was concerned and wanted to be sure this was not an unbreakable pattern. He blurted out abruptly to his mother, "Charlotte is hesitating about our marrying because I went to some prostitutes"! We were sitting in the kitchen of her apartment overlooking Lake Shore Drive. I was surprised that he would talk with her about this. She was, after all, a woman in her mid-seventies. He earnestly assured her that it would never happen again, and explained to her that his loneliness as a single man for nine years, on top of a "loveless" short first marriage drove him to it. She did not seem to be fazed by this news. I was surprised by her calm reaction, and years later, wondered if she 'knew,' what she knew. His mother turned to me. "Oh, he may have done that once when he was single for so long, and so lonely, but I am sure he never did again, and certainly won't after you are married. Charlotte, I am satisfied he will never do this again. Are you?" I promised her I would think about it, and discuss it further with him.

I decided I wanted more professional assurance. When we returned to New York, we went to a therapist who told us that Jon needed help. Jon agreed to begin therapy. I still decided to break off the relationship. That summer, I went to a resort in the Caribbean. He went to his mother's. He was inconsolable about the breakup, and he called me from his mother's. His mother got on the phone, telling me she thought he "could not live without me." He met me at my return flight, and we resumed our relationship.

The following summer, we broke up again when I went to Mexico for seventeen days, a ten day conference in Ixtapa, and then with a group of friends to see Mexico City and other sights. From there I went to Los Angeles to see my sister, brother-in-law, and nieces. My niece Joni had married and was expecting a baby. From there I planned to travel up the coast to San Francisco to visit friends. When I arrived at the Beverly Hills Hotel, there were two dozen red roses in my room which Jon sent me for my birthday. He called to tell me that he had gotten the help he needed, was no longer in therapy, and would I see him again. He said that the therapy made him realize that he wanted to leave his position as Dean of the School of Sacred Music at Hebrew Union College in New York, and take a position as a rabbi of a congregation. He said that he accepted a position in a town in Connecticut. He thought that this position afforded him the possibility of a stable life in a small close knit community, and would give him an income with which he could support himself, which he had not been able to do in New York. He said that, with the help he had gotten in therapy, he had stabilized his life; that he had not seen any more prostitutes, and never would again; and that he was getting out of the debt which he attributed to his many years of schooling.

(I was to learn after our marriage that that was not the reason for his continuing debt. There was the much more appalling reason that he had never stopped frequenting prostitutes. An additional reason was that he was an addicted gambler. I learned a great deal about addiction because of this marriage, including that addicts usually have multiple addictions. I was to learn that he was also addicted to pornography in any form. He rented videos, bought magazines, audio tapes, went to peep shows in Times Square. I eventually learned, and it eventually became clear to me that he also was addicted to lying.)

Jon continued making his case about why we should get married. He reported that he had written down a list of reasons and would read the list to me on the telephone. First, and most important he said, was that we had "a deep love for one another that was rare," and that we were "soul mates." This was of utmost importance to him. He had

59

despaired of finding his "soul mate" until he had met me, and reminded me that he had even told his mother about this. He also reminded me that she had "come around to the idea of our marriage." She had been much opposed to our relationship from the beginning because of the age difference, and because he had never had children of his own. As a mother myself, I understood her opposition. When we were on one of our many visits to Chicago to see her, she admitted to me that she thought I was "very good for her son," and she pressed me to set a wedding date.

He reviewed all this, and offered to go with me again to any therapist of my choice to discuss the advisability of our getting married. He conveyed that he had been in therapy for some time; he was clear about what he had done and why, and would not need or want to do it again. He continued with his "list" about why we could and should marry. With his increased income from his salary as a congregational rabbi, and from the extras he made by officiating at weddings and *Bar Mitzvahs*, and other events for people outside his congregation, and the lower cost of living in the area of Connecticut where his synagogue was, he said that we would have more than enough to live comfortably. He remarked about his knowledge of my desire to leave my children my savings, and that we wouldn't have to use them, or to use my income for our lifestyle in the community where he had taken a position. He expressed his desire to support me financially. He went on to say that the *Talmud* said that, "A man's home is his wife. A man should clothe himself with what he has on, eat and drink what he can afford, and honor his wife with more than he can afford." He promised that it was his desire to support us both financially and have me put my income in my savings. He offered to sign any prenuptial agreement that I would have drawn up. He thought I could commute to New York a few days a week to continue my work there, and, gradually, build a practice in the new community. He urged me to come up to see the community, to attend services and meet the people who were members of his synagogue, to see for myself.

He continued, quoting from the *Talmud* that "God counts a woman's tears, and if a husband could not hear his wife, he should bend down to listen." He was sure, he promised, that he would never be unfaithful to me, that he would always listen to me and make sure that he heard me, and would not "cause me any tears." The way he spoke to me reflected so much of what I loved about him. He could be so organized, realistic, intellectual, and spiritual, sensitive, loving, and caring, all at the same time.

While I did not agree to cut my trip short, I agreed to come up to Connecticut when I returned to "see for myself." He met me at the airport. I started going to Connecticut on weekends. We had such loving, joyous times together. The values and interests I thought we shared included our desire for a close family; our love for Judaism and sharing this love in a close knit community where we could inspire people's participation and spiritual growth; helping people to overcome life's problems and to grow - to become part of *Tikkun Olam*, or repairing the world; music of all kinds (we loved singing together at the piano, or while he played his guitar, and he always sang our special songs to me, including "One Alone," and "Cuando Caliente El Sol," or "Love me With All your Heart;" cooking inventive and unusual dishes (we had taken a "natural gourmet" cooking course together early in our relationship) and inviting friends in for the delicious meals we created, good conversation, and singing together at the Fun Machine or playing his guitar.

He talked to me at length about how he hoped that my adult children would accept him as their stepfather, and that we could have a "close, involved, Jewishly identified family." He knew of my deep desires for a close family life, and to be a part of a Jewish community, and expressed his similar desire. He knew that my sisters were scattered all over the country and that we were not close, and that he and his brothers, who lived in Chicago, were never close. He talked about his and his brothers' differing values in life - that they were "into making lots of money," that they and their families were "not Jewishly identified," and lived "shallow, materialistic lives." He said that he felt that he never "fit in", with them. He had already met my daughter the first Spring we were together when he invited her, his mother, and me to a Passover Seder he was conducting for the synagogue where we first met on the Eastern tip of Long Island. My daughter expressed her liking for him at that time, and again when we went up to visit her the following year at the college she was attending in Massachusetts.

He thought that it was significant that we first met when I went for the first and only time to the synagogue in the community where I was staying for one month to say the *Kaddish* on my mother's first

Yahrtzeit (anniversary of death) when he was guest rabbi at that synagogue. He thought it was *"Bashert"* - fate- that we met there, and on such significant occasions for us both.

During one of these exploratory weekends in Connecticut, during the High Holy Days, his mother came in from Chicago, and the three of us spent a happy and joyous time talking about the prospect of our getting married, and of her desire to become involved in what she, too, hoped would become our wonderful, loving family. After seven weeks of his demonstrating that he was true to his word, and establishing what I thought was an honest, loving, and committed relationship, and trusting his promise that we would have a monogamous marriage, I agreed to marry him. (By that time, I had known him for over three years.)

He announced our engagement to his congregation from the pulpit at the next Friday night *SHABBAT* service. He beamed, "My mother always wanted me to marry a Jewish doctor. I want to announce that Dr. Charlotte Schwab and I are engaged to be married"! The people at the service clapped their joy and approval. I had gotten to know many of them over the weekends I was going up to Connecticut. They broke 'protocol' to get up and flock around me to express their delight. I was sitting in the front row, directly in front of him, where he always wanted me to sit and where I sat for the duration of our marriage.

I started proceedings to finalize my divorce from my first husband. I had been legally separated for three years by then, and it only took two weeks to get the divorce decree.

The night I received my divorce decree from my first husband, we celebrated by going for a hansom cab ride in Central Park. It was Christmas Eve. The lights of the city were especially beautiful. It was snowing lightly. He sang to me in the hansom cab. Then we went to the Plaza Hotel's Palm Court, an especially romantic place with violinists. He got up to tip them so he could sing. They told him it was their policy not to do this. This did not faze him, and he returned to our table and sang to me softly. The song he chose was "One Alone." I have come to believe that the choices of songs he sang to me were significant. Although I was to learn only years later, after our marriage, that I was not his "one alone" sexually all through our dating period and our marriage, contrary to what he promised me, singing these songs to me may have been a way of his to throw me off the track of the truth about his life, to convince me, and maybe even to convince himself. He would say, much later, when he admitted the truth prior to his assaulting me to threaten me not to expose him, that sex with me was different, that he loved me, had married me, and that this had "nothing to do" with his other sexual activities! I believe his "Dr. Jekyll" personality partially believed this. However, I later learned and now know that he knew this was not true, that he knew what he was doing, that he was lying to himself, me, and everyone else.

I wanted to be thoroughly convinced of his stability. He had seen a Ph.D. cognitive/behavioral therapist. Now, I wanted us both to consult a psychiatrist recommended to me by a friend who was the head of the sex therapy clinic at a leading hospital. He agreed.

The psychiatrist, whom I'll call Dr. "R", interviewed us together and separately. His opinion was that my prospective husband suffered from depression, and that he should take medication for it. Furthermore, Dr. R's opinion was that this illness probably caused him to go to the prostitutes when he was so lonely as a single man. Jon did not tell this psychiatrist, or me, that he had never stopped going to prostitutes or having sex with every woman he could. Dr. R believed that this would not occur again, especially if he took the medication and was "monitored." Dr. R also said there was "no reason" for him to oppose our getting married. He thought he/we would be "fine." He prescribed the medication and set up a schedule to "monitor" him. With these assurances, we decided to set a date for our wedding. We set a January date for our wedding. He wanted it to be on the same day that his parents were married.

MARRIAGE TO RABBI H

Our wedding was a spiritually beautiful, loving ceremony held on the *Bimah* at a historic landmark synagogue in Manhattan, Central Synagogue, where we had gone to *SHABBAT* services together when he lived in New York. I had become a friend of the senior rabbi there, Rabbi Sheldon Zimmerman. I wanted him to officiate at our wedding but he had to be out of town. Jon asked the cantor at Central Synagogue, who was a friend of his, and a rabbinic classmate of his from Hebrew Union College to officiate. We decided to invite only immediate family members and a few friends.

My husband-to-be planned the entire wedding ceremony, including the music. He found a harpist and flautist, and, in addition to Pachelbel's "Canon," they played "One Alone" from the operetta The Desert Song, which he sang directly to me. In planning our wedding he exhibited one of the characteristics I loved about him - the ability to get things done while not being afraid to be romantic. "One Alone" became 'our song' after we saw a performance of the operetta. He promised me after seeing that operetta that that I would always be his "One Alone."

At our marriage ceremony, which he audio taped, we each said beautiful, spontaneous vows to one another. Our wedding was an expression of the spirituality, tenderness, gentleness, and creativity I loved about him. He asked me to walk down the aisle of the very large synagogue, promising that he would come down the stairs to bring me up to the *Bimah* himself. I protested that it was too long a walk to reach the small number of people who would be present up at the *Bimah*. With no people planned for the seats of the huge congregational space, I would have to walk past hundreds of empty seats. He said he wanted to savor my walking to him the length of the beautiful synagogue. Because it meant so much to him, I agreed. Starting down the aisle, it seemed like miles away to get to the *Bimah*. The synagogue was dark. The only lights were up at the *Bimah* where he and our families and friends were waiting for me. He, too, realized how difficult it would be for me to walk the entire length of the synagogue in the dark, alone. He quickly walked down the stairs from the *Bimah* to walk hand-in-hand with me the rest of the way. Yet again, I was touched by his thoughtfulness and gentleness, which I greatly valued. I let him know my gratitude for his thoughtfulness, and observed, "Many men do not understand that gentleness, tenderness is strength. I cherish you for that."

We left Central Synagogue in a silver stretch limo my husband wanted me to arrange for and pay for. He said he wanted his brothers to see him getting into the limo. I was happy to make him happy. I planned, arranged, and paid for our reception at a beautiful restaurant on top of a building overlooking Manhattan, the Rainbow Room at Rockefeller Center, because we both felt "on top of the world." We had two tables next to the windows overlooking the lights of the city for our wedding party. The walls seemed to be all of glass, all windows. It was a magical setting. The restaurant had a wonderful dance orchestra, and when we got up to dance, it seemed that all of the hundreds of diners applauded, along with our own families and friends. We cut our wedding cake at the windows high above the glittering lights of the city. My daughter took pictures of all the special moments. It was an enchanting celebration for both of us.

We flew to a resort called Dashene on the Caribbean island of St. Lucia for our honeymoon. It was the place in the "Superman" movie where Christopher Reeve as Superman flies to pluck an orchid to bring back to Lois, played by Margo Kidder.

Upon our return to the new home I purchased for us in the community where my new rabbi/husband had his synagogue, we settled into what was called in the headline of an article about us in a local newspaper, The Newington Town Crier, "A Successful Commuter Marriage." (I was the one commuting the 110 miles each way to work, and, in winter, in ice and snow.) The headline was not to be prophetic. In the article, which was published along with a photograph they took of us "relaxing at home," I was quoted as saying that my new husband "inspired me in my life and my work." He was quoted as saying that, "I consult with my wife and learn a great deal from her; she reinforces me and makes me a more effective rabbi."

I was working in New York City, putting in a full week's work in the short space of three days, and spending four days with my husband. During the time I spent with him, he expected me to attend all the services at his synagogue, every other event at which he officiated - baby namings, bar mitzvahs, weddings, funerals - for congregants, and for non congregants who hired him, as well as every social event relevant to his work. He said that he needed my advice and support to handle his work and to handle the extensive personal interaction.

At first, I enjoyed these events very much. But, he often officiated at events for people who were not presently his congregants in distant places, requiring that, on top of the more than two hours drive to get to our home, I also had to drive us there. That became very stressful. He needed me to drive so that he could review his notes, or relax, because he said it was very stressful to officiate at these life cycle events. I soon learned that he became highly anxious before any event at which he officiated, including conducting services at his own synagogue. He needed me to calm him.

I asked him why he felt he had to do so many events for people not involved in our lives, especially since this was so difficult for both of us, although in different ways. He said he needed the money to get out of debt. I believed him, and admired him for what I believed was wanting to straighten out his financial affairs. So I continued to "be there for him" at those times. Later, it began to be extremely stressful for me to do all this and commute 110 miles away to my own work. The driving was becoming exhausting. Also, the commuting distance necessitated that I sleep over three nights a week in the city where I worked. While I found the commuting and living separately quite difficult, my husband did not. I only learned much later why he liked the arrangement.

After we were married a few months, at my husband's suggestion, I swapped my three bedroom, two and a half bath apartment in New York for a one bedroom where I could stay the three days a week I was in the city and also see my therapy clients. I was paying a hefty rent for the larger apartment. He said the smaller apartment would be adequate, since I was only there three days a week, and it was big enough for us both to stay over when he wanted to come into New York. He wanted me to use the difference in rent for us to travel and go to the theater, opera. His cantorial professional organization was planning a trip to Israel that summer, and he wanted me to go with him and pay for the trip. I paid the down payment and closing costs on our new home. He was paying the carrying charges as he promised. He transferred the deed, which had to be purchased in both our names to my sole name, also as he promised. He said that he believed that a woman should own the home in a marriage, because, as the *Talmud* said, anyway, "A man's home is his wife."

Because I believed that he was not only egalitarian, but as generous as he could be, at his request, I bought him a new wardrobe for his new position. I also paid for the new furniture and household items we needed in Connecticut beyond the ones I brought from my larger apartment. I paid for most of our cultural events, and our travel. I also paid all my own expenses, including the new car I had to purchase to commute, and all of the expenses for my office/apartment in New York. So, the smaller, less expensive apartment seemed a wise decision. I paid for all the moving expenses to move my own things and furnishings to Connecticut when we were first married, and again, four months later when I moved additional furniture and other belongings to Connecticut on the swap to the smaller apartment. (I also paid to furnish the second, much more expensive and much larger home we were to purchase when he moved to a new congregation, more about which, later.)

We were living in our new home a few months when my husband announced that he thought it would be important that we entertain his congregants. I agreed that this would be a nice thing to do. He asked me to plan and pay for a housewarming 'open house' to which he wanted to invite the entire congregation, some three hundred families! He finally settled on "the most important members." It was a wonderful party. He enjoyed it so much, that I decided to give him a surprise party for his fortieth birthday the following month, inviting those people who seemed to be becoming our friends at the synagogue, as well as friends of both of us from the New York area.

I enlisted the aid of some of these friends to pull off the surprise. We were invited to the Connecticut shore overnight to stay with a couple from the synagogue at their condominium. I arranged for the caterers I retained to be let into our home by some friends to set up the party. My husband had absolutely no idea. When we got home, the garage door opener would not work. Unknown to both of us, one of our friends disconnected it so that we would have to walk in the front door. My husband, as he always did, went first. Our guests had positioned themselves inside the front door, and, when he opened it, they shouted "Surprise"! He was totally, delightfully surprised.

We had a wonderful time celebrating his fortieth birthday. My daughter and her husband, who at that time lived only 45 minutes away, drove down for the party. I invited his family from Chicago, but none of them came. We were so happy to have so many of our friends present - forty people! People made connections, the conversation went on and on, in the living room, outdoors on the patio - everyone was having a fun time. We ended the celebration with many of us singing around the Fun Machine, his electric piano my husband loved to play.

One night my rabbi/husband brought me home a gift of a red lace teddy. He expressed that I was the most "delicious, beautiful, sexiest woman he had ever been with." He communicated that he delighted in my "full, yet firm breasts," couldn't "get enough of them," marveled how "gorgeous" they were, "especially as a mother of two now-grown children." He loved my toned body. He would gently run his hands along what he called my "smooth, firm, aquiline neck," my face, and then my entire body. He told me often how much he loved my soft, delicate, fair, satiny skin. He said I had the "sexiest, most beautiful, sensual, curvaceous, voluptuous, yet, slim, statuesque, dignified bod" he ever saw. He wanted me to show it off in this way to him. I was happy to comply. While I had worn what I thought were sexy, lacy, black or white nightgowns before I gave up trying to tempt my first husband to make love, and wore white, ivory, or black lacy nightgowns with my rabbi/husband, I never had anything like this before: red, what I felt was a "blatantly" sexy teddy. I probably did think that it was 'cheap,' but this was my rabbi/husband whom I adored asking me to wear it.

I was enraptured by my husband who expressed so much delight for me, with me, sexually and otherwise. I was delighted by how much he appreciated, adored me. I returned his compliments, telling him he was the "sexiest man alive," how much I loved his "bod" (I used his term,) and that he was the best lover I could have ever imagined. Sometimes he took my breath away. He was larger than life to me, effusively affectionate, sexually generous, giving. I loved him passionately, actively, with all my heart. He returned the compliment in kind, telling me that I "blew his mind." He especially was "turned on" he said, by how "dignified you are, how serene, how peaceful, calm in every setting, what a loving presence you are, such goodness you emanate, and yet how passionate, sensual, sexy you are, how active a lover, how giving" I was with him. He said that I was the first woman into whose eyes he looked, wanted to look, while making love. He said, "Your eyes are the "window of your beautiful soul." I felt exactly the same about him in so many ways, and told him so as frequently as he told me.

I believed then that he was not afraid of intimacy, as many men are, that he was not afraid of mutual "into-me-see," truly knowing one another, a term which in one of my psychology trainings I learned to identify intimacy. He agreed when I expressed to him my opinion that intimacy was not just sex, certainly not casual sex. That only along with "into-me-see," and only with sacred, committed marriage could a couple realize and enjoy deep, passionate, God-given, sacred sexuality. He was especially desirous that I experience "multiple orgasms" with him in this sacred, passionate place we had found together, and that we find my "G spot," both concepts I learned when I studied sex therapy and brought this information to my clients. He was clearly familiar with these concepts and wanted me to have these experiences with him as often as I desired.

He quoted, and even gave me a copy of a 'resource sheet' called, "Sex is for Women Too," which he said was from *The Mishnah*, the "Oral Laws" of Judaism, stating that the "Bible catalogues three primary obligations of husbands to wives: food, clothing, and sexual rights. The *Talmud* then singles out sexual rights as the most important of these…. "The printout went on to quote, and he read it to me, the instruction from a marriage manual usually attributed to Nachmanides, "…. Engage her first in conversation that puts her heart and mind at ease and gladdens her…. Speak words which arouse her to passion, union, love, desire, and Eros - and words which elicit attitudes of reverence for God, piety, and modesty…. Speak with her words, some of love, some of erotic passion, some of piety and reverence…. Hurry not to arouse passion until her mood is ready; begin in love; let her orgasm take place first…. "I never dreamed that I would have such a satisfying sex life when I came out of my first sexually barren marriage. I was delighted by and with my rabbi/husband, and eager to please him sexually too, which he said I did, beyond what he had ever experienced or ever dreamed himself. I made love to him with passionate abandon. I felt safe, loved, loving, home. When we made love, I felt as if our souls met, were one. I felt that we shared the deep joy of a God-given blessing. He always insisted that we fall asleep in each others' arms.

At about this time, my husband asked me to co-lead a class at his synagogue about sex. I agreed, and we led a class which congregants seemed to find informative, satisfying, and in keeping with the goals of their congregation. I believe that many of them thought that my rabbi/husband and I had the utmost loving, passionate, yet sacred marriage. Some of them told me so.

I reveled in my rabbi/husband's charisma, his outgoing, effusive, energetic gregariousness. I tended to be shy in social crowds of strangers, which we often had to be with when he officiated at weddings and *Bar* and *Bat Mitzvahs* which were for non congregants. I was content to enjoy and watch him 'shine'. He said he reveled in our differences, and he used a term I often used to teach my clients to love one another, especially couples, families who came to me in strife: I "celebrate" our differences. I, too, celebrated our differences, and let him know how I felt about him. I truly believed that our love was sacred, unique, the love of two soul mates, two complimentary soul mates, the sacred, passionate love of married lovers. I loved him with all my heart and soul. I believed he loved me the same. He said to the reporter who interviewed us for the <u>Newington Town Crier,</u> and wrote the article called, "A Successful Commuter Marriage," and as she quoted in the article, "We are not in competition." He related to her that he felt equally comfortable being introduced as "Dr. Schwab's husband," as I did with being introduced as "the rabbi's wife." To me at that time, he was "the" rabbi, my rabbi, my rabbi/husband. Although I did not mind or correct people who referred to me as "the rabbi's wife," he often did, proudly informing them that I was "Dr. Schwab," and exulting about my accomplishments.

After my rabbi/husband brought me the teddy, I took great care to find beautiful, sexy teddies and other sexy lingerie myself. He showed me the store, not far from where we lived, where he purchased them. Subsequently, I took one of his congregants there at my husband's suggestion. She shared with me and my husband that her marriage was "on the rocks," that her husband did not make love to her anymore. I helped her pick out a teddy that I assured her her husband would love, and assured her that she looked sexy in it. Of course, having come out of a sexually barren marriage myself, I knew that this congregant and her husband probably needed more than a sexy teddy to impassion their marriage. I did suggest that she and her husband find a counselor to help them. [I did not know at the time that this congregant, who had been taken to a mental hospital in a strait jacket, would later testify untruths against me in court at the trial at which my rabbi/husband sued me for alimony!]

I had never been so happy in my life. I was thrilled by my new husband. I basked in the terms of endearment, admiration by which he referred to me, including: *Shandele* (my Yiddish name, which means little pretty one, which no one but my parents had ever called me,) and "Face," because, he said, I had the most beautiful face, more beautiful than any woman he ever hoped to be married to. I was thrilled that he always wanted to sleep in each others' arms. I rejoiced in the spiritual, intellectual, communicative, affectionate, passionate marriage I thought we had.

We went to Israel on the two week trip with members of the American Conference of Cantors and their families six months after our wedding. Again, I paid for the whole thing. I loved Israel. We traveled through much of the country. I was shocked when I saw with my own eyes how small a country Israel is, starkly realized how closely surrounded it is by so many unfriendly Arab countries. I was deeply affected by the strength of the Israeli people.

Tzefat (Safed) was especially meaningful and spiritual to me. Safed sits high on a mountain top, more than 3000 feet above sea level. It is one of Israel's four sacred cities. It is known as "City of Mysticism," because it is the location of the founding of *Kabbalah* - a philosophy created in mediaeval times about direct communication between human beings and God. Rabbi Isaac Luria, also called "*Ha'ari*," or "The Lion," was the founder and chief exponent of *Kabbalah*. Safed also is home to a colony of artists, sculptors, and crafts people. They are attracted by Safed's clean, mountain air and picturesque scenery, including narrow, stepped streets and vine-covered courtyards, and wonderful panoramas of the mountains. I found a necklace handmade by an artisan there depicting the Ten Commandments, and still love to wear it often to *SHABBAT* services. I bought one like it for my friend Bernice, who hosted us for a few days at her beautiful home in Easthampton, Long Island, before we left for Israel.

I was deeply moved when praying at the Western Wall, although I hoped that the rules not allowing women to be included in prayer services there would be changed.

I was also greatly moved by Masada. In fact, much about Israel was extremely moving and meaningful to me. I admired the Israeli people, who seemed so strong in the face of so much strife. We stayed at a kibbutz called *Kiryat Shmoneh*, named for the national hero, Joseph Trumpeldor, and his companions. It is one of the sites where children were murdered by a terrorist attack. I was especially, repeatedly struck during this trip by how close the surrounding, hostile Arab countries are to Israel.

In Tel Aviv, I had a gold necklace made with my name *Shandele* in Hebrew letters. I still treasure it and wear it, often.

My rabbi/husband wanted to stop in Paris for a week on the way home. Because we had not made reservations, the only hotel available was the Hilton. He insisted we go. I paid for all of that, too. I loved him very much. I strongly believed in egalitarianism in marriage, but he complained to me that he was in debt because of all his student loans, and was "working hard" to get out of this debt. I trusted that he was getting out of debt, and that everything would become more financially equal in time. (I did not know that he wanted to find prostitutes in Paris. One evening, when I was tired and wanted to stay in, order room service, he said he wanted to go out, and left me alone in the hotel room. I did not learn until much later that he went to find, and found prostitutes that night, in Paris.)

Much to my relief, after we had been married about seven months, my husband began talking about looking into getting a congregation closer to New York. He revealed that he felt the people at the current one were very "simple, uneducated, unsophisticated," and he found them "boring." He wanted more of a challenge. I asked him how he would cope with the challenge a more sophisticated congregation would present, since he experienced such anxiety with his current one. He said that he felt he wouldn't be anxious with more of a challenge. I had always encouraged him, and buoyed his self-esteem, telling him that he was far more capable than he believed. When I praised his sermons, and all his efforts with his work, he would become self-deprecating, disclosing to me that he plagiarized most of his sermons. I encouraged him by assuring him that I knew when he spoke extemporaneously he was brilliant, and that when he prepared sermons on subjects he loved, he didn't need to plagiarize, and that they were also brilliant.

In the December of our first year of marriage, my husband said he wanted to take a trip for several days to Vermont over the New Year holiday. Not to ski, he was not at all athletic, just to "get away." I paid for that, too. Again, I didn't mind at the time, because I believed him that he was "getting out of" his "student debt." He promised that he would pay for "things" in the future, and I believed him. Vermont was a resplendent, white, winter wonderland. One of the highlights of the trip for me was meeting Christopher Reeve on the lift line. I had seen all his Superman movies and enjoyed them. I told him that, and that we had gone to Dashene for our honeymoon, the place on the island of St. Lucia where he, as Superman, 'flew' to get the orchid for Lois. My favorite Christopher Reeve movie, though, as I told him is "Somewhere in Time," about a man (played by Reeve) who falls in love with a 70 year old portrait of an actress (played by Jane Seymour, also a favorite actor of mine,) and travels back in time to meet her. Leonard Maltin calls this movie a "superficial tearjerker," with "stilted dialogue, corny situations," although he does grant it "pretty scenery (on Mackinac Island)." I don't always agree with Leonard Maltin, and I was pleased to have the opportunity to tell Christopher Reeve how much I like his work. In person, I found him to be a beautiful human being, his eyes electrically magnetic, radiating empathy and compassion, which, because of his subsequent tragic accident, the world has come to know.

Snowmobiling was one of the highlights of the trip for my husband. He found it to be "one of the most exciting things" he ever did. He liked being able to speed, and the sense of power the machine gave him. He liked me to be on the seat behind him, although he gave me a short turn driving it. I could tell why he was exhilarated by it, although I felt it was too bumpy, and much too risky at the speed he drove.

A highlight for both of us was New Year's Eve at the hotel. The orchestra was terrific. They played tunes from the '40's, which I love, and we danced the New Year in. I loved dancing with my husband. Although he claimed he didn't know how to dance when we met, and asked me to teach him, particularly, the rhumba, and other Latin dances, once he got going, he was great, especially in the Lindy Hop. He was never secure about his body and his ability to do anything he thought was "athletic." Because I did a lot of ballroom dancing during my college years, danced with a professional partner on the

University of Michigan Hill Auditorium stage in a dance exhibition, and performed at proms, my husband felt more confident after I taught him what he called, "the moves," and because I always praised his dancing.

For our first anniversary, my rabbi/husband wanted to take a trip to another island in the Caribbean. Our honeymoon at Dashene had turned out to be at a place in a rain forest, something the travel agent neglected to tell us. It rained the entire week. We never got to a beach. Also, Dashene had become very run down. He wanted to have a second honeymoon in a better place. We chose a place on British Virgin Gorda. We were assured (by a different travel agent) that it was a "beautiful, quiet, romantic, informal, small resort, with private bungalows in excellent condition, right on a gorgeous, secluded beach." The pictures certainly seemed to promise just that. I made reservations.

Jon wanted to spend a couple of days in New York before we flew to the Caribbean. He arranged for us to have dinner with another rabbi and his wife, a rabbi of a synagogue on the Upper East Side of Manhattan. At dinner, he told this rabbi, whom I was meeting for the first time (in front of me and this rabbi's wife) that he did "not want a monogamous marriage." I was aghast. I could not believe what he was saying. When he went to the men's room, I asked this rabbi for help to deal with this. I didn't know what to make of it. This rabbi told me that it was "none of his business," that he would "not get involved." I could not believe what I was hearing. (Much later I learned about the rabbinic "old boys network," about rabbis covering up for other rabbis engaged in sexual misconduct.)

When we got home, my husband told me that he "didn't mean it," and to "forget" what he had said. Being very practiced at denial, and wanting to believe he did not "mean it," I was glad to accommodate his request.

We had a wonderful time at Tradewinds, the resort on British Virgin Gorda. Tradewinds was splendid, gorgeous. Our elegant, comfortable cottage was a little bit up a hill, on the beach, tucked into beautiful tropical landscaping. It had an outdoor, yet enclosed private shower room, extensively planted with luscious, exotic flowers and foliage, open to the sky. We were alone for most of the time. It was like a second honeymoon. No, third, because Vermont had also been like a honeymoon. We swam in the sea, went sailing for an entire day with a 'skipper' on a 32 foot sailboat, sailing through Drake's Passage, a breathtakingly beautiful area of the Caribbean Sea. We tried our skill at wind surfing, and swam in the pool, which we had all to ourselves. We were taken to a private beach and explored the huge and unusual rock formations. We made love a lot. He told me over and over that I was his "soul mate," called me by all the pet names he coined, including, "Face," and "Princess Summer Fall Little Face" because he said he loved my beautiful face. I told him over and over, too, that he was my soul mate, and I called him my *zeesi neshumah* (sweet soul), one of the the pet names my mother had called me. The hotel dining room was open to the sky and sea, very romantic, and served delicious food. Our trip was truly a honeymoon. Until the last day.

The last day of our trip, after breakfast, my husband discovered an office worker in the hotel, a single blonde in her thirties. He flirted with her outrageously in my presence. I was hurt and shocked, and told him so. He apologized, and promised me it would never happen again. Of course, I wanted to believe him. He was so convincing. He looked at me with his beautiful brown eyes which seemed so tender, caring, loving, honest. He told me he loved only me, that he married me, that he did not want anyone else. Then, he made love to me. He was a wonderful lover, passionate, tender, considerate, taking much time to please me, affectionate, verbal. He told me I was beautiful, sexy, brilliant. He said he had never been with a woman as beautiful, sexy, and brilliant as I, and that he would always love only me. He compared me to the beautiful flowers surrounding our secluded cottage, that I was "luscious, gorgeous." That I was "delicious." That I was his one alone, his one and only. I melted, believed him, and accepted his apology. There was nothing I would not do for him. This pattern became well established.

When we got home, because Dr. R told us he would "not give me any trouble as long as he stayed on the medication and continued in therapy," I asked him if he was taking the antidepressant medication, and continuing to see the psychiatrist. He assured me he was, and, again, I believed him. I also supported his interest in finding another congregation. I, too, would be glad to have him at a synagogue closer to New York, because I would have a shorter commute, and hoped that I would not have to stay over in New York at all. I learned much later that he had discontinued the medication shortly after he began, and that he had not continued his treatment with the psychiatrist. I also learned much later the real reason why he had to change his congregation.

In July of that year, we went to the rabbinic conference in Snowmass, Colorado. He much preferred to go to the cantorial conferences, even though he had been a rabbi for several years. He felt "intimidated" by most other rabbis, and did not feel this way about cantors. He said he had "a lot more in common" with cantors. However, because he was now a congregational rabbi, he decided to go to that conference. Also, I was constantly praising his ability as a rabbi. I did, indeed, believe that he was a wonderful rabbi. I admired his work on the *Bimah*, the way he interacted in synagogue with his congregants, how supportive he was to them. I did wonder why he had to hug the women so closely, and, it seemed for so long a time. I liked so much that he was warm, outgoing, affectionate, communicative, that I thought this kind of behavior went with such a personality. He was so opposite of my first husband in so many ways. It was a refreshing, wonderful change for me. I cherished his expressions of affection, his warmth toward me, and, of course, he was my husband, making love to me, giving me what I had never had in my life from a man, a husband, and I wanted to do nothing that might put a damper on that. I had no suspicions at the time that he was having sex with women congregants, many women, even prostitutes.

I always sat in the front row at services, directly in front of him, where he insisted I sit, smiling up at him, with the joy I felt about his role, about my being his wife, the *rebbitzin* as he would teasingly call me in private. He said he needed me there to be able to perform his role on the *Bimah*. I loved being there, feeling so connected to him, with him, that we were one. I radiated love. My smile was so radiant I got the nickname "Vanna," after Vanna White, the star of the television show, "Wheel of Fortune." I had never seen this show, but now, tuned in to see a beautiful woman with a truly radiant smile. I was happy to be called Vanna, because I knew this expressed that my husband thought I was beautiful.

The nickname "Face," which he said he called me because I had the most beautiful face he had ever seen and he was so lucky to wake up to it each morning was his favorite. He sang "The First Time Ever

I Saw Your Face" to me often, serenading me in bed, at breakfast, at the Fun Machine in the living room. He made a tape of himself singing this and other songs to me so that I could listen to him in New York, when I was there alone and missing him. He also called me *Shandele*, often, which means "little pretty one," the Yiddish term of endearment by which only my parents had ever called me, because, he said, "You are my little pretty one."

I was pleased that he called me these pet names, that he loved me so much and that he showed me in the many ways that he did. I believed I now had a marriage with an active lover, with a man engaged in active loving, with an open, honest husband who wanted intimacy - into me see - as I had taught to so many clients. I denied his growing intermittent cruelties, and my growing suspicions, and believed that I felt very happy with him. The fact that he was a rabbi contributed to my denial. I could not believe a rabbi would/could be anything but honest, loving, open. I also needed to believe that he was honest. I could not face the possibility that I was in another dishonest, cruel marriage, this time to a dishonest, cruel rabbi.

I was delighted by his knowledge of Judaism, Jewish music, many kinds of music, his love of fun, food, cooking, his gregariousness, entertaining together, going to parties, traveling, on short or long trips, spending time alone, talking, making love on our down quilt in front of our fireplace, singing at the Fun Machine, listening to music we loved, going to concerts at Lincoln Center in New York, or in Hartford, which was near our home, sharing so much, just the two of us, that we both loved.

My husband was romantic in myriad ways. He brought me a little vase with one perfect rose, a candle in a cut-glass, heart-shaped covered dish, and, for our first *Chanukah* as husband and wife, he bought me a beautiful red wool knit dress because he said that the *Torah* says that a man should "clothe himself with what he has on, and buy his wife beautiful clothes." This was the only garment (besides the teddy) he ever bought for me. His attitude that a husband should buy his wife beautiful clothes, and clothe himself with what he has on, which he said was in the *Talmud*, was not borne out by his asking me to buy him a wardrobe, but I ignored these inconsistencies. I wanted to believe him. Anyway, I wanted my wonderful husband to look well dressed, and to make him happy.

He said he bought me the fitted, yet tasteful dress to "show off your gorgeous bod." He often said complimentary things about my figure, or "bod" to use his term, expressing his wonder at how slim, shapely, and fit I was, even though I had had two children, and was so much older than he. By our first *Chanukah* as a married couple, I was 52 years of age. I told him that being fit had a lot to do with nutrition and exercise. I taught him about eating healthy foods, tried to get him to walk around the track at the local high school with me, and bought him an exercise machine (he wanted a rowing machine), so he could exercise at home. All this was to no avail. Jon complained he is too "oral," that he is a singer, and that "all singers are oral."

He argued that Luciano Pavarotti is hugely overweight, probably a hundred pounds heavier than he; that he is in good company. We knew this 'first-hand,' because after we were dating for only a short time, he asked me the question, "If you can have, do anything at all that you want in New York, what would it be?" Without hesitation, I said, "I want to meet Luciano Pavarotti." Incredibly, a short time later, he called to tell me to get out my "black tie." "We are going to the Metropolitan Opera Gala in honor of Carlo Bergonzi's 25th anniversary. Pavarotti is singing." The wife of a student at Hebrew Union College sang in the Metropolitan Opera chorus. She gave Jon two house seats, and as a surprise, arranged for us to go backstage at intermission to meet Pavarotti. Jon took my picture in Pavarotti's dressing room with Pavarotti's arm around me. I was delighted. Later, he had the picture enlarged to 12"x14" and beautifully framed. It hangs in my foyer to this day. We were invited to go to the party at the Opera Club after the performance, and, when Pavarotti made his grand entrance into the packed room, he came directly across the room to me, again putting his arm around me. I have that picture in my album. Years later, in Snowmass, I played a tape on my Sony Walkman, of Pavarotti hitting high C's, as my rabbi/husband and I soared over the Rockies in a hot air balloon. The combination of soaring over the majestic Rocky mountains while listening to Pavarotti was glorious!

My rabbi/husband often stated that one of the biggest enjoyments in his life is food, especially greasy food (he was not a lover of sweets); that he loved fried chicken, bacon, anything greasy. In New York, every time we passed a fast food place with greasy chickens in the window, he stopped just to stare, and savor thinking about eating them. He told me that he thought fried chicken skin was the most delicious, best treat in the world. Nothing I could do: tempt him with healthy dishes, give him articles about the importance of nutrition for health, could get him to change. His one concession was that many Monday nights, when we did not have to be anywhere else, we stayed home and cooked tofu, garlic, onions, ginger, many other spices, and many vegetables in our wok, and ate this dish, which he had to season heavily for him to enjoy, over steamed brown rice. He liked variety in food, as in everything, he would say, and spice, heavy spice. One of his pet names for me was "Jalapeno pepper," and another was "chili pepper." He was satisfied that I was "plenty of variety and spice" for him. He often expressed his appreciation of how "serene and dignified" I was, "especially in public," and yet, how "passionate" I was in our lovemaking. I bought a pair of earrings with red chili peppers on them, telling him I was his "chili pepper."

In Snowmass, at the rabbinic conference, a good friend of his, a rabbi who was single, arrived with a young, single woman who he said was a Protestant minister. She was clearly his 'date.' They stayed together in one room. I thought this was entirely inappropriate at a rabbinic conference and mentioned this to my husband. His response was that he "envied" this rabbi his ability to "sleep around" and that they had done much "swinging" together, including having a "threesome" with a Park Avenue matron in her apartment and in her home on Fire Island. I was horrified. I asked him if he wanted 'out' of the marriage. He quickly assured me that he hadn't meant what he said, and, of course he did not want out of the marriage. He reassured me that he had not been unfaithful to me since our marriage, let alone done "swinging." He became very loving to me, and, as was now an established pattern, made love to me, and I forgave him. However, from them on, this kind of behavior escalated. First, he would tell me how he wanted not to be monogamous, and then he would apologize and become very loving and attentive. I would deny what he had told me and go along with him because I wanted to believe him, and because he was so convincing. Remember, I also had experience with denial of the abuse of my first husband. It was an easy habit to fall back into, and, of course, it provided Jon with the opportunity he wanted for what he was really doing, which I still did not know at that time.

Ironically, now, because of the recent news as of this writing, about Rabbi Sheldon Zimmerman,[32] whom I knew when he was a rabbi at Central Synagogue in New York, before he moved to a congregation in Dallas, I danced with Shelly, jitterbugged, at the CCAR conference in Snowmass. He was a great dancer. We had a wonderful time. Shelly did not make any inappropriate movements or gestures or suggestions to me. I never suspected he would come to the disgrace he has at this writing. I am very sad, shocked about his reported transgressions. He was the last rabbi I ever would have thought would be guilty of sexual misconduct, even with all the cases, the tragedies, I have come to know with my research and working on this book for the last ten years. I always had the greatest respect for Shelly, looked up to him and came to wish during my marriage to my rabbi/husband that he would be the kind of husband I thought at that time that Shelly was.

From Snowmass, we went to a spa in southern California for a week. I welcomed the pampering at the spa. I enjoyed the mud baths and the massages. I loved being in the sun. I am a 'sun person,' although I am careful and do not sunbathe because I am so fair skinned. At the spa, my rabbi/husband and I met a man involved in venture capital. We told him about our dream to open a Judaic retreat center in the Catskills, if possible at Lake Minnewaska, or somewhere beautiful, pastoral like that, where we could put on cultural (especially musical) and spiritual programs, and which would be a combination spiritual, human development and spa center. My rabbi/husband would direct the Judaic programming, and I, the human development programming, although we would both offer programs in each. This venture capitalist was very excited about the prospect, and promised to look around for other investors. We discussed the project in detail, and we were very excited about realizing the prospect of this dream.

From the spa we went to a hotel in Laguna Nigel. I wanted to visit my sister and brother-in-law. They lived in Laguna Hills. I also wanted to stay where my niece Joni could drive down from L.A. for

---

[32]See Part Two, in which I discuss Rabbi Zimmerman's resignation as President of Hebrew Union College and suspension from the CCAR because of allegedly sexually abusing women at his former congregation in Dallas.

the day with her eighteen month old son, whom I had never seen; and where other friends from the L.A. area could drive down to visit with us. My husband picked the hotel, an elegant "Leading Hotel of the World" and very pricey, the Ritz Carlton. Again, I paid. I went along with it because I loved making my husband happy. As soon as we got to the hotel, my rabbi/husband informed me that we were "close to Las Vegas." He claimed he had always wanted to go there. He would "fly there overnight to spend all night gambling," and I could have more time visiting with my sister. I told him I did not want him to go to Las Vegas. I did not like the idea of his gambling. I pointed out to him that he could not afford it. I also knew that Las Vegas was a place where there were prostitutes. By this time, I was getting suspicious of him.

He went despite my objections. He returned the next night and took a taxi up to my sister's to join us for dinner. He hadn't returned on time to go with me. He apologized profusely for being "late." He behaved in a most loving and attentive way to me in front of my sister and brother-in-law, which was unusual for him. Since our marriage, he disliked "public" displays of affection to me, although he always loved this before our marriage. But now, often, after he behaved badly, he was especially affectionate, loving, verbally so, demonstratively so. (I was to find out much later he did go to prostitutes on this trip to Las Vegas and that he had been a gambler for many years; that these two things were really what put him into debt, not his college loans.)

My sister and brother-in-law thought he was a "prince." They liked him very much. They knew what I had suffered with Mort, and they thought I now had the wonderful husband I deserved. They were happy for me. They, of course, knew nothing of what I was going through with Jon. My brother-in-law was suffering from a life-threatening illness, and I did not want to burden them with my problems with my husband, which seemed to pale in the light of theirs.

My niece, Joni, drove down to the Ritz Carlton in Laguna Niguel from her home in Los Angeles with her baby of 18 months, Danny William, whom I had not seen since his birth, to spend the next day with us. I was delighted to see them. It was a pleasure to play with my great-nephew, who was a beautiful baby. He looked so much like Joni. As we watched him playing in the sand, I revealed to her what

Jon had been doing, how he had been behaving toward me. I told her of my suspicions, how worried I was. She and I had become very close over the last nine years. We had become more like sisters and best friends than like aunt and niece, even though I was 17 years older than she. Her mother, my sister Ronnie, was 14 years older than I. My sister Ronnie and I had been very close for most of my life, but over the course of her husband's illness, which he had been suffering for several years at that point, and since they had moved to California from Massachusetts nine years before, that closeness had been diluted. On the other hand, my niece had lived with me for five months in New York several years before. She came to New York for several subsequent visits. I went to California when she was 8 months pregnant, and we spent a joyous time together seeing the sights. We spoke frequently on the telephone.

My niece Joni was quite worried by what I told her about my rabbi/husband. She agreed that we should find professional help for him as soon as we returned home. Unfortunately, her premonitions proved to be true.

THE FIRST ASSAULT BY MY RABBI/HUSBAND

When we returned home, my husband disclosed to me that he had a venereal disease, and that his doctor told him to tell me that I should be examined. I was shocked and frightened. It turned out that he had given me this disease, called condyloma, and it took many painful treatments for me to become disease free. I asked him if he had indeed gone to prostitutes since our marriage. He insisted that he hadn't, and that he had contracted this disease before our marriage. I insisted that we tell certain people whom I thought at the time were our friends, including the rabbi and the cantor who officiated at our wedding, and my daughter and son-in-law. My daughter was married for over three years by this time, and lived about 45 minutes away from us). I wanted to ask their help and support to get him back into psychiatric treatment. I wanted an extended family and friends 'intervention.' I knew I/we could not handle this alone. I told him I would call them. As I was going up the stairs of our home to make the calls from the study, he accosted me and hit me. I was shocked. This was the first time he had ever hit me.

Along with most people at the time, and in spite of my experience with my first husband, I had the belief that Jewish men, and <u>especially rabbis,</u> did not hit their wives. I believed in *Shalom Bayit* - Peace in the Home. I grew up in such a home. My father loved and respected my mother, and I know would never have dreamed of hurting her. When we were married, I expressed regret to my rabbi/husband that my parents, who had both died years before, would never know that I married him. Although I knew my parents would have been very sad about my first marriage, and that it ended in divorce, I believed they would have been very happy that I married a rabbi who I believed was a wonderful man and with whom I was very happy. Judaism was central to my parents' lives. Mine, too.

By the time I married Jon, a Reform rabbi, I was passionately interested in women's issues and egalitarianism between men and women. Reform Judaism seemed somewhat egalitarian to me. Women had been ordained as rabbis since 1972. The Reform seminary where Jon was trained, had been receptive to my egalitarian ideas when I lectured there. Jon was continually giving me articles about Judaism and feminism, continually professing that he was a feminist. Because of all this, I could not believe that he would hit me.

When my rabbi/husband hit me, I had been a practicing psychotherapist for almost 15 years. I had been extensively involved in the women's movement. I was familiar with the "battered woman syndrome," a misnomer for what I believe should be called the "battering man syndrome." I had been the victim of my abusive first husband for many years. Even though it was hard for me to believe that Jon, my rabbi/husband could be a batterer, and even though I did not want to believe what he did, that he hit me, there was no way now I was going to ignore what he did. I managed to get away from him and call the local police.

The sheriff who came was a friend of his. They both attended the same civic organization. The sheriff said my husband was the "upstanding local rabbi" who "could not possibly have hit me." The sheriff talked me into "forgetting it." The sheriff said that he believed that "whatever happened would never happen again." Intellectually, as a psychotherapist, I knew I should not be allowing him to talk me into "forgetting it." I would have counseled any client not to, to take action to stop it; but I suspended this knowledge to believe in the rabbi/husband that I adored. I did not follow my own advice to clients. It was a case of the 'shoemaker going barefoot.'

I wanted to believe he would never do such a thing again, and said I would forget it. However, I was quite frightened at the time, and told a couple who, although they were congregants, I believed were my/our friends. I did not understand the politics of synagogues then. I mistakenly thought that these 'friends' would be supportive to both me and my husband, and help us to get the help needed. They did not choose to do so. I was to learn subsequently that certain members of this congregation already knew at that time what my husband was up to, and was why, I was told by some members of the congregation, his contract was not renewed. I was never to be able to "forget it."

I had to have more than one surgical procedure for the removal of the condyloma, which my rabbi/husband had 'given' to me. The last procedure, at the office of a doctor at a hospital in Connecticut, resulted in my being taken to the emergency room. My rabbi/husband swore up and down in the emergency room, in the presence of my doctor, and my daughter, who had come with me for the procedure, that he would never go to prostitutes again, that he would be monogamous.

My daughter, who believed she had almost seen my demise when I went into shock on the emergency room table, and she had been removed from the room while a team worked on me, was in horror at what he had done to her mother, and furious with him. She wanted him no where near me or her.

They kept me in the hospital overnight. The next morning, my daughter insisted that she drive me to New York, and that I not go back to him. She stayed with me in New York overnight, trying to convince me to leave him. She was very angry at Jon. My husband called me in New York several times, pleading with me to come back to him. He swore over and over that, in spite of what he had admitted in the emergency room in front of my doctor, that he was not now going to prostitutes, that he had been faithful to me.

I stayed at the office/apartment in the city to rest. I had to work there in two days anyway. My rabbi/husband kept calling and pleading with me to come home. He said he wasn't sure his contract with the synagogue would be renewed, and he did not have any prospects for another post. He said he needed me, that he "could not make it" without me.

Then his mother died. He called to tell me, and asked me to meet him at the airport to fly to Chicago for her funeral. He didn't believe he could get through it without me. I agreed to meet him at the airport. He was very grateful to me, apologetic, loving, attentive. He disclosed to me he feared that I would leave him.

In Chicago for his mother's funeral, I got a clearer picture of how my husband's two older brothers treated him. They acted as if he were a 'third wheel' in the family. The lawyer/brother was autocratic toward him, and treated him as if he were a child. This brother, the middle one in birth order, and not that much older than my husband, told him in my presence, what "would be done." The older brother was president of his own advertising company, and he behaved distantly with my husband, even to the point of disdain. He had never had a word to say to me, nor had his middle brother. My husband complained to me bitterly about their treatment of him. He said he felt "alone" in the family now, as his mother and he had been so close, but he was never close with his brothers. They looked down on him and on his profession. My husband told me that he knew his middle brother was "carrying on a sexual affair." He said he knew this brother had "no love lost" for his wife, who was obese and whom he found "distasteful." My husband did not think much of his brother for this. He liked his sister-in-law, and identified with her.

He battled being overweight his whole life, and often was put down about it by his brothers, neither of whom was "overweight." My husband often referred to himself as "fat." I disagreed with him, and told him often that I loved him and his body. I know that the things I told him helped him not to be so hard on himself. He often told me how much he admired my "svelte, slim, shapely, sexy body," and what he would give to be less heavy, and as "graceful" as I. He told me often that he loved my "long, slim neck," my "tall, gazelle-like" bod. He said that I looked like a blonde "*shiksa* goddess," which, though I did not like the term, he thought was the ultimate compliment. He hated what he called his "fat, short neck," and his "fat, clumsy" body. I showed him the exercises I did every morning to maintain my figure, and asked him to do them with me, but he would not. He said he "couldn't," that he was "intimidated" by what I could do that he could not. I tried other ways to get him to exercise with me, and, sometimes, he would go with me to the neighborhood school, which had a track, to walk briskly with me for as long as he could. He told me that if he had a rowing machine, he thought he would do the rowing, because it was "fun" to row. He asked me to buy him one, which I did. He used it a few times and then it languished in our bedroom, where he put it because he wanted me to watch him row.

He empathized with his sister-in-law because he, too, loved eating, food of all kinds, way too much. Especially fatty foods. As much as I would try to cook healthy meals, peel carrots, prepare celery sticks for him and put them in baggies for snacks, or encourage him to order healthy food when we ate out, he told me that he would "pig out" in private. In fact, a restaurant opened up in New York near my apartment called Pig Heaven, and he was enamored of it. I later realized that food, too, is one of his addictions. He chose not to stop gorging himself on all kinds of, especially fatty foods, going to "Pig Heaven" metaphorically, all the time, even though he loathed his body. He knew and we talked about how much fat, cholesterol, carcinogens were found in these foods. Yet, he would not stop his eating orgies. So he took his sister-in-law's part over his brother's in private to me, and did not like that his brother cheated on her.

The only carte blanche his brothers gave my husband was the eulogy which he wrote and delivered at the funeral. My husband spoke about his mother with reverence, humor, and a great deal of knowledge. He had been *very* close with her, even to the point of consoling her that her other two sons, although they lived not far from her in the Chicago area, hardly ever came to see her, and had little contact with her. She spoke with my husband frequently on the telephone. He went to Chicago often to visit her, staying with her in her home, and spending all his time while there with her. She also came to New York or Connecticut several times since I had known my husband. They shared a mutual love of music. It was she who introduced him to music when he was a child, taking him to the opera, and other live performances. She also played the piano, right up until she died, and often would play while my husband sang, various types of music, including operetta, Broadway show tunes, and pop. The three of us spent many happy times together this way. She played and my husband sang her favorites, and then, she played "romantic" tunes which he sang to me. One tune she always played while he sang to me was, "Have I Told You Lately That I Love You." We continued this practice in our own home after his mother died, singing at her beautiful, white, baby grand piano which she left to him.

In Chicago, my husband leaned on me to get through his mother's funeral, and, as he told me, "to be able to take what his brothers dished out." He declared that he thought I was going to leave him. He told me he needed me now more than ever. He swore to me that he was faithful to me, and that I "would not have to worry about him ever again." He pleaded with me to stay with him, to stay in the marriage. I told him that I would stay on the condition that he would find and see a psychotherapist, and that he would take the medication that Dr. R said he absolutely needed. He promised that he would. We also discussed his looking for a position nearer to the city so that I would not have such a long commute and we would not have to be apart several nights a week.

The following months were a nightmare. My husband learned that he would indeed not be asked back by his synagogue after the current year was up. He became extremely negative and self deprecating, much more than usual, even hopeless about his life. He did see a therapist, but it did not help. He fluctuated between being suicidal, and being 'up,' and abusive. He blamed all this on his mother's death coming at such a difficult time for him: not knowing where he would be employed the following year. I spent my time with him trying everything I could to get him out of the suicidal depressions he went into, often calling his doctor, often taking him out to walk around the track at the local school, since physical, outdoor exercise could help him; and then, alternately, doing everything I could to calm him down, deal with his abusiveness, and try to help him to get some sleep when he became extremely agitated and flipped into unbelievable 'highs.' I also spent a lot of time and energy doing everything I could to build up his self esteem. He constantly went on about how he was "sure" he would never get another post as a rabbi, going into long monologues of lament.

I reminded him repeatedly at these times of how much he complained he did not like the current position and the people of this community anyway, and that he *could* look at not being asked back as getting what he wanted: an opportunity to find a position and a community that he would feel "challenged" by and happy in. During all of this stressful time, for *me* as well, I was driving the 110 miles each way to spend three days working in New York, jamming a week's work into the three days so I could spend four days with my husband, four days which were increasingly being entirely spent dealing with his suicidal lamentations or out-of-control 'highs.'

He begged me to drive up earlier and earlier on Fridays, which were his most stressful days, so that I could be there to support him. He wanted me dressed and ready to leave for synagogue for the *SHABBAT* service, whether he was home and ready to leave or not. He claimed that he could not "function" if I was not in the front row in the seat in front of him when the service started. He also claimed that he could not deal with his "boring" congregants unless I was there by his side after the service at the *Oneg SHABBAT*. He went on and on about how they were "uneducated, unexciting, unattractive, unaccomplished, narrow, bottom end of middle class people." No matter how much I pointed out to him the education of many of his congregants, and, more importantly, what I saw as their commitment to Judaism, their synagogue, and their close, sharing community, and commitment to one another, he still mercilessly put them down. I did not like that my husband put people down, especially his own congregants. I attributed it to his lack of self esteem, and I worked hard to help him build up his self esteem so that he would not have a need to do this. It was/is such a contradiction to me that he could preach about family, loving one another and all the values of Judaism on his *Bimah*, act in caring ways to his congregants, and then, put them down.

Now, I know that the reason he puts people down, was/is judgmental of others was/is because he himself was transgressing, pursuing a nefarious double life. He was/is "a person of the lie,"[33] and a good way to take the spotlight off himself was/is to judge others.

Eventually, he was offered a position at a synagogue closer to New York. It was half the distance from New York. This synagogue had just been through a difficult experience with their previous rabbi who was accused of embezzling a great deal of money from them. There had been a physical altercation between this rabbi and a large donor to the synagogue which became a scandal in the town. They wanted a rabbi whom they thought they could trust and who would not give them any scandals. After he interviewed with them alone, we were interviewed together by them. They liked us both, trusted us both, and believed that my husband would not give them any scandals. They were very afraid of more scandal. They revealed to us this was a town which had been quite inhospitable to Jews, if not anti-Semitic. They were extremely concerned about being accepted by their non-Jewish neighbors.

My rabbi/husband prevailed upon me to stay in the marriage, to move with him, to buy a new home with him. He pointed out that, while this post was not an easy commute from Manhattan for me, it was half as far as the previous post had been. He observed that the people in this congregation were more educated, wealthier, and that I probably would have a much easier time relocating my practice and business there than was possible in the Hartford suburb. He promised he would be a good husband, and that I would not be sorry I stayed with him. He said his mood swings had been all because he did not

---

[33]M. Scott Peck, MD. <u>People of The Lie: The Hope For Healing Human Evil.</u> New York. Simon & Schuster. 1983

know where or if he would be employed. He promised emphatically that because he had inherited money from his mother he would put down half the down payment on a home with me, and that he would continue to pay the mortgage and carrying costs as he had done in our previous home. He promised that the home would be in my name only, that he would give me a quit claim deed after the closing as he had done for our current home because he believed a woman should have the home in her name, and that what happened to me with my first husband would never happen with him. I would still pay for my New York space, commuting, and supporting myself there for the three days I worked there. I would pay for furnishing the new home. He promised repeatedly that the new home would always be my home, that I would "never have to worry about having a home."

He was attentive and loving to me, remarking how we "fit together" in so many ways, exemplified by how we slept in a "perfect spoon" position as one. He said he could not imagine life without "cuddling" with me, that this gave him much comfort, sustained him, along with everything else I brought to him. We would still not be able to be together three nights of the week. I hoped this would soon change. Little did I know then that this was a part of the marriage that suited him - the geographical distance, my commuting; that this arrangement made it easy for him to pursue his nefarious double life in my absences. I did not know about this then. He persuaded me to go with him.

We began looking for a place to live near the synagogue where he was to become rabbi. I paid the entire down payment on our first home because my husband had no savings. I accepted his explanation that loans for his years of schooling took all of the limited salary he had made as Dean of the School of Sacred Music at Hebrew Union College. Looking back on it after things became clear to me, and I began to study rabbis and sexual misconduct, I realized that his money was going to prostitutes, his other nefarious sex actions, and his gambling habit. I learned that often, people who are addicted to one destructive habit, usually have other addictions as well.

For our first home, a condominium, my husband offered to put the home in my name, with my paying the down payment and other costs and his paying the carrying charges. He said that it says in the *Talmud* that, "A man's home is his wife." He quoted *Talmud* to me often with

90

regard to our marriage. He told me that he would never make me cry, as, "God sees a woman's tears." "A man must listen to his wife: if she is short, he must bend down to hear her." He told me that a man must respect his wife, there must be "*Shalom bayit*"- peace in the house. He wanted me to feel secure and to feel I would always have a home, no matter what. I believed him and adored him. I thought he adored me too. He promised to give me a quit claim deed for this second home, the same as he had done for our first home, as soon as the closing took place, so that, although when we bought the home it would be in both our names, I would end up owning it, as I had our first home. Because he had given me the quit claim deed with the purchase of our first home, I trusted he would do the same with this one. This home required a much larger down payment than the first home, almost five times as much. I was concerned about putting so much of my savings into the down payment for it. Because of his inheritance from his mother, my husband told me he had been able to pay off all his debts and that he "would have no trouble putting down half the down payment on this home and paying the carrying charges on it. After the closing, I expected my husband to give me the quit claim deed as he promised. When he did not, I asked him for it. He kept promising me that he would. He never did.

His payments on the home amounted to less than half of what I was paying for the place in New York. Our goal was for me to build up my practice in Connecticut and, as soon as possible, to live there full time. He promised that even then he would not ask me to pay half the carrying charges on this home, as he would be making up for the considerable sums I had spent on his wardrobe, furnishing our homes, travel, commutation, and other things. And he promised me that once I moved to Connecticut full time, he would financially support us, with my earnings going into my savings for my children. He said he wanted to do this, that a husband should do this, that a home should be in a wife's name; that the Talmud says that "a man's home is his wife." Perhaps because he repeated this so often, I should have been suspicious. But, I was not. I was elated. I thought I now had a real husband, a husband like my father had been to my mother. I believed him.

My husband inherited a large sum from his mother. He wanted us each to put down an equal amount on a much more expensive, much larger, more luxurious home. If we both put down an equal amount, we could move into the kind of home where he wanted to be able to entertain his new congregants. These people lived in beautiful single-family homes in a section of Connecticut that was quite "posh," as he described it. He wanted a place to show off his mother's baby grand piano. We found a beautiful brand new town home, a condominium. It was twice the size of our previous home. It had a two story ceiling in the large living room, with an imposing fireplace and skylights; a large master bedroom and bath, also with skylights, on the second floor, along with second bedroom and bathroom, which he wanted as his study. There was a large room and half-bath, which was to serve as my office/study on the first floor where I could see clients. There was a large dining space which Jon thought would be perfect for entertaining; a huge, eat-in kitchen; and a patio. It was on a lake with a clubhouse, tennis courts, and pool. It certainly was an elegant home where my husband would be able to entertain his "rich, posh" congregants and friends. It seemed like Paradise to me. I would have to endure only half the commute, driving 55 miles each way, instead of the 110 miles each way I had been logging.

Although it meant another large outlay of money for me (I would have to buy more furnishings), I believed my husband would give me the quit claim deed, would keep his promises to me; that as he told me, he wanted me to feel secure and to feel I would always have a home, no matter what. I believed him and adored him I thought he adored me too. He had gone back to the loving way he treated me before we were married and when we were first married. The nightmare of his 'swings' from suicidal depression to manic 'highs' seemed to have vanished. (Unfortunately, I was to learn that this was only temporary. He was to get much worse). He seemed very happy, and I was very happy, too. Although he kept promising me that he would give me the quit claim deed, this promise, like many of his others, proved to be a lie.

My rabbi/husband asked me to buy the additional furniture and appliances he wanted. I did as he asked. Along with many other items, I bought a refrigerator, since this new home did not have one, kitchen furniture and additional appliances, patio furniture, an expensive dining room set with six silk custom upholstered chairs, bedroom furniture, and a queen sized sofa bed for the study so family and friends could sleep over.

I thought my husband would be overjoyed at being offered this position. These were much more sophisticated people than those at his first congregation, more educated, and wealthier, which was all important to him. Instead, after he assumed his new post, he found things to criticize about these people, too. He declared that while they were wealthier than those in his former congregation, and, even though it was a smaller congregation, and they would pay him a larger salary, which he liked, that they were "shallow," and were more like "*goyim*" than Jews. I was horrified at his judgementalism.

However, after my rabbi/husband accepted the position in Ridgefield, he seemed to come out of his negative mood. He promised me he would be a good husband and I would not be sorry I stayed with him. Indeed, he was very attentive and loving, more so than he had ever been.

He wanted to go to Maine for vacation before assuming his new post. He had never been to Maine. We could visit my father's *shul*, he could pray at my father's lectern, which was still maintained by his congregation, and we could visit my relatives who had remained there, and my parents' and sister's graves. I would be pleased to show him where I grew up. We decided to take a trip to Maine.

I was very proud to show off my rabbi/husband to family and people I knew who still lived in Bangor. The rabbi in the Orthodox *shul* honored my husband by calling him to the *Torah*. I had on my biggest "Vanna smile," beaming from ear to ear. I was proud to have my rabbi/husband praying at my father's lectern. It was one of the proudest and happiest moments of my life. The only thing that would have made me happier would have been for my parents to have been there.

We flew from Boston to Bar Harbor in a small twelve seat plane. The view of Mt. Desert Island and the smaller islands around it, off the Maine coast, was breathtaking. I took my rabbi/husband to the last place I walked with my father before he died, a place I feel my father's presence, his *neshama* (soul) when I go there: the top of Cadillac mountain in Acadia National Park, Bar Harbor, Maine. It is my most favorite place in the world, a place where the Atlantic Ocean meets the mountain, where you can see for miles, even to Mt. Katahdin, the highest mountain in Maine, where I had gone to Girl Scout camp and walked across Knife's Edge when I was ten years of age. My parents took me to Cadillac mountain many times as young girl, and I have gone there often as an adult. My husband loved it, too, and we walked the paths together.

At the cemetery in Bangor, my rabbi/husband said the *El Molay Rachamim* at my parents' graves and the grave of my dear sister Lillian, who died the year after my father did. She is buried next to them. I 'talked to them,' telling them I was happy with my husband and knew they would love him, too.

I showed my rabbi/husband the house where I grew up around the corner from the *shul*, the Jewish Community Center, my elementary school, my junior high school, and my old high school (Bangor High has since moved to new, larger quarters,) and the Bangor Public Library, where I spent so many hours, expanding the boundaries of my sheltered, small town life by reading every book I could.

We returned to Connecticut and settled into our new home. My rabbi/husband gave me a birthday party, as I had done for him in our first home. He invited congregants from the synagogue, and friends of mine, his and ours. He also planned a Musicale, which he knew I loved. He invited a pianist, baritone, and soprano to entertain. He, himself, sang my favorites, both with guitar and playing the Fun Machine, and, although I felt embarrassed that he played and sang songs Elvis Presly used to sing, and did the Elvis 'gyrations,' I delighted in the live performances in my honor. One of our guests videotaped the party and Musicale. My husband also traveled a good distance to buy a birthday cake from a special caterer who catered a wedding at which he officiated. I had remarked on how delicious the cake was, and he wanted me to have it. I was delighted that my rabbi/husband seemed now to be 'doing' for me, as I had for him for so long.

I felt wanted by my husband. I felt appreciated by him. I felt pretty, sweet, beautiful, and I looked it. People commented on how beautiful I looked, and on my radiant, beautiful smile. Once again, I buried my suspicions. I denied my doubts, the truth about how badly he had behaved toward me about the condyloma and during the period after he found out he had not been invited back to his first congregational position as a rabbi. I told myself it was 'understandable' that he would have behaved so badly with all the stress he had been under. Now that he had a new position, in a synagogue more to his liking, and we had a beautiful, large, elegant new home, he seemed to have put all that behind him. He was 'being a husband,' the husband he had promised he would be. I told all this to my daughter. She accepted it, and she and her husband came down for my party, and for *SHABBAT*. Then, along with his parents and two grandmothers, they came down again for Thanksgiving dinner, which my rabbi/husband and I cooked together. We were being a family, as he had promised he wanted. I was happy.

That December, we went to England for two weeks, one in London and one in Oxford. My son had become engaged to a girl from Oxford, and I wanted to meet her family and celebrate their engagement. We had a wonderful time, celebrating New Year's eve at the ballet, and then dancing at our beautiful hotel, the Meridien, with my children. My husband was thoughtful, attentive, caring with me and my family. He behaved like a loving stepfather to my children. He remarked, as he had done often, that he "marveled" at what a good mother I was. He admired me very much for that. I was very happy. We enjoyed ourselves immensely, seeing all the sights in London and then in Oxford.

I told my rabbi/husband of the difficulty I felt commuting. To help me to relocate my practice and business from Manhattan to where we lived, my husband arranged for me to give a seminar for the Men's Club of his synagogue. He advised me that many of the members were executives with large corporations in the area or owned their own businesses and that they would make good clients for me. He often touted my work, accomplishments and expertise, and seemed to be my biggest champion, as I was his. In order to facilitate this career move, I bought a franchise with the Success Motivation Institute, and marketed their programs: cognitive behavioral trainings on audio cassettes, with lesson manuals in motivation, goal setting, time management, management, sales skills, and sales management. I planned to utilize these programs to consult to companies and organizations as well as with private clients.

In January, my niece Joni died. She had not told anyone how sick she had become or even that she had lymphoma. When I spoke to her in December before we went to England she sounded fine. She put her little boy, then three years of age, on the phone to speak to me and to hear my voice. I had not seen them since we had been in California over a year ago. I was in total shock, grief, inconsolable, sobbing out my grief. Jon was quite loving to me. He organized a *minyan* to say *Kaddish* at the synagogue that night. I grieve for Joni to this day. I still miss her. She was a light in an often dark world, a beautiful, loving young woman. She was only 36 years of age when she died.

Not long after this, my husband started being verbally abusive again. He criticized me and put me down mercilessly, just as he did his congregants, but with me, it was to my face, the "Face" he had always said he loved. If I did not get the key in the door immediately, he would grab it out of my hand and say, "What's the matter with you, can't you do anything?" I stopped unlocking the door as he always wanted me to do, and instead, handed the keys to him so he could do it. He criticized how I chopped vegetables, so I told him he was the best vegetable chopper. He criticized me for all kinds of ridiculous, trivial things. There was no reasoning with him about any of this; he would just get more critical, so I found ways of easing out of the situations he created. I did not like his cruel behavior, and knew I did not want to go on this way, but did not know what to do about it.

He started leaving women's names and telephone numbers around the house that were clearly not congregants. He seemed to be totally out of control. He drove so fast that I stopped riding in the car with him. I insisted that either I drive or we go in separate cars. Depending on what was happening we did both of these. He previously gave me his calendar every week so we could check each other's schedules and make plans accordingly. He no longer did this. He hadn't done so for some time. When I asked him for it, he said he left it at the synagogue.

He stopped wearing his wedding ring, the wedding ring he insisted I pay for along with my own because he wanted a double ring ceremony. We picked out the rings together on 47th Street in the diamond district in New York. The rings were engraved with, "I am my beloved's and my beloved is mine," in Hebrew letters. When I asked him about his ring, he said he lost it playing touch football on the lawn at the synagogue, and, although he searched and searched, he could not find it.

One day, in April, we drove up to the town where his previous congregation was located to visit one of his former congregants, a woman we both loved who was terminally ill with cancer. She was at home, with nurses, because she wanted to die at home. He brought along his guitar to play and to sing to her. He could be a very loving man when he chose. But I was beginning to think he was a Jekyll/Hyde personality. He would be loving one minute and then, critical and cruel. When we left Bea's home, he drove into Hartford. I asked him where he was going as this was in the opposite direction from our home. He said he wanted to show me something. He drove to a street which he then told me was where he often "picked up prostitutes." I was in shock. I asked him why he was telling me this. Was it true. He said, "Yes, it's true." Then, abruptly, he said "No, it's not true. I just wanted to see how you would react"! I was incredulous and asked him why he did this. He had no explanation.

Before his 'Mr. Hyde' seemed to take over his personality completely, I wanted to do something special for him and his new synagogue. At his suggestion, in loving memory of my niece, Joni, I donated enough copies for the congregation of the new <u>Gates of Song</u>[34] prayer book to his synagogue. He had worked on the committee which produced it and his name was in it. I also fund-raised for a music fund I established in his name at the synagogue. I planned a birthday party and concert for him at the synagogue to inaugurate the music fund, and arranged for a professional violinist and pianist I knew to come up from New York. I arranged for a caterer to donate the food and serve, and I invited friends of his he never would have expected to be there. I rented a baby grand piano to be delivered to the synagogue. The rabbi who officiated at our wedding, and who was rabbi at a congregation nearby, over the border in New York, came with his wife. My husband was overjoyed at the entire celebration.

But his behavior became erratic. He would be loving one minute and critical and cruel the next. He continued to leave women's names and numbers on little slips of paper around the house, which he would alternately say were prostitutes, and then change that and say they were "synagogue business." He did officiate at weddings and other ceremonies for non-congregants. I wanted to believe him. He continued to refuse to allow me to see his calendar. He also wanted

---

[34]<u>Gates of Song: Music for *SHABBAT.*</u> Congregational edition. American Conference of Cantors, by committee. New York. Transcontinental Music Publications. 1987.

me to stop driving to the city, and, instead to take the train from Brewster. He said he would drive me to the train very early Tuesday morning and pick me up late Thursday night, that this way I would only have two nights to sleep over in the city instead of three. He promised he would not speed, but would drive carefully to the train station. I wondered what the real reason was that he did not want me to drive, to become dependent on his picking me up at the train, but I went along with his request. I wondered why he started driving my car. First, I thought it was because my car was only three years old and was a top of the line Toyota, a Cressida, what people called the "poor man's Mercedes," and his was a battered Buick Skylark. I later surmised it was because he did not want his car, which was known to synagogue members, parked at women's homes or at prostitute's places of "business."

I had been staying in New York three nights a week and cramming all my clients and business into three days. Because of his increasingly erratic, cruel behavior, and because I knew that he had "gone to prostitutes" in the past, I became quite suspicious. Also, my rabbi/husband now flirted unashamedly with women wherever we went, congregants included, right under my nose, flaunting this behavior. He told me they "expected" him to do it. Indeed, many of these women draped themselves around him shamelessly and in my presence. He said he wanted to make them "feel good." "I love women, all women, but I love you in a different way," he explained. He cherished me, adored me, he said. He was married to me and I was his wife, he had chosen me for his wife, he maintained. He swore up and down that he did not "do anything beyond the flirting."

But his behavior became increasingly alarming and suspicious. One night, at an event for teens at the synagogue, which he asked me to chaperon with him, he told me how "hot" the daughter of the President of the synagogue was, especially because she was half Puerto Rican, and that he would "love to pork her." This was a phrase he used constantly now. I had never heard this term before. He had to explain to me what it meant: he said it meant that he wanted to "f——her." (He said the word, but I do not write it out here.) I was horrified. I told him that his behavior was out of control and that he needed help.

One week, I told him I wanted to drive instead of taking the train. Then, instead of coming home Friday mornings as I would when I drove, I came home Wednesday night, planning to take the train back to New York early Thursday morning. When I arrived home, I parked the car in the garage and started up the stairs. My husband shouted, "What are you doing here?" I was shocked at this greeting. I called, "It's my home. I'm home." He met me at the living room landing. He was naked. I was sure I heard the kitchen patio door open and close. I asked him who was there. He said no one. But when I went into the house, the sofa bed in my study was open. I was very suspicious. He insisted no one was there, but he acted guilty. I was fearful and felt devastated.

I also found out that during this time my husband was renting and watching pornographic videos. He disclosed to me that he had done this prior to our marriage and had never stopped. He disclosed that he thought he had been seen in a place to rent these pornographic videos in the prior community we lived in, the one where the congregation did not renew his contract. In June, I planned to go to England for my son's wedding. He was not to go. My first husband and my daughter were going over with me. I was very fearful to leave him alone. I feared that he had gone back to prostitutes and that he was also pursuing other sex addiction practices and that we needed to seek expert help. When I asked him about this, he denied it vehemently. However, he was more often cruel to me than loving at this time.

He did agree to go to a Sex Addicts Anonymous (SAA) meeting with me. I had started researching information about sex addiction, a term I was not familiar with until that time. In fact, it was a fairly new term, one that Patrick Carnes wrote about in his recent book.[35] My rabbi/husband denied up and down at the SAA meeting that he was a sex addict even though the others at the meeting saw through his denial and tried to help him to admit it and face it so he could change. I was in tremendous fear about what this all meant. We were beginning to learn about AIDS at this time, and this information produced enormous fear for me. I had already suffered one STD (sexually transmitted disease) because of my rabbi/husband. Fortunately, that was a disease which could be and was cured, although painfully. The American public was just beginning to learn about AIDS. From that time until many years later, I lived in mortal

---

35 Patrick Carnes. The Sexual Addiction. Minneapolis. CompCare Publications. 1984

fear that he had given me AIDS, and had myself tested every year for ten years after the last time I had sexual relations with my rabbi/husband, until my gynecologist insisted that there was no reason to take any more tests, that I did not have AIDS and was not going to have it.

When I returned from England, I pressed him about his calendar. I suspected there was an iniquitous reason for his not wanting me to see it. On July 4th, he officiated at a wedding in New York. It was at a very beautiful place on the Queens side of the East River. We were able to stand on the terrace and see the fireworks directly in front of us, with the New York City skyline across the river. The bride and groom and others were standing on the terrace around us. My rabbi/husband began whispering loudly into my ear the sexual things he wanted to do to the bride. I was horrified. I asked him how he could say those things, even think them, when he was the rabbi who just officiated at her wedding. I asked him how could he say them to me, his wife? I also asked how he could say these things in such close proximity to the bride and groom and other guests gathered around us to watch the fireworks. Wasn't he afraid they would overhear? I was shaking in fear. When we got home, I asked him to go to see a psychiatrist with me.

Finally, he agreed that if I could find one someplace like Mt. Kisco, New York, not where we lived, not in Connecticut, he would go. I found a psychiatrist at the hospital in Mt. Kisco and we went to see him together. This doctor interviewed both of us together and then each of us separately. He told us that my husband was a sex addict, had bipolar disorder, also known as manic depression, was in a manic state, and needed immediate treatment. He said he would have to be an inpatient to be treated properly. My husband pounded his fist on the psychiatrist's desk, shouting that he was a rabbi, had a *SHABBAT* service to conduct that evening, and there was no way he was going into some hospital. He stormed out of the psychiatrist's office. I was sick with fear. I was afraid of him and for me. I felt as if I were in a terrible, terrible nightmare. We drove to the psychiatrist's office in separate cars. I hesitated, not knowing whether I should drive to our home, or to my office/apartment in Manhattan. I drove home.

That night, I could not go to the *SHABBAT* service with him. I could not be there for him as I was used to doing, looking up at him adoringly, playing the role of "*rebbitzin,*" wife of a rabbi, a "holy" man, a man who stood on the *Bimah* and preached about God, Torah, family, and who behaved in such cruel, immoral, abusive ways, and lied about it.

That Sunday, July 10, the fateful day, he finally brought his calendar to me. He was on his way to a baby naming. He asked me to go with him. I almost always accompanied him to the weddings, *Bar* and *Bat Mitzvahs*, and baby namings at which he officiated, sometimes four events on a weekend. It was exhausting for me, not only because I worked in the city during the week, and was commuting long distances, and I also did much of the driving to these events, but especially because he needed me to bolster his confidence and self esteem to be able to officiate at these events. There was nothing I would not do for my husband. I loved him unconditionally.

But now, not only because he had returned to his frequent practice of driving recklessly, speeding, pounding on the steering wheel, and shouting, and I knew I should not allow him to drive us both, but also because he was behaving in such immoral, cruel ways, and because of what the psychiatrist had told us, I could not bring myself to go. I could not go and act as if everything was all right when he was so out of control. I told him I did not feel up to going.

I was very grieved and fearful about his behavior, feeling a sense of foreboding. I knew I could not go on this way with him. I told him this. He ran upstairs to his study, came quickly down to the kitchen, where I was standing, and shouted, "O.K. Here it is. You might as well see this now, too, and know the truth so that we can have some peace." With this, he slammed the calendar book and a red box down on the dining room table.

THE ASSAULT and MY RABBI/HUSBAND'S THREAT TO KILL ME

When my husband returned from the baby naming, I got up from the kitchen table where I had sobbed for some time. I had remained there, not knowing what to do.

Now, carrying his calendar book in my hand, I greeted him in the hallway between the kitchen and dining room. I gestured with the calendar. "What are all the whiteouts?" It was easier for me to start with the calendar than the contents of the red box. He admitted he had "whited out prostitutes' names and appointments with them," and that the little pieces of paper he left around the house with women's names were those of prostitutes and women he had sex with. Shocked by all of this frightening information, shaking, I told him we had to get expert help. He shouted that he would not go again to anyone for so-called help, that he did not need or want any help. He said he "liked" what he was doing. "Don't rock the boat and you will have a marriage, the same marriage you have had. I have never stopped going to prostitutes, never stopped having sex with many other women, any woman I want! Anywhere I want! I never will! The list in the box, 500 names of women, are women I have had sex with, students, congregants, single, married, any women, prostitutes!" he shouted. "Yours is the only name not on the list. I married you, didn't I. Don't rock the boat, and you will have the same marriage we have had." I was shocked, shaking. I could not believe what I was hearing. But, I knew I had to believe it and to stay rational, calm. I mustered up all the strength I could to stay calm. I spoke to him in a soft but firm tone of voice. "If you will not go for help, then I must take all this to people who *can* help to get their help without you," gesturing toward the red box and lifting the calendar.

He grabbed the calendar out of my hand, tore at its pages, grabbed me, and slammed me hard, repeatedly, against the wall, shaking me, and shouting, "If you tell anyone about this, I will kill you, and I will be exonerated because I am a rabbi"! He continued slamming me against the wall. "I will put you in a wood chipper so no one will ever find you," he continued shouting, a reference to a Connecticut woman who was killed and put in a wood chipper by her husband. The case had been in all the news. I was in mortal fear for my life. He finally stopped slamming me against the wall and let me go. He turned and walked into my study and turned on the television as if nothing had happened. Although in shock, extremely frightened, quite dazed, in pain and bruised from his slamming me against the wall, I slowly and quietly went upstairs to the telephone in our bedroom and called the police. I was physically hurt. My husband had used a great deal of force in all his fury. I was afraid for my life. Quietly, I went downstairs and out the front door to meet the officers who answered my call.

The officers asked me what was going on. I told them what my rabbi/husband had shouted, threatened. I told them that two days ago we had been to a psychiatrist who wanted to hospitalize him. I told them about his repeatedly slamming me against the wall. They informed me that the law in Connecticut now mandated them to arrest my husband because they saw signs of violence against me; that they saw red marks on my arms and neck, that they saw bruises and abrasions. They wrote down my statement and asked me to sign it. I begged them not to arrest my husband, but to get him to a psychiatrist. I again told them that we had seen a doctor in Mt. Kisco who wanted to hospitalize him. I asked them if they could take him to a hospital. I did not want him arrested. I wanted to get him help. I believed at that time that he could be helped. They told me that it was not their job. Their job was to arrest him because they had seen evidence that he had hit me. They again told me about the law that took effect in Connecticut Oct. 1, 1986 (after the first time my husband assaulted me, and the sheriff did not arrest him) requiring police to take suspects into custody if they see evidence of violence. Then, they went into the house to arrest my rabbi/husband. I waited outside numb, in shock. They handcuffed him, took him into the patrol car and left. The police allowed him to take some personal things with him but they made him give me his house keys and car keys. They told me he would be at a motel awaiting arraignment in the morning.

My husband called me repeatedly from the motel begging me to help him, to go to the police station to get the charges dropped. I did everything I could to get the charges dropped. I called the police station, but they said I could not get the charges dropped, it was "out of my hands." My husband kept calling me. He wanted me to take him to a hospital where he knew people on the staff and which was near his synagogue so he could sign himself in and get out of being arraigned in the morning. I was very fearful to do this, but I loved him very much and wanted to get him help. I called the hospital and they said I could bring him in. I tried to get a neighbor to go with me because I was afraid to drive him there alone, but I was not able to do so.

I drove him to the hospital, Four Winds. I warned him that now that the police knew he hit me it would be in his best interest if he did not hurt me any more. I made clear to him that the hospital knew what he had done and that I was driving him there. The ride to this hospital was harrowing. I was in pain from his assault on me. He pounded on the dashboard and shouted the entire way. By this time, it was dark. I had never been to this hospital before, was not sure exactly where it was, and the directions they gave me seemed complicated. It was located along a winding, country road. It seemed pitch black out. It was the longest, most frightening drive of my life. Somehow, I stayed calm.

Somehow, I made it there. I was numb, and at the same time, in spite of the physical pain from his assaulting me, mustered up the strength to drive him to the hospital, much the same way as a parent, when a child was trapped under a car, lifted the car.

They interviewed us both, individually. Then, they told me they were admitting him. I drove home. I felt frightened, exhausted. I prayed for him, that he would get the help he needed, that the rabbi/husband I loved and cherished, not this dangerous man, would be coming home.

The next day, I called the hospital. They scheduled an appointment for me. I went in to see the psychiatrist who was treating him. He informed me that it would take "time" before they knew what his prognosis would be. I visited him a few times in the hospital. He alternately proclaimed he told his congregants that I put him there, or that he signed himself in to get away from me. Clearly, he had not divulged the truth to them. Certainly, I could not "put him" in a mental hospital. Obviously, they would not keep him in the hospital for two months as they did, for him "to get away from" me.

By August, my dear friend Bernice, whom I had known for almost eight years (from Central Synagogue in Manhattan), asked me to come out to her summer home in Easthampton, Long Island, to spend some time with her and to get away. I loved Bernice. She was a kind, generous person. She hosted me at her beautiful home several times, and hosted Jon and me for a few days before we went to Israel. I found it very relaxing to be at her home, to swim in her pool, to lie in her hammock under the trees. Bernice was always a caring and gracious host. I thought that it would help me to cope with what was happening to be with her. I went to Easthampton.

I called the hospital from Easthampton and spoke to the chief psychiatrist whom I was informed was now his doctor. This doctor announced to me that, "Jon is a sociopath, a person who lacks a sense of moral responsibility or social conscience, is a sex addict, has a character disorder, and is manic depressive. He is in a manic state." He said that while they would do their best to treat him, there was very little hope that he would change, and that he was dangerous to me. He urged me to change the locks on my home, and to arrange for an alarm system to be installed immediately because this hospital was open, not locked, that Jon could walk off at any time. He also told me to get a Court Order of Protection against him. I was reeling, struck mute with intense shock. I could not believe what I was hearing, that this was happening.

I decided to return to New York to my office/apartment immediately so that I could take the steps the psychiatrist urged me to take. I did not know how to proceed. Because my first husband was/is a lawyer, I called him. By this time, he had been practicing law in Brooklyn where he had returned to live, for some time, and was doing quite well. (It seems that once he did not have a father-in-law and wife to provide him with funds, he was "able" to work). He told me how to proceed with the steps necessary to request an Order of Protection. He instructed me that I had to serve Jon with papers to proceed with obtaining a Court Order Of Protection, and he found a process server to do this for me.

I returned to Connecticut to get the locks changed on the house and to have an alarm system installed. I was doing all of this in a semiautomatic state, putting one foot in front of the other, doing what the psychiatrist told me had to be done. I was praying and hoping that the psychiatrist was not right, that Jon would be helped, that he would return, that my "soul mate," the man I loved, my rabbi/husband would come home, that he would be 'cured,' and that we would have a loving, normal life together.

THE ORDER OF PROTECTION HEARING

The transcript of the Order of Protection hearing is a matter of public record. Dr. Newt Schiller, a psychotherapist from White Plains, New York, went with me for support. He knew Jon before he knew me, had come to our housewarming at our first home, and he and I had become friends. He was aghast at what Jon had been doing, what he had done to me. He was very supportive of me, and he helped me to get through the hearing. Unfortunately, Newt was not able to come the next day to guide me not to agree to the deal pressed upon me by a local rabbi emeritus from another synagogue near our home. The deal which this rabbi emeritus proposed was for me not to press charges against Jon if he promised not to pursue contesting the granting of the Order of Protection for an additional day. I agreed to the proposal under this pressure.

I regret this decision. The rabbi who pressured me, I now know, did not have my interest at heart. I went to his house the evening before the second day of the hearing and asked him and his wife for help. I brought some of the contents of Jon's red box. He examined the pictures at length. His interest seemed prurient. He told his wife not to look at the articles from the box which I had brought. He agreed to come to court the next day to "help" *me*. Then, he followed me out to the car, got into my car, which I thought was strange, leaned over, and tried to kiss me on the mouth! A man in his late '70's, a rabbi 'emeritus' whom I thought I could trust, who had offered to support me. I managed to turn my head away. I was very grateful that my car had bucket seats and not a bench seat. He was not able to move over and press himself on me, as it seemed he was trying to do. I got out of the car on my side, and said I thought he did not mean to do what he did, and that his wife was waiting for him in the house.

As I feared, this rabbi 'emeritus' did not come to the hearing to help me as I requested, and as he promised. He had his fellow rabbi's interest at heart, not mine. When this rabbi 'emeritus' came to the hearing the next day, in the corridor outside the courtroom before the hearing was to start, he said that if I agreed not to press charges against my rabbi/husband for assaulting me, that he could get my rabbi/husband to stop contesting the granting of the Order of Protection and that this was in my best interest. I was in a state of fear of my husband. I now had to contend with a rabbi 'emeritus' whose advances I had spurned and whom I could not trust. I did not challenge him or stand up to him. Again, I was 'like a lamb to the slaughter.' Under the pressure, I agreed not to press charges. The Order of Protection was granted.

The Order of Protection probably would have been granted anyway. The policeman who had arrested my rabbi/husband and had seen the bruises he inflicted on me by his assaulting me came to testify. My rabbi/husband admitted to his frequenting of prostitutes on the stand the previous day. I had given evidence to the court to substantiate the granting of an Order of Protection against him. The monstrous "old boy network" reared its ugly head. I now could not press charges against my rabbi/husband for assaulting me.

My rabbi/husband was ordered not to go on the property where our home was, or anywhere near me.

Would that I could have had the strength at that time in my own life that I taught my clients, men and women, to have, and which I exhibited in sessions with them. I do believe that my suffering, although unknown by them, made me trustworthy to them. One of my male clients was a prestigious Park Avenue attorney; one had a seat on the stock exchange; a few were wealthy stock brokers; others were a professor, an academic department chairman, an advertising agency president, executives, owners of multi-million dollar businesses. I was very strong with them. I 'called' them on their behaviors in private sessions or in joint sessions with their wives, or wives-to-be. I was far from naive with them and not intimidated by them. Instead of being a 'lamb to the slaughter' with them, I was like a lion, or like Daniel in the lions' den, strong and unafraid.

After the Order of Protection hearing and for some time afterwards, I went to a group in a town in Connecticut about 30 minutes drive north of our home for women victims/survivors of domestic violence. They helped me, we helped each other to cope with what we had been through. I was able to emerge from the experience with renewed strength and a determination to help other wives and ex-wives of rabbis and victims/survivors of rabbis' domestic abuse. I did not yet have the knowledge to understand the concept that the women on my rabbi/husband's list of women with whom he had sex for at least thirteen years before our marriage and all during our marriage, and which list was presented as 'evidence' to the court, single, married, divorced or widowed women, were abused by him. Some would even say that the prostitutes on the list were abused by him. In some places the men who frequent prostitutes, ironically called 'Johns' are the ones arrested for prostitution, not the women prostitutes. This knowledge came later.

I was to suffer further abuse by my rabbi/husband. The hospital he had been admitted to kept him for two months. As soon as he got out, he found a lawyer to represent him in a legal suit against me for alimony! The doorbell rang one morning at 7 AM. I looked through the window before I answered it, as I was still afraid of my husband and been told not to let him in, if he showed up. It was a process server. He served me with papers for the legal suit my husband instituted. <u>He was suing *me* for alimony and to obtain my half ownership of our home</u> *so that he would be the sole owner!* He was also suing me for the entire contents of our home, and one half of any other assets I owned!

I was in such a state of shock from the threat these papers posed to my life that when I ran down the stairs to get in the car to drive back to New York where I had to see clients, I fell, missing the last several stairs. I was still in back and neck pain from the assault by my husband. Because of this pain, along with the intense surprise of, and the threat of the legal papers, I did not negotiate the steps. I was numb with shock and fear. I did not know I had suffered a fractured ankle until hours later when I was sitting with a client in a therapy session. I only knew that I had clients who needed me, expected me to be there for them, and that I wanted to be there for them. I was unaware that I had a swelling the size of a baseball on my ankle! My client saw it as we were getting up at the end of the session. I had trouble standing on my left leg. I went to Lenox Hill Hospital Emergency Room by taxi. Indeed, my ankle was fractured. I had driven 55 miles and conducted a therapy session with a fractured ankle! I was put in a cast and on crutches, which further aggravated the neck and back injury from my rabbi/husband's assault of me.

My rabbi/husband called me and told me that it was my fault that he had been in the mental hospital, that I had "humiliated" him by calling the police, that it was my fault that they had handcuffed him, and that he was going to make me <u>pay</u>, that he would make my life "miserable."[36] I had to find a lawyer to represent me in the legal suit my rabbi/husband filed while I was on crutches and in a cast. I spent six weeks quite immobilized. The only thing that kept me going was that I had my clients. Concentrating on them and what they needed allowed me to forget the horrible nightmare I was living in my private life for the hours a week that I was with them and worked with them and helped them. I stayed in Manhattan until I was able to get off the crutches and got on a cane. Fortunately, I was able to work in the office/apartment while on crutches. I was able to order food delivered, and friends helped me get through this difficult time.

My rabbi/husband pursued legal machinations against me for almost two years. He tried everything he could think of to harass me and cost me more money. He had his lawyer file papers against me for one thing after another. One of the maneuvers he tried, causing me much anguish as well as expense, was to ask the court to order me to give him a list of my clients' names and their records, (any clients I had ever had!), ostensibly to prove that I could pay him alimony, but probably so that he could harass them. The court did not allow this. My lawyer said that my rabbi/husband wanted to get the court to give him the entire equity in the house, even though I had paid half of it. This, after spending years telling me that he quoted the *Talmud* to me when he said that, "A man's home is his wife. He should eat and drink what he can afford, and honor his wife with more than he can afford," and, promising me that I would never have to worry about having a home; that he would make sure, no matter what, the home we shared would be mine. Now, he wanted not only to take away my home, but to get the court to order me to pay him alimony as well.

My lawyer cautioned me that, although my husband was employed, at this time, making more money than I, if I did anything to bring about his losing this position, the court could order me to support him financially. My lawyer said that even if I did not do "the something" to make him lose his position, but that if he lost it through

---

36An Expert social worker, as quoted on page 291 in Shattered Dreams, by Charlotte Fedders and Laura Elliott, states that, "Mental health professionals who are knowledgeable about the dynamics of family violence know that physical abuse is accompanied by psychological control and that when the victim takes action to end the violence, the assailant often turns to the court system to regain control and continue the harassment."

some other means, I could still be ordered to support him. I lived in fear that this could happen.

When I married this rabbi, I gave up my large apartment in New York to take a small one bedroom. I used it both as an office and to sleep over for three nights, then going back to my home in Connecticut. Most of my furniture and belongings were in my Connecticut home, including all the new furniture, kitchen equipment and other items I had bought to furnish it. If I lost my home, I would have nowhere to take these belongings, as they would not fit in my small quarters in New York. I would also have to work and live full time in a small one bedroom apartment, as the legal machinations along with everything else the marriage had cost me had depleted my savings. I could not see how I could ever financially support my rabbi/husband if the court ordered it, nor did I see how this would be legally fair or morally right. I felt that I was living an unreal nightmare that my rabbi/husband had created for me. The only thing that kept me 'grounded' was the time I spent on my clients' needs and with them to help them. I was only able to work part time, because of the strife my rabbi/husband was causing in my life; but, at least for those hours, I could immerse myself in my professional pursuits and help others who needed my help. I was most honored, privileged, and gratified to be able to help them.

I discussed with my lawyer the idea of my contacting the CCAR, the Central Conference of American Rabbis, the Reform rabbinic organization. I wanted to ask their help to get him to stop the legal suit against me for alimony. I was desperately afraid that with all the legal and court costs I would become destitute. I knew that most women who go through divorce, especially if the divorce is contested, end up destitute, or very close to it, according to studies which have been done.[37] I also wanted to inform the CCAR about what my husband was doing in order to protect any future victims from his abuse. My lawyer agreed that I should call them. He cautioned me to request that they not tell his synagogue board until after the divorce was final, because if he lost his job, the court could order me to support him financially. I was incredulous that this could be true, but I decided to follow his advice.

---

[37]See for example, Lenore J. Weitzman. The Divorce Revolution. 1985. New York. Macmillan.

First, I called and made an appointment with the rabbi who officiated at the *Bar* and *Bat Mitzvah* of my children. He was a "distinguished member" of the CCAR. I prepared a written statement on the advice of my lawyer. Rabbi Stern listened to me, looked at the statement, and then stood up. "This does not concern me," he said. "You have a lawyer." With that, he started toward the door of his office, indicating that my appointment was over. I was shocked. How could it "not concern" him! Did he mean to just sit back, do nothing, allow Jon to continue his abuse? I could not believe that this rabbi, whom I had looked up to and respected all the years I was a member of his synagogue could turn his back on me and on this shocking information.

I called the CCAR. I spoke with the rabbi then in charge of this kind of report. He said I must submit it to him in writing, which I did. Nothing was done. Unbelievably, they did not want to know about it! While my husband's sexual misconduct and his abuse of his wife were committed by him alone, his ability to continue this misconduct after rabbis in the rabbinic organization were informed was aided by the inaction of these men, and by a lack of effective controls over rabbis by this rabbinic body, the very body which places them in positions as rabbis, and governs their rabbinic lives.

No wonder my rabbi/husband thought he could get away with anything, even murder! I felt vulnerable, alone in a fight for my health and life, as well as for my financial safety. A rabbi whom I interviewed some years' later when I was researching my book, Arthur Gross-Schaefer, told me that these rabbis were as guilty as my husband by turning their backs on me and by ignoring what my rabbi/husband was doing. By the time I contacted the CCAR, my rabbi/husband had been perpetrating sexual abuse of women for 16 years, thirteen years of which were before I married him.

My rabbi/husband's legal maneuverings went on and on. Each one required my lawyer's response, and, of course, I had to pay for his time. His clock kept ticking. I called my rabbi/husband and begged him to stop this madness he was causing, to meet with our lawyers to try to settle this out of court. I pointed out that the trial could be covered by the press and I was sure he did not want his nefarious double life to come out in the newspapers. I did not know he was taping the call. He gave the tape to his lawyer to try to use against *me* in court!

During the trial, my lawyer told me that he had read a book I might know about since it was more in my field than his, called, The People of the Lie, by M. Scott Peck.[38] He said that my rabbi husband was one of "the people of the lie," that he knew he was a liar, living a life of lies, perpetrating evil. In spite of this statement, my lawyer was not willing to 'go the extra mile' for me so that the judge might be more inclined to order my husband to pay my legal and court costs, which were the result of my husband's actions, not mine, and to reimburse me for the considerable amount of dollars I had spent on him. If anyone were entitled to 'alimony,' I surely had to be the one. My lawyer stated to the judge that this rabbi/husband had duped me, assaulted me, and pursued prostitutes while married to me. But, while I was not ordered to pay him alimony, he did not even have to pay the legal and court costs he had caused me.

My lawyer, who was Jewish and male, would not go 'the extra mile' for me because he was very concerned with "how this all looks, a rabbi doing what he does." He wanted to prevent the information about this rabbi/abuser from getting out to the wider community in Connecticut, or into the Ridgefield Press or other local newspapers. He did not want people in the town to know about it because he wanted to "protect the good name of Jews in general and of rabbis in particular." He would not call certain witnesses I wanted called. For example, he would not call the police officer who had come prepared to testify at the Order of Protection hearing. He would not call the psychiatrist who had told me that Jon is a "sociopath," a "sex addict," and is "dangerous to (me)" and who instructed me to get the locks on the house changed and to pursue the granting of the Order of Protection. And, he would not refute the testimony and character of "character witnesses" my husband paraded before the judge. He said the judge would not "fall for this ploy." In one case, my lawyer allowed to stand false testimony by a woman I knew and told him had been taken to a mental hospital in a strait jacket. He told me he "saw no need to embarrass her" and that the "judge would see through her." I protested to my lawyer that he was allowing this woman to break

---

[38]M. Scott Peck, The People of the Lie: The Hope For Healing Human Evil New York. Simon & Schuster. 1983.

one of the Ten Commandments by allowing her to perjure herself, that he was injuring my case, injuring me. Nevertheless, he would not refute her testimony or expose her as an incompetent "character" witness. This was a case of the "old boy network" again hurting a woman, of the legal system stacked against women.[39]

I had tried to find a nonsexist or feminist lawyer in this Connecticut town, but was not able to do so. This wealthy lawyer was not on my side to the end of the case. He actually held up the sale of my house when I was finally able to put it up for sale. The market had dropped, and the price I was able to sell it for was far less than the purchasing price. I also had to give my now ex-husband/rabbi half of the money realized from the sale. My lawyer knew I desperately needed the funds. He claimed he was due additional fees, and would not release my house to be sold until he was paid these "additional fees." The Coalition for Family Justice,[40] a nonprofit organization which helps people (who are mostly women) with unfairness in family courts regarding divorce, now says this is unconscionable for divorce lawyers to do. This is a practice, an abuse which they are now working to change, to make it illegal for divorce lawyers to perpetrate this practice on their women clients. I was fighting for my survival against a rabbi/husband whom this lawyer had called one of "the people of the lie, evil," and yet, he was perpetrating his own form of evil against his client.

While my rabbi/husband was not granted the alimony he unbelievably, outrageously sought from me, nor was he granted the sole ownership of our home, my half of the home, the judge did not order him to pay my legal and court costs or to reimburse me for any of the considerable amount of money I had spent on him during our marriage. My lawyer calculated the amount that I had spent on this rabbi/husband perpetrator to total over $150,000, including his clothing, the travel he wanted us to do, the furniture and kitchen equipment he wanted, everything else he wanted which I paid for, and

---

[39]Karen De Crow. Sexist Justice: How Legal Sexism Affects You. New York. Vintage Books. 1975. See also, Charlotte Schwab. "External Causes of Depression in Women," a paper presented to The American Psychological Association. New Orleans. 1989.

[40]National Coalition for Family Justice. Monica Getz, President. Irvington, New York 10533.

the cost of commutation for me. This amount increased because of the legal fees I had to pay for the suit my rabbi/husband instituted against me to collect alimony from me, and because by the time I was able to sell the house, which I was legally prevented from doing during the trial and, later, by my lawyer, the real estate market had dropped, and I had to sell it for far less than we paid for it. This man, this rabbi/husband, deceived me, assaulted me, had gone to prostitutes, cost me most of my life savings, and did not have to pay me for what this so-called marriage had cost me.

I now regretted that I had agreed not to press charges against him for the assault in return for his stopping the contesting of the Order of Protection. The only one that benefited from my agreeing to this course of action was him. Had I not agreed, there would have been a second day of hearings, with all the evidence coming out about his sexual misconduct and his abuse of me. There is no doubt that the Order of Protection would have been granted, anyway, and I would have been free to press criminal charges against him. I was suffering physically, financially, emotionally, and otherwise from the havoc this rabbi had wrought in my life.

My rabbi/husband admitted to his iniquitous, predatory sexual activities on the stand. The judge found the contents of the red box of great interest: the picture of my rabbi/husband with the naked prostitute exposing her genitals to the camera with his hand on her breast, and the rest of the contents: other pictures, books and audio tapes about prostitution, articles about S&M prostitution, his 'membership card' in a known place of S & M prostitution in Manhattan, and Screw magazines. Yet, all this did not make the judge do the fair thing and order my rabbi/husband to pay my legal and court costs. I believe my lawyer bears some of the responsibility for this decision.

FREEDOM

Since my divorce from my rabbi/husband, and everything he put me through, I have worked hard to be like a lion, or like Daniel in the lions' den in my private life. My birthday is in August, which according to the astrological chart, makes me a Leo, Leo the lion. I have a lithograph of a painting by an Israeli artist which I found in Israel. It depicts the lion and the lamb. It hangs in my office/study. I look at it often, and it inspires me: to be the lion in my own life when needed, not always the lamb. I work hard in my life to maintain a sense of safety, empowerment, validation, and emphasize my strengths - the same principles I have taught clients, men and women clients, but especially women clients. Because of sexism in society, women do not have a sense of safety, are not empowered, are not validated, and are not usually aware of their strengths.

Since freeing myself from the entanglement of my rabbi/husband's abuse, and then, finally, from my first husband's hold on my life, I have used my freedom to achieve a spiritual independence, a true "I/Thou"[41] with the universe, giving to myself what I need so that I can give to my family, friends, community, the universe: to do God's work, *Tikkun Olam*. I am extremely grateful for my life, for the gift God has given me to bring a feminist spiritual healing to the world. I had always been troubled by how to reconcile my spirituality, my Judaism, my belief in God, my belief in the sanctity of marriage and family, community, with my feminism. I always wanted a spiritual, sacred relationship, marriage to a man. I still do.

I believe that women need connection. My friend, Dr. Judy Jordan, has studied and written about this with others at the Center for Research on Women at Wellesley College. But I will never compromise my spirituality, my feminism again to achieve connection, a connection which is spurious at best, and harmful and abusive, at worst. I find my 'connection' with my family, my spiritual groups, and with my friends, both women and men.

---

[41]Martin Buber. I And Thou. Touchstone Book published by Simon & Schuster.1996.

Since my freedom from abusive marriage, I have been a 'lion,' spreading this word, learning ways to help victims of rabbis' sexual harassment and abuse all over the country, helping women (and men) all over the world to heal from such abuse. I can give you only a few examples in this book.

In 1990, to better aid victims of rabbis' sexual abuse, I took a training at The Milton Erickson Institute of Hypnosis of New York with Daniel R. Lutzker, Ph.D., and received Certification in "Modern Hypnotic Techniques." Often, victims of rabbis' sexual abuse have difficulty talking about the abuse. Utilizing hypnosis can help them to talk about what happened and to heal. I have found the techniques I learned from Dr. Lutzker very helpful.

In 1992, I took a training with the College of Physicians & Surgeons of Columbia University in, "Innovations in the Treatment of Depression." I received a Certificate for "A.M.A.'s Physician Recognition Award," for completing this training. Often, victims of rabbis' sexual abuse suffer from depression. I want to be current with all the available techniques so that I can best help them. **Also, in 1992,** I served on the committee to create the conference at Hunter College, "Women Tell the Truth." I gave a seminar at the conference on how to handle sexual harassment at work. **Later, in 1992,** I lectured at the <u>AWED (Association for Women's Economic Development)</u> conference at the Marriott Marquis in New York on "Successful Negotiation Strategies for Women." I had given this lecture previously for several hundred women at a Women Business Owners of New York (WBONY) conference. The room was packed at the Marriott. Several thousand women attended this conference.

In 1993, I was invited to go to Russia as a 'citizen diplomat' to help women there to become entrepreneurs. They had lost their positions as doctors, psychologists, mathematicians, teachers, and in other professions. Several hundred women attended the conference in Moscow, and others in St. Petersburg. When I gave a small workshop on "Positive Self Identity: Achieving Self Defined Success" in Moscow, the women were ecstatic. I taught them how to do mirror work utilizing the tools of affirmations, visualizations. I had them stand on a chair and look into the mirror over the fireplace in the room where our workshop took place. This was the only way we could do this in the old building where the conference was being held. As each woman learned to call out her affirmation with strength, I taught the rest of the women to shout it back to her, to validate her. All this was done with a Russian translator at my side. It was one of the most elevating experiences of my life, and they told me, of theirs. They asked me to stay in Russia. They all wrote me letters at the end of the workshop, in Russian, thanking me, telling me what I had meant to them, the courage I had given them. I was extremely moved and honored.

When I returned from Russia, I gave a seminar/workshop at the New York Open Center, called "Women and Men: Achieving Successful Relationships." I taught the participants about gender differences, how to honor them, celebrate them, how to communicate and negotiate, taking them into account, how to keep love, spirituality alive in the relationship.

Later in 1993, I appeared on a panel on the "Brian Lehrer Show," on WNYC-TV called, "New York Men." I spoke about gender differences, the need to be aware of them, acknowledge them, honor them, celebrate them.

In 1994, I published an article in Ask Women for Success, called "Achieving Positive Self Identity and Self Defined Success,"[42] outlining a "Ten Step Program" for accomplishing this goal. My work emphasized the importance for women of not sacrificing self, and of working to achieve one's life's purpose.

Later in 1994, I gave a lecture/seminar to the "top 65 rabbis and executives" of the UAHC, (Union of American Hebrew Congregations) - the congregational organization in the Reform Judaism movement - about sexual harassment. I was asked to help them because there were "many congregations being sued because of sexual harassment of women by their rabbis." At this seminar it became clear that many of the men did not 'get' or want to admit that sexual harassment by rabbis even exists in the movement. The women saw it; the men did not. I describe what happened at this seminar elsewhere in this book.

In 1995, I traveled throughout Italy for a month with the daughter of a friend of mine with whom I had become friends. She was living in Florence, studying architecture. I had three primary destinations. I wanted to see the painting in the Uffizi, Botticelli's "The Birth of Venus." I loved this painting since I had first seen it in a book in my

---

[42]Available from the author.

teens and purchased a reproduction which I framed. It hangs on my wall and I look at it every day. I identify with Venus, not only as a beautiful goddess of love, but as an independent, self-defined, spiritual woman. I believe I am finally giving birth to my 'Venus.'

The second destination was to see Michaelangelo's "David." I have sometimes felt like David fighting Goliath in my life. Although David won, he went on to experience trials and tribulations, and to do some <u>not</u> spiritual deeds in his life, for which he made *Teshuvah*. In the end, his greatness prevailed, his spirituality prevailed. David's life has always inspired me.

The third destination was to see Michaelangelo's "Moses." Many people wondered why I wanted to see this sculpture, pointing out to me that Michaelangelo depicted Moses as having horns, an anti-Semitic belief. I do not regard the horns on this sculpture that way. To me, while Moses was the great leader he was, he also had faults, 'horns.' The life of Moses inspires me to continue to fulfill my life's purpose, to make my contribution to *Tikkun Olam*, accepting that what happens on the journey may include loss, pain, and that we are all, like Moses, human. God did allow Moses to fulfill his purpose of leading the Jewish people out of Egypt, leading them to the promised land. But, God did not allow Moses to enter the promised land. I pray that God helps me and allows me to fulfill my purpose of helping to 'clean up the rabbinate,' of helping survivors of rabbis' abuse to heal, of helping Jewish religious denominations and organizations to come from integrity with regard to their rabbis, to be open, honest, not to hide the truth, to tell the truth. Elsewhere in this book I write about what I believe they need to do.

In 1996, I presented my "Schwab Mind/Body/Spiritual, Conscious, Connected Breathing Total Method for Achieving Positive Self-Identity and Self-Defined Success" tm also known as "PSI/SDS" tm at the New Life Expo in Manhattan, teaching people how to "say good bye to anxiety, fear, depression; promote health; realize successful, loving relationships, increase energy, joy, and aliveness, and achieve a balanced, constant state of growth, harmony, and satisfaction in all six major life areas: Spiritual/Ethical; Loving Relationships (including in one's family and home); Physical/Health; Mental/Educational; Financial/Career; Cultural/Social." In addition to helping countless others learn these skills, developing and teaching this method was a further step forward on my own path, my own journey toward creating balance in my own life, toward achieving the 'I/Thou' as a 'child of God,' with God, and with others in my own life, and toward assuring that the 'shoemaker does not go barefoot.'

Also in 1996, I traveled to Ireland, England, and Scotland. I stopped for several days in the country of Robert Browning, and at the Lake District in England to visit the home and burial place of William Wordsworth. Browning and Wordsworth are two of the many poets who have inspired me. My favorite poem of Browning's, which I memorized when I studied Browning at the University of Michigan, is Rabbi Ben Ezra. I recited the first verse recently at a *Basherte* conference at *Elat Chayyim* (a Jewish spiritual retreat center in Accord, New York), and again at a Kripalu Consultants Consortium (KCC) conference in the Catskills. KCC is an organization which exists to bring spirituality to the workplace.

> *"Grow old along with me!*
> *The best is yet to be,*
> *The last of life, for which the first was made:*
> *Our times are in His hand*
> *Who saith "A whole I planned,*
> *Youth shows but half;*
> *Trust God: see all, nor be afraid!"*[43]

I am in the "last of (my/this) life." I truly believe that the first (part, half) of my life was made for this last part. I believe "the best is yet to be." I "trust God," pray that I "see all," am not afraid.

I read Claire Bloom's book, Leaving A Doll's House. She displayed courage by telling the truth about the abuse by her husband, the author who is acclaimed in many circles, the author whom I always knew is a misogynist. Her memoir encouraged me, strengthened my resolve to finish writing my own book, my own exposé of misogynist men, of misogynist, abusive rabbis. Claire Bloom's book, in which she describes Philip Roth's alternating cruelty and tenderness to her helped me to write about my rabbi/husband's dual cruelty and tenderness, alternating good and evil, God and evil; helped me to help shatter the myth that Jewish

---

[43]The Shorter Poems of Robert Browning. William Clyde DeVane, editor. New York. Appleton-Century-Crofts, Inc. 1934. p. 234.

men, rabbis, are not abusive to women. Just as Bloom's book helped in my own healing, in my own path of *Tikkun Olam*, I pray that my book will help others.

In 1997, for research on my book, I traveled to California to meet with Rabbi Arthur Gross-Schaefer, who had published articles about rabbis' sexual abuse. He was very supportive of me and my writing this book. The information he gave me was/is invaluable. I also met with victims/survivors of rabbis' sexual abuse and ex-wives of rabbis to help them, let them know about my work. I gave support to them, and obtained support and information from them. I also met with Michelle Samit, the author of No Sanctuary: The True Story of A Rabbi's Deadly Affair. She shared her experience with me and tried to assist me in any way she could to find a publisher for my book.

Lilith magazine published a listing about my work in their *"Tsena Rena"* pages, and, as as a result, I received many more inquiries from women wanting help to recover from the sexual abuse they suffered from rabbis. After I talk with women, counsel them (pro bono, for one in person or telephone session) I try to find them a counselor where they live.

In 1998, I was invited by Rabbi/Dean Allan Kenski to give a lecture/seminar at the Jewish Theological Seminary in New York about rabbis' sexual misconduct, about rabbis' abuse of women. After the lecture/seminar, I was able to help women students at the seminary who reported to me they were being sexually harassed by both faculty members and male rabbinic students. I was gratified when some student rabbis and faculty who attended this lecture/seminar told me that the information I gave them changed their approach to the rabbinate.

I know my work has already helped countless others.

A conundrum I struggled with in my mind, in my own life, and in writing this book, was how to reconcile my feminism with my spirituality, and especially with the sexism in Judaism, with abuse by rabbis, with the ubiquitousness, and what seems to be the proliferation of battering (Jewish) men. In 1998, I came to a resolution of this puzzle when I read the book by Carol Lee Flinders, At the Root of This Longing. I often felt like Isaac, struggling with the angel. Just as Isaac awoke from his 'dream' to 'become' Israel, I found release from my struggle in Flinders' book. Flinders writes about what it means to her to be a woman on a spiritual path, provides the framework for a reconciliation of feminism with spirituality, a means for creating a life of balance between a social voice that is effective and a strong contemplative spirituality. Flinders' book helped me to clarify, to affirm, to rejoice in my belief that feminism and spirituality are one; that organized Judaism must become both spiritual and feminist.[44] Women's full empowerment, women's true equality within organized Judaism is essential. Women's empowerment within a context of spirituality is essential for *Tikkun Olam*, for a spiritual world to come to exist. Women's need for connection is not only with men (or with women, for that matter), but, most significantly, women's 'connection' is with their own souls, and with God.

In 1999 I took a training at the Jewish Healing Center in New York to hone my healing skills, especially to be able to better relate them to Judaic prayer, ritual, etc. At this training, I saw the rabbi who brought the young woman Protestant minister to the rabbinic conference in Snowmass, the one whom my rabbi/husband said he had done "swinging with." I greeted him, but he could not face me, and shortly afterward disappeared from the training.

Also in 1999, I took a training in, "New Advances in the Treatment of Depression" with Albert Einstein College of Medicine, and received a Certificate for an AMA Physician's Recognition Award.

Later in 1999, WGRZ/TV Buffalo came to Manhattan to interview me on camera about rabbis' sexual exploitation and abuse of women. They told me they knew that several women in the Buffalo area had called me for help about the sexual abuse they suffered from a rabbi there.[45] The president of that synagogue also called me for advice. As a result of this interview and the information and articles I gave to the news correspondent, WGRZ/TV Buffalo produced a two part news program about that Buffalo case and about rabbis' sexual misconduct in general.

---

[44] I have been following with gratification the increasing interest in and practice of meditation, interest in *Kabbalah*, and the movement toward a deeper spiritual context both within organized Judaism and in separate, complimentary efforts. I also note with keen interest the ongoing creation of new ritual by women's spiritual and prayer groups and publication of books in these areas by women.

[45] I discuss the case of this rabbi in PART II.

In 2001, I designed and taught a course for the Cooperman Academy for Adult Education at Congregation *B'nai Torah* in Boca Raton, Florida, "Celebrating Women's Wisdom: A Woman's View of Torah, Liturgy, and Ritual." I taught my students about creating prayer and ritual for women's experiences, including healing from abuse, and how to 'read *Torah*' and include women's experience, which is a very important step for making Judaism inclusive of women's experience, which is an important foundation for working toward elimination of rabbis' sexual abuse.

In 2002, I taught two courses at the Cooperman Academy, "Women and *Torah*," and "The Rise of Egalitarianism in Conservative Judaism: What the Future May Hold." I included information and discussion in these classes about rabbis' sexual abuse of teenagers and women. In the latter class I showed them the video of the <u>WGRZ-TV</u> program. I also gave them each a copy of my article which was published in the <u>Jewish Journal</u>[46] about rabbis' sexual misconduct. The discussion was spirited. Three people invited me to be a guest speaker about rabbis' sexual misconduct for a meeting at their homes of their study groups, agreeing, "We need to know."

I was still struggling with whether to include my memoir, my story, in this book, whether to make it solely a work of nonfiction, and include only other women's stories, other cases of rabbis who abuse women and wives. I asked Richard Marek, the former president and publisher at E. P. Dutton, to read my book and give me his opinion. He wrote me a two-page letter, telling me that he read it, "….with great interest. It is intelligent, moving in its autobiographical details, and important. What's more, it is well written and persuasive….your personal story….should be paramount…." I made my decision. Others who have read my memoir reinforced that decision by telling me, for example, that my "story is important for the survival of Judaism"!

I had one question about men who batter and abuse women, raised not only by my two marriages, but also by women I have seen in therapy: why do these men usually not batter and abuse women until after marriage? Lenore Walker, considered an expert on men who batter and on the women they batter, answers this question. She states

---

[46]See the "Newspaper Articles" section of the Bibliography.

that <u>most men who abuse women do not do it until after they are
married and have control.</u> This was certainly true of both my
husbands. Although, now we are seeing more cases of abuses like
stalking, date rape, and men battering women they are not (yet)
married to and don't live with. Walker does state that one out of two
women will be battered by a man who loves them. Learning these
facts has helped me to understand my experience. But, my experience
and learning these facts also raised the question: how can a woman
trust a man, be sure she will be safe with a man?

Many women remain single out of choice. Others, while they
might enter into and maintain relationships, or even live with a man,
say that they would never marry. They believe that they can better
maintain a sense of their own power by remaining single. I pray that
we soon see the day when women <u>know</u> they can trust a man,
especially one who is a rabbi.

I also asked myself the following question when I thought about
my rabbi/husband while researching and writing this book. "How
could so much good exist with so much evil in one person?" The
answer that repeatedly comes to me is that God created us with
choice. The choice to do good or evil; the choice to choose life or
death; the choice to live or die. As it says in Deuteronomy, "I have
placed before you the blessing and the curse, life (good) and death
(evil), therefore choose life that you may live." My rabbi/husband
chose, chooses to do good *and* to do evil, at the same time. As M.
Scott Peck wrote, and as my lawyer stated, he is one of the "people of
the lie." Why do I say, "chooses," the present tense? As another rabbi
told me, "<u>A wife is a good cover for a rabbi who wants to live a
secret, nefarious double life.</u> " Most important, he chooses not to, has
never, made *Teshuvah*, <u>never</u> acknowledged what he did, does; <u>never</u>
apologized; <u>never </u>made restitution; <u>never</u> made amends. All of the
experts I spoke to told me that because he has never acknowledged
what he did, never made *Teshuvah*, never made amends, that he is
most likely still doing his evil, still living his secret, double life.

I do not believe, and I object to, the description of my
rabbi/husband as an 'addict.' Addiction implies illness, that one can
not help himself, and engenders compassion. His behavior was/is
cruel, due to lust. I do no believe my ex-husband/rabbi stopped his
sexual abuse of women. He admitted he "likes it" and had/has no
intention of stopping. As his psychiatrist told me, he is "a sociopath, a

person who lacks a sense of moral responsibility or social conscience." He is not insane, however. He knows what he is doing. He is a mixture of 'God and evil.' He was/is fully aware of what he does. He makes a choice. He chose, chooses, both his sexual abuse of other women and his verbal, emotional and physical violence toward his wife.

I am making sure that now, in my own life, the 'shoemaker' does not go barefoot. What I have taught, teach my clients, I now succeed more often in doing for myself. Instead of hiding my suffering, hiding my pain from, and the truth of, what my first husband and my rabbi/husband perpetrated, I am telling - telling the truth, as I have done by writing this book. I offer my healed broken heart to others, the wholeness I have achieved, my healing to others, in the hope that they may acknowledge their own broken hearts, tell their truths, and heal themselves.

Returning to my Judaism, prayer, the support of my family and friends, my work, and researching and writing this book, counseling women survivors of rabbis' sexual abuse, working to effect a healing, a cleaning up in the rabbinate and true egalitarianism in Judaism have all sustained me.

Recently, a friend sent me the following e-mail:

"A beautiful and profound quote from Rebbe Menachem Schneerson (the beloved *Lubavitcher rebbe* who recently died):"

For hundreds of years - perhaps since the beginning of Creation -
a piece of the world has been waiting for your soul to purify it.
And your soul, from the time it was first emanated and conceived,
waited above to descend to this world and carry out that mission.
And your footsteps were guided to reach that place
And you are there now.

I was deeply moved by the synchronicity of receiving this quote as I was preparing this book for publication. I have believed this myself for a long time. This quote from *Rebbe* Schneerson, whom I regard as a truly holy man, validated my belief, and, somehow made it totally clear, totally true: the suffering I went through had a purpose, a purpose which I was not able to see at the time; a purpose which has become clear to me over the years of my own healing, over the years of researching and writing this book, over the years of helping other women victims/survivors of battering men, victims/survivors of rabbis' abuse; namely, the purpose of effecting a healing of the victims of rabbis' sexual abuse, effecting a healing of the rabbinate, of Judaism, effecting *Tikkun Olam*.

Charlotte Schwab

PART TWO

Cases Of Rabbis' Sexual Abuse

Charlotte Schwab

Women Tell The Truth
Composites of women's stories: their experiences of rabbis' sexual abuse, as told to me

Since I started working on this book ten years ago, women victims/survivors of rabbis' abuse have contacted me from all over the country, Canada, and Israel. They have heard about me by word of mouth, from the listing that appeared in <u>Lilith</u> magazine, from lectures and seminars I have conducted on this problem, from my television appearance, and from many web sites which have listed my work. At last count, I have over two hundred cases in my files. These include women who have called me, consulted me by telephone and in person, written to me via e-mail or U.S. mail, spoken to me at conferences, seminars, or at my lectures, or whom I have read about in newspaper and journal reports or in books. I have listed many of these published resources in the Bibliography.

I interviewed many of the affected parties in cases published in newspapers and articles, including victims/survivors of rabbis' sexual abuse, parents of victims/survivors (in these cases the victims/survivors were teenagers at the time of the abuse), ex-wives of rabbis who endured their husbands' sexual abuse of other women, rabbis of other congregations in the same denominations as the rabbi-perpetrators, and affected congregants and members of the Boards of Directors of affected synagogues.

I have created composites of many of these cases, changed names, and disguised locations and other information to protect these women's privacy. The composites I have created may include cases from different locations, including California, the Southwest, the South, the Midwest, the Northeast, and the Mid Atlantic States, from large cities, and from small towns; cases involving rabbis from the Orthodox, Reform, Conservative, and Reconstructionist denominations, and from the Jewish Renewal movement. Most of these cases involve rabbis affiliated with synagogues, Jewish organizations, and rabbinic organizations governing their denominations; a few are unaffiliated. In some of the cases which have been written about in newspaper articles, I identify the rabbis.

129

In my own case, as an ex-wife/ survivor of my rabbi/husband/perpetrator's sexual abuse of other women, and his resultant emotional, verbal, and ultimate physical abuse of me, his admissions are a fact of public record: he admitted them in court. He admitted to perpetrating physical abuse by stopping his contesting of the Order of Protection hearing when I agreed not to press criminal charges for his abuse. The Order of Protection was granted. He again admitted to sexual misconduct on the stand in the court trial described in PART ONE of this book.

Some people asked me if I believe the women who told me their stories. My answer was/is, that of course I believe all the women who told me their stories. It is impossible not to believe them.

Judy was abused by the rabbi of her synagogue when she was, as a young girl, attending Hebrew school. This happened in the large city in the mid Atlantic state where she grew up. He would call her into his study, always saying to her that she was more "knowledgeable," more "intelligent" than the other girls, that he "respected" her and "admired her." He told her to sit on his couch, and then he would put his hand inside her blouse and up her skirt. Then, he would take her hand and put it on his crotch, outside his pants. While he kept her hand there, he put his finger in her vagina. He seemed to writhe around while he did this. She sat frozen in fear and shock. He was 'the rabbi'. She was taught to look up to him, never to question him. Her parents respected him. She did not dare say anything, let alone scream; mostly she held her breath.

She did not dare tell her parents or anyone. She suffered this abuse in silence for two years, believing for years afterward that something was wrong with *her* for him to do this to her. She never thought that there were other girls suffering the same humiliation, fear, degradation that she was. She never told anyone until after she was married. She did overcome the abuse enough to marry and have children. She approached the birth of her first child with much fear. She was afraid that somehow the gynecologist, everyone in the delivery room would know about what the rabbi did to her, that she was somehow dirty, 'spoiled'. She was very relieved when no one said anything to her about this. She told her husband about the abuse she suffered at the hands of this rabbi some years into their marriage. Her husband was supportive and understanding, telling her that it was the rabbi's fault, his doing, not hers. However, she still feels shame. She was never able to attend a synagogue. Her children are approaching the age of studying to become Bar and Bat Mitzvah, and she thinks about whether she is depriving them if she does not allow them to realize this important step in Jewish life. She not only does not want to deal with any rabbis herself, but also, she does not want to risk her children being abused.

Judy learned about my work on the Internet and called me.[47] I supported her in an hour's telephone session. I recommended several healing rituals for her, including going to a body of water and immersing herself and imagining herself cleansed.[48] I recommended that we sing Debbie Friedman's *"Mi Shebeirach"*[49] together, which we did, and that she sing this every day until she no longer needs to. I recommended that she read The Primrose Path,[50] a fictionalized account of a rabbi's sexual abuse of teenagers, written for teenagers. She called me again a month later. She still wanted to come and see me even though it was many miles and she would have to fly. Flying had scared her since this abuse happened.[51]

Judy did come to see me months later. Her husband drove her up in their car. When Judy consulted me, we worked on several healing steps which seemed to help her.[52] However, she said that she thought

---

[47]Since beginning this work, I have offered a free one hour therapy session either in person or on the telephone to all women who call me. I then try to find them a therapist where they live who has experience working with women survivors of sexual abuse (preferably of rabbis' sexual abuse; however, I have found few of the latter).

[48]Marcia Cohn Spiegel, who has written about new healing rituals for women, recommended this ritual to me (similar to going to a *mikveh*) in a conversation with her about women needing to cleanse themselves of rabbis' abuse.

[49] *"Mi Shebeirach"* c 1988 by Deborah Lynn Friedman, ASCAP, Music by Deborah Lynn Friedman. Lyrics by Deborah Friedman and Drorah O'Donnell Setel. Sounds White Productions, ASCAP.

[50]Carol Matas. The Primrose Path. Winnipeg, Canada. Bain & Cox. 1995.

[51]Often, women who have suffered abuse become phobic. I wrote about this in an article called, "The Making of Phobic Women" when I wrote a column for Majority Report See Bibliography.

[52]See Part Five.

she would never feel "closure," never be able to stop remembering the horror unless she could see this rabbi/perpetrator again and confront him, accuse him, stand up to him.

She came up with the idea that she wanted the head of this rabbi's rabbinic organization to go with her to confront him, thereby somehow proving to herself that there is a rabbi who will "do the right thing", and making her feel less trepidation about allowing her children to study with a rabbi. This was the one thing she thought might help her to put the constantly relived memories to rest. The rabbi who abused her is now retired, and, again, she would have to travel by plane to see him. I explained to her that she might be able to heal the phobia about flying as well by doing this. I supported her in this plan. I cautioned her not to see him alone, but to have her husband or someone else with her whom she considered a person who would give her unconditional support. We talked about her calling the rabbi-head of the denomination with which he is affiliated and asking him to arrange this for her.

When she got home, she called the rabbi-executive she was referred to in this rabbinic organization. He promised to arrange a meeting. She called him many times since then, over the next two years. This is a denomination which claims still to be "working on" a sexual policy for their rabbis. I know them to be "working on" this policy for the past four years at least. They have not agreed to release the "working policy" as of this writing.

The rabbi who abused Judy is a member of the same denomination, same rabbinical organization as a rabbi in Buffalo, **Charles Shalman**,[53] who <u>was accused</u> of abusing **several women.** Rabbi Joel Meyers of the Rabbinical Assembly did travel to Buffalo to try to convince Shalman to resign. Several women called me to tell me that Rabbi Shalman sexually abused them. I counseled them by telephone. One of these women told a news correspondent of WGRZ/TV Buffalo about my work. This correspondent, Rich Kellman, traveled to Manhattan to interview me about this case and

---

[53] I name Rabbi Shalman because he was named on the news program listed below.

cases of rabbis' sexual abuse of women in general. I subsequently appeared on their news program,[54] which was aired in two parts.

One of the women who called me told me that she knew seven women who had been abused by this rabbi. She told me that she consulted this rabbi for solace after having been told she would have to have a hysterectomy[55] and would never be able to have children. She said that Shalman came to her house when he knew her husband and children were not at home, and without calling her first. She thought it was odd, but, she rationalized, *"he is the rabbi."* He sat beside her on the sofa. Before she knew what he was doing, he placed one hand on her abdomen and one on her breast, and rubbed his hands over her. She sat frozen in horror, not being able to move for several minutes. She cried out, "Why are you doing this?" and got up and moved away from him. She told him this was inappropriate behavior. He told her there was "nothing wrong" with his doing what he did. That it would probably "help to heal her," make her feel better.

She protested to me that, not only did it not make her "feel better," but that she was shaken, shocked, shaken in her belief in Judaism, unable to return to synagogue, unable to face him again. She told me that one of the women reported the rabbi's abuse on the telephone to Rabbi Joel Meyers, an executive of the rabbinic organization of this denomination. She told me that she reported this rabbi's abuse to an officer on the synagogue's board of directors. "As a result," she related, "her name is mud" in the community.

She reported that women she knows support this rabbi and do not believe her, even though she knows six other women who have been abused by him and she believes most, if not all of them, have reported the abuse to Rabbi Meyers and the synagogue board. I validated her, promising her that I believe her, and explaining to her that what he did was sexual abuse. That it had nothing to do with "healing her" or "making her feel better." I went on to explain that a rabbi who sexually abuses a woman does so because of his prurient interest in her and other women, his lust, his sex addiction, his evil, his being one of the <u>People of the Lie</u>, his using his position and power, and

---

[54]<u>WGRZ-TV Buffalo</u>. "A House Divided," by Carol Kaplan and Rich Kellman. August, 1999.

[55]I have altered certain facts about these women and created composites of the women who consulted me to protect their identity.

access to her and other women because of his position, to sexually abuse her and other women. I pointed out to her that he was betraying a "sacred trust" by doing this, that he was hurting her, her family, the synagogue, the denomination, the community, all Judaism, and even the wider community. I suggested several steps to help heal her from this rabbi's abuse and to restore her faith in Judaism. We did a few healing processes on the telephone and I suggested she continue to do them.

Neither I nor she could find a therapist in her area, and she remains a "victim," unable to heal.[56] Because she told me her husband was not supportive to her, that he was more worried about his position in the community than about her, and that she was especially upset about what this would do to her marriage, I suggested she ask him to call me and that I would speak with him, educate him about the facts concerning rabbis' sexual abuse. I would talk with him regarding his fears about his position and try to help him to see that his best interest would come from a spiritual and ethical place, not from pride and not from a materialistic place.

Subsequent to this woman's call to me the troubled President of the synagogue called me for my advice. The rabbi refused to resign, and the Rabbinical Assembly, the rabbinic organization in the Conservative denomination allowed him to remain with certain restrictions. I suggested that the synagogue board consult a lawyer to find out their rights, that they might be able to fire him for cause. The board president told me that there was "terrible division" among the congregants, with "constant arguing, letter writing campaigns, anonymous threatening letters;" that the congregation has been in a state of "upheaval." He feared that there would be a breakup of the synagogue, with those wanting to fire the rabbi leaving if the rabbi remained. The rabbi had a contract for four more years with the synagogue amounting to some $500,000. There was to be a vote by the congregation the following evening on whether to fire him. He thought that 60% would vote to keep him and 40% would vote to fire him. He told me in anguish that he did not think he could remain with

---

[56]I use the word "victim" to refer to women who have not recovered from rabbis' abuse, and the word "victim/survivor" to indicate women who have recovered enough to be able to lead productive lives, although they may be plagued by recurrent frightening images and memories of the rabbis' abuse.

the synagogue, let alone remain president of the board should they vote to keep this rabbi.

I suggested several courses of action to begin with: 1) Play the video of the TV program, "A House Divided" at the congregational meeting. 2) Ask the women who had come forward to speak at the open meeting, assuring them support. 3) Give a copy of the Rabbinical Assembly's letter to each congregant and have a professionally trained person (not a rabbi) lead an open discussion. 4) Ask the rabbi if he is willing to admit to wrongdoing and willing to go into therapy with a person trained in rabbinic boundary violations (not a rabbi); willing to apologize to the women and their husbands in the presence of an impartial professional; willing to make *Teshuvah* to the women and their families, including paying for any therapy that may be necessary for them; willing to apologize to his wife in the presence of the impartial professional and to the congregation; and, that he have no contact alone with any woman in his capacity as a rabbi.

The congregation voted to retain this rabbi. The president informed me he resigned as president and also resigned from the Temple. He wrote me that about 50 families left the congregation. To this date, according to this inside source, the rabbi has never admitted publicly to any of the charges for which he was accused. According to this source, Rabbi Shalman did admit to these charges when he was questioned by representatives of the Rabbinical Assembly in a closed, secret meeting attended only by those few invited, including this source, who was a "witness to these admissions." This source also wrote me that at least one woman sued the rabbi and the temple. The actual settlement amount of this legal suit was never made public.

This case sharply underscores the need for the education of synagogue congregants about rabbis' sexual abuse. Without this education, and especially without the knowledge of the extent of these cases, congregants are too apt to believe that the women who do have the courage to come forward and report rabbi-perpetrators are "trouble makers," "misfits," and to blame the women and do nothing about the rabbi, who is then free to stay on and keep on perpetrating his sexual abuse, whether on teenagers or women.[57] Rabbi Gross-

---

[57]Rabbi, Dr. Arthur Gross-Schaefer, J.D., C.P.A. "Rabbi Sexual Misconduct: Crying out for a Communal Response". Working Together. Winter 1997. pp. 3-5. Also see, Gerald L. Zelizer. "Why do Parishioners

Schaefer writes that, "The victim becomes victimized again and again as his/her reality is denied. This sense of isolation and denial can lead to the injured blaming themselves. With everyone telling them that they are "wrong" and with feelings of being isolated, they sometimes doubt their own perception of what happened. They may even start to believe that they, in some way, were 'guilty' of what happened. Through the powerful tool of silence, we continue the pain and abuse of the victims."

Women in Buffalo who told me they were victims of the rabbi there (as well as many other victims of rabbis' abuse who have consulted me) confirm to me that that has been exactly their experience. The majority of the congregants do not want to believe their stories. They do not want to believe that the rabbi is guilty of sexual misconduct. It is easier to deny than to confront this troubling information. It is easier to ostracize the women who claim they are this rabbi's victims than to hold the rabbi accountable. The women are voices crying out in the wilderness of the silence of denial. They are like trees which fall in a forest with no one there to hear. Do those trees make a sound? Are the women making a sound?

Marcia was 42 years of age when she turned to the rabbi in her community for help. Their children went to the same public school. Her husband had just been fired from his job, and they were in grave financial difficulty. He was looking for a new job. They did not have the money for the mortgage payment, and Marcia feared they would lose their home. The rabbi asked her to meet him at the synagogue after hours, because this is "the only time" he "was free," and that he would "try to help" her. She rarely went out alone at night, and especially not at such a late hour, but she felt desperate for help. She knew that rabbis had "discretionary funds," and thought that maybe he could lend her money to pay the expenses that were due. She fully intended to pay him back.

When she got there, they went into his study/office. The synagogue was dark. No one else was there. She felt strange. He asked her to sit on the sofa, and sat beside her. The next thing she knew, he pushed her down, climbed on top of her, and forced his

---

Stick by Clergy Who Commit Crimes?" <u>USA TODAY</u> May 24, 1999, pp. 27A.

penis into her mouth. She was in shock, extremely frightened, and began gagging. She thought she would suffocate and die. When he finally stopped and got off her, she could not look at him. He said nothing. She managed to get up, somehow got to her car, and somehow drove home. She felt ashamed, humiliated. She did not know how she could face her husband, how she was going to go on with her life. Only because of her children, did she manage to pull herself together. She never told her husband what happened. She never told anyone. She felt worthless and that it must have been her fault. He was "the rabbi." She trusted him. She felt she could never trust any rabbi again. She did not want to see the inside of a synagogue again. She did hear some years later that this rabbi had cancer. He was still a comparatively young man. She couldn't help wondering if it was his 'payback' for what he had done.

Marcia learned about my work from one of the listings on the Internet. When she talked with me, I helped her to understand that what happened was in no way her fault. That the responsibility for his actions was solely this rabbi's. We did some rituals for cleansing and letting go of the sordid experience. I told her about the seven step healing program I developed, and about the literature I know which does exist about rabbis' sexual abuse. I did not know of any therapist I could recommend to her where she lives. Therapists who are knowledgeable about rabbis' sexual abuse of women and who are capable of helping women to heal from the sexual abuse they suffer from rabbi-perpetrators are desperately needed.

Sarah had just given birth to her first child. She could not stop crying and spent most of the day in bed. She could hardly cope with the care of her new baby daughter. She knew she could not go on this way, and thought that maybe the rabbi of their synagogue could help her. She made an appointment to see him.

When she got to his study, he pulled a chair up in front of the desk to sit beside her, facing her, very close. She thought it was too close, but did not say anything. She did not dare question what he did. She looked up to him. He had performed the 'baby naming ceremony' for her baby daughter. When he stood on the *Bimah* preaching about the holiness of a family, about the sanctity of the *Torah*, and that the core of Judaism was to be found in the words written on the wall above the ark: "To love mercy, do justice, and to walk humbly with thy God," she always looked upon him in awe. He would expound about how this meant that ethics are the core of Judaism, to behave ethically, morally was more important than *Halacha*, or keeping the 613 commandments, or to be observant of the rituals and laws. She felt he could do no wrong; that he, himself, was holy.

Sarah had been brought up in a very religious family. Her parents were very observant, and they were highly ethical and moral, even righteous. The rabbi asked her to tell him what was bothering her. He looked directly into her eyes. He seemed to care, to want to help. She thought that she could confide in him. Hesitantly, she told him that she constantly thought about death, and yet, that she was afraid to die, that these feelings, this sense of dread, had happened since the birth of the baby. The birth had been very difficult, and she thought she would die. She had to have induced labor, the doctor said, because she was "a risk." The drug the doctor gave her to induce labor produced violent contractions. Then, he gave her a drug to put her to sleep and he had to take the baby with forceps. The baby had colic. The doctor was not able to find the right formula for her. She was almost three months old, and for all this time, she had been fussy, very difficult. Sarah vacillated between wanting to run away, being afraid of death, and wanting to die. So she stayed in bed, often putting her hands over her ears so she wouldn't hear the relentlessly crying baby. She was worried about the baby as well as herself, and did not know what to do, where to turn. Her parents lived 3,000 miles away. She and her husband had no relatives in this city. Her husband worked very late hours, trying to "make partner" in his firm. She had no one to turn to for help. She felt so alone, so abandoned, like a baby herself. Indeed, she had married so young, right out of high school, and the baby had come less than a year after the marriage. She needed help.

The rabbi listened intently to her, his eyes never leaving her eyes. Then he took his hands and rubbed them along her thighs, toward her "privates"! He kept rubbing them, up and down, each time getting closer to her "privates." She was frozen in horror. He said something about flesh being temporary, life being temporary, that we all die. He continued to rub his hands on her thighs, as she remained frozen, unable to speak, unable to move, unable to breathe. When she could move, she stood up and ran out of his office. She felt that if she had been able to cope with things this would not have happened to her. She blamed herself. When she got home, she made a resolution to change what she had been doing, and to try to forget what had happened with the rabbi.

She got up every day, took the baby out in the carriage, and pushed the carriage briskly around the neighborhood for hours to forget. The exercise and fresh air seemed to lift her spirits and got her out of the depths of despair she had been feeling. The hours in the carriage also must have helped her baby, because she stopped fussing. Or maybe she had grown out of the colic and the need to fuss. The bad thing that came out of the experience was that she never went to synagogue again, never wanted anything to do with this rabbi, or any rabbi. Her daughter is now ten, she told me, and she has been feeling guilty about not belonging to a synagogue where she could train for her *Bat Mitzvah*.

Sarah finally told her husband about the horrible experience with the rabbi when he started insisting that they join a synagogue and enroll their daughter to study for her *Bat Mitzvah*. While he was supportive about her feelings of antipathy toward this rabbi, toward rabbis and synagogues, he still wanted their daughter to become a *Bat Mitzvah*. She was in terrible conflict about what to do.

We did some prayers and rituals together to help release her from the frightening memory of the experience with this rabbi. I told her that while some experts estimate that between 18% to 39% of rabbis may be guilty of some form of sexual abuse, that left 41% to 82% who may not be. We also discussed her trying to find a synagogue with a woman assistant rabbi or female *cantor* for her daughter to train for her *Bat Mitzvah*. She decided to pursue that direction.

Barbara is 34 years of age. She went back to school to study social work after her divorce. She was able to go at night and leave the children with her mother. Her ex-husband paid some child support and a small settlement to her. She needed to prepare to go work to financially support herself after 12 years of marriage and being a housewife, which was what her husband wanted. Judaism had always been important to her, but not to her husband. She started going to synagogue after the divorce. She chose a synagogue near her home, and her mother, again, agreed to stay with the children. When she called me, she had been attending services at this synagogue for six months. She said the rabbi would come up to her in the hallway on her way to the ladies' room and "bump" into her, touch her buttocks, even pinch her. He said things like, "You're so soft." He would wait for her to come out of the ladies' room and block her exit. He positioned his body close to hers and stared at her at close range. She had to push past him. She could not understand how he would risk this behavior with other people in the synagogue. She asked him to stop doing this. She did not know what to do. One day, when she was speaking to the woman president of the synagogue, she decided she seemed like a sympathetic woman and told her what the rabbi had been doing. This woman called her a "troublemaker," and told her not to come back to the synagogue. She was hurt, shocked. Why did this woman not believe her? She had never done anything to indicate she was a "troublemaker." She had attended services on *SHABBAT* faithfully for six months. She left with her mind whirling. Maybe her ex-husband was right. Maybe she should do what a friend of hers had done and join an Ashram.

I talked with Barbara and validated her hurt and pain. I explained to her how, often, even 'just' verbal sexual harassment by a rabbi can be the worst sexual abuse. This rabbi had emotionally and physically harassed her as well. I told her that whatever religion she sought out, there was no guarantee that the clergy would not be sexually abusive, informing her about the guru who had been let go "for sexual transgressions," from the Kripalu Center For Yoga and Health and "spiritual attunement," a retreat center in Lenox, MA. I informed her that experts believe that male clergy sexual abuse of women is found in other religions at about the same percentage rates as in Judaism. I also talked with her about the common practice of blaming the women victims for rabbis' sexual abuse, and how prevalent it is that congregations and boards stand by the rabbi when many women have come forward, and when the abuse is much more 'serious.' I encouraged her to try to find an egalitarian synagogue where she might feel more welcomed. I suggested she look for a synagogue which has a woman rabbi or at least a woman associate or assistant rabbi, or a woman *cantor*. She agreed with this suggestion. She also decided to report this rabbi to the rabbinic organization of his denomination. As of this date, she has not found a suitable synagogue in her town. The rabbinic organization has not responded to her letter reporting this rabbi.

Cases Which Have Been Reported in the Media

Some of the victims in these cases have also talked with me. Because these cases are matters of public record, I name the rabbis and, in some cases, where their names also appeared in the press, the women they were reported to have sexually abused.[58]

The Case of Rabbi Fred Neulander

The New York Post calls this case, "A BIZARRE and chilling saga of lust and murder, of sex and betrayal, hidden passions and labyrinthine deceit...."[59] Rabbi Fred J. Neulander, now aged 60, as of this writing has, some say, "finally" been imprisoned and is awaiting retrial for allegedly hiring a 'hit man' to murder his wife, Carol Neulander. The first trial ended in a hung jury. It took almost six years for Rabbi Neulander to be suspected, investigated, charged, and imprisoned to await trial. According to people I interviewed about this case, and the abundant media reports, Rabbi Neulander is believed to have hired a 'hit man' to murder his wife when she found out about his sexual "involvements" (what I call abuse) with other women.

According to one of these women, Elaine Soncini, a woman who sought counsel from Rabbi Neulander when her husband was dying, and who testified before the grand jury, and was quoted in many newspaper articles over the past several years, and whom I also spoke with on the telephone, Rabbi Neulander implied to her that he would be free to marry her after a certain date, the date it turned out that his wife was murdered. Rabbi Neulander lured her into a sexual involvement within two days of her husband's funeral. According to Soncini, they had a two year sexual "involvement" often conducted on synagogue premises.

The murder of Carol Neulander and the subsequent news that came out about Rabbi Neulander's sexual misconduct sent the affluent, tight-knit community of Cherry Hill, New Jersey, into shock.

---

[58]Some of the media articles reporting these cases, and other articles reporting other cases are listed in the Bibliography.

[59]Peter Fearon. "Thou Shalt Not Kill or Commit Adultery." The New York Post. Tuesday, August 22, 2000. Pp. 26 & 27.

It divided the congregation. Unbelievably, some congregants still support Neulander, even after the first trial. Others want him to "disappear." Some people were relieved that he was "finally" suspended by the CCAR, and that he resigned as rabbi of the synagogue he had helped found and led as rabbi for some 25 years. Carol Neulander is dead. Many people: the family, congregants, the community, people in the denomination, in all Judaism suffer because of Rabbi Neulander's actions.[60]

The Case of Rabbi Arnold Fink[61]

One of Connie Rappaport's sons was being counseled by Rabbi Arnold Fink. One day, when her husband and sons were out of town, Rabbi Fink called her and asked to come over to swim in the lake which was nearby her house. Connie thought she was welcoming someone who had "been part of my religious family life for a long time". She served ice cream sundaes.

Suddenly, Rabbi Fink shoved his spoon into her mouth. Then, he grabbed her, pulled her over to him, locked her in a tight hold, and passionately kissed her. Connie says that she did not invite this to happen or expect it. She was caught off-guard. She was in a "troubled" marriage, and the rabbi knew this. He also knew that she was coping with grief concerning the recent death of her mother. She was vulnerable. She said she didn't know how to refuse this rabbi, to reject him, that he was the most "important authority figure" in her life at the time. She ended up having a six month sexual "involvement" with Rabbi Fink. To use a more appropriate description: Rabbi Arnold Fink sexually abused her for six months.

---

[60]Rabbi Robert J. Gluck of Congregation Ahavath Shalom, Great Barrington, MA, told me in a telephone conversation in November, 1996 that, "Sex between rabbi and congregants or other members of the community who look up to them as rabbis is destructive of community."

[61]Because this case has been reported by several news sources, including in an article by Debra Nussbaum Cohen, released in the Daily News Bulletin of the Jewish Telegraphic Agency, Inc. New York, September 18, 1996, and the names were published, this rabbi's name and the name of Connie Rappaport appear here.

Rabbi Fink took advantage of, used his sacred power, his position as a rabbi, as a trusted authority figure, and of his resultant privileged knowledge about Connie's life to abuse her sexually, to lure her into a sexual "involvement" with him. The responsibility for this sexual involvement, this sexual abuse of Connie Rappaport lies solely with Rabbi Arnold Fink. He was the one with power, sacred power, not Connie. He is guilty of rabbi sexual misconduct, of rabbi sexual abuse.

The Case of Rabbi Robert Kirschner

Rabbi Robert Kirschner's case has also been publicized in newspapers; hence, I publish his name here. Rabbi Robert Kirschner was the rabbi of the largest synagogue in Northern California, Temple Emanuel in San Francisco. Rabbi Kirschner was a married father of four children. He was considered to be a "rising star" in the movement. Some thought Rabbi Kirschner was destined to become the leader of the Reform movement, to succeed Rabbi Alex Schindler to lead the UAHC, the Union of American Hebrew Congregations. Rabbi Kirschner was accused, according to some sources, of sexually harassing, exploiting, abusing 40 women, one who was reported to be anorexic at the time of his abuse. Reports have stated that at least a dozen women came forward to complain, and at least three women settled out of court with the synagogue and its insurance company. Yet, though Rabbi Kirschner was finally forced to resign as rabbi of Temple Emanuel, he retains the title "rabbi." With this title, he was given a position as program director of the Skirball Cultural Center in Los Angeles which is affiliated with the Reform movement's rabbinical seminary, Hebrew Union College-Jewish Institute of Religion. There, he is reported to have access to young women, women of all ages.

One man who was outraged by this appointment picketed the Skirball Center and demanded that Rabbi Kirschner be fired. They ignored his demand and Rabbi Kirschner remained in his position. Rabbi Kirschner eventually made a public apology, in newspapers, but when I spoke with victims/survivors of his abuse, they told me he had never apologized to them directly, nor had he made any amends to them. One of the women I spoke with is Deborah Warwick

143

Sorbino. She was a student of his. She survived, and went on to be a counselor of victims/survivors of clergy abuse in her California city.[62]

When I spoke with Jerome Levin, Ph.D., a professor at the New School for Social Research in New York, and a psychotherapist with over twenty years of experience identifying and treating addictions, including sex addiction, and the author of seven books on addiction, he stated that sex addicts try to lead split or 'double' lives under the delusion that the risk taking behavior will not 'spill over,' will not affect their other life. However, all of the cases I describe here, including the case of Rabbi Kirschner testify to the failure of these men to keep their double life secret, fortunately for any of their possible future victims. Unfortunately, they are aided and abetted in the goal of keeping their secret by their rabbinical organizations' cloak of secrecy. When their cases are not made public, and especially when they are given positions in another city as a rabbi, the rabbinical organization facilitates their being able to continue their sex abuse, their split or 'double' lives. This tragic fact was sharply illustrated to me by a call from a reporter at the L.A. Times, who telephoned to interview me about rabbis' sexual misconduct and about my/this forthcoming book. She said she had never heard about the case of Rabbi Kirschner; yet, she works for a major newspaper in a city in the same state as the city where he perpetrated the abuse of women (for which he publicly apologized to the press), and in the city where he was "shuffled" to a position where he retains the title, "Rabbi."

Rabbi Steven Jacobs

According to people I interviewed when I went to California in 1997 for research on my book, Rabbi Steven Jacobs was known to have many sexual involvements with women. Anita Green, the president of the synagogue, had raised funds to build the synagogue for Rabbi Jacobs. Anita Green was married, unhappily married. People told me that, instead of counseling her to deal with the unhappy marriage, or advising her to get professional counseling help, Rabbi Jacobs became sexually "involved" with her. She moved into

---

62 Bill Lindelof. "Her calling: Aid clerics' sexual abuse victims." Sacramento Bee. 9/5/93. p. B1. See also, Jennifer Bojorquez. "The healing hand." Sacramento Bee. 2/1/94. p D1.

Rabbi Jacobs' home. The morning after she moved in with him, (had she just left this rabbi's bed?) she went to her husband's place of business to see about collecting funds he owed to her. She never made it. She was murdered by a 'hit man' in the driveway outside of her husband's business.

One of the people I interviewed in California was Michele Samit, who wrote a book about this case, called, No Sanctuary: The True Story of a Rabbi's Deadly Affair.[63] Ms. Samit told me that when she wrote an article about the case for a Los Angeles magazine, and then when she published the book, she became persona non grata in the community where she lived and was a member of this synagogue. People attacked her verbally for casting suspicion on the rabbi. They made it so unpleasant that she and her family eventually moved to another community. When she went to Israel a few years later, she saw one of the women members of this synagogue at Masada. The woman screamed at her that she "destroyed Rabbi Jacob's reputation," and that, "If my teen aged daughter has to learn about sex from someone, I would rather it was from Rabbi Jacobs"! Ms. Samit was incredulous, as was I when I heard this story. What this woman's attitude illustrates is how congregants often believe that rabbis are (like) God, that they can do no wrong. This is one of the biggest stumbling blocks to cleaning offenders out of the rabbinate.

Rabbi Jacobs was never investigated as a suspect in the murder of Anita Green. Some people I interviewed believe that he should have been investigated. (Rabbi Fred Neulander was not investigated in relation to the murder of Carol Neulander for years after she was murdered.) They told me that they thought that by the time Anita Green moved in with him, Rabbi Jacobs was "tired of her," that "with her living with him," it would not have been "as easy for him" to have other sexual "involvements." Before the case came to trial (Anita Green's husband was charged with her murder), Rabbi Jacobs remarried. I was told he married a very young woman whom he converted to Judaism, and that he did not tell her anything about Anita Green or the trial coming up.

When she found out about it, she went to the court to hear what was going on. That day, she went home, packed her bags and moved

---

[63]Michele Samit. No Sanctuary: The True Story of A Rabbi's Deadly Affair. New York. Carol Publishing Group. 1993.

out, leaving her husband, Rabbi Jacobs. Anita Green's husband was tried and convicted of hiring the 'hit man' to kill her, some say on "circumstantial evidence and hearsay." The 'hit man' was never found.

The Case of The Student-Rabbi.

This case is about a rabbinic student at Hebrew Union College in New York who had a placement as a student-rabbi in a synagogue in a suburb of New York City. His father was a prominent senior rabbi in another nearby suburb, beloved by his congregation, and by many in the Reform movement. Shortly before this student-rabbi was to be ordained, he was accused of sexually abusing teen aged girls at the synagogue where he was a student-rabbi. Criminal charges were brought against him. Even so, he was to be ordained. However, there were too many protests for the college to ignore.

I interviewed rabbis of the denomination which was to ordain this student-rabbi who knew about the case, as well as members of the community and synagogue where he was student-rabbi, and a parent of one of the molested girls. I was told that, although he was not ordained, rabbis who were powerful and influential, whose names I will not repeat here, found him a position as rabbi in a city in the South where people had not heard about the charges brought against him. The parent of one of the girls he allegedly molested told me that his daughter had never recovered from the abuse even though she was now an adult, and that it had an enormously "injurious" effect on her life, leading her in a direction that she may not have taken without this abuse. According to this parent and the other people I interviewed, this student-rabbi never acknowledged the abuse, let alone apologized, or made any amends for this abuse. It is chilling to imagine him as rabbi in an unsuspecting community.

The Case of Rabbi Sheldon Zimmerman

Sheldon Zimmerman was rabbi at Central Synagogue in Manhattan for many years. I knew him in that capacity for several years. I know him as Shelly, as did his friends and congregants. Shelly never behaved in any questionable way with me. We had lunch sometimes at a coffee shop on 57th Street a couple of blocks from the synagogue and across the street from the health club where I swam a few days a week. On several occasions I met with him in his synagogue office to discuss matters such as my teaching at Hebrew Union College, and ways I thought people could be attracted to and be more involved at Central Synagogue.

Rabbi Sheldon Zimmerman was the last rabbi, in spite of my knowledge of the estimated high percentage of rabbis who sexually abuse women, and of my first hand knowledge of the numerous cases of rabbis' sexual abuse, whom I ever thought would overstep his bounds, would be guilty of sexual misconduct. He is descended from venerated rabbis. I always thought him to be a righteous man.

Now that the news has come out about Shelly's transgressions, it jogged my memory to a time in his office when he asked me why I was "with" Jon (who was to become my rabbi/husband.) I had been dating Jon for over a year at the time. Shelly went on to say, before I could answer, that he could arrange dates for me with "substantial" men, congregants and non congregants; that I was "so attractive, accomplished," had "so much to offer," that he was sure I could have my "pick" of many great "catches." Why did I want Jon? I thought it was strange of him to say these things at the time. I told him I loved Jon and that he loved me. I did share with him that I did not know where we were going with our relationship because of the age difference, that Jon was so much younger than I. Shelly then said that "the age difference is the least of it." He would not elaborate. I forgot about this discussion until after Jon and I were married and the truth about his leading a double life became clear to me. I wondered then if Shelly knew about Jon's "double life" before I married him and could have told me and protected me. I never asked him. I did call him in Dallas when Jon sued me for alimony to tell him what Jon was doing, had done, and to ask his help. He told me to "get a lawyer."

Now that the news about his own transgressions have come out in the newspapers, I wonder again, did Shelly know about my husband and not tell me, not tell anyone? If he did, he is as guilty as my now ex-husband/rabbi, as guilty as the other rabbis who knew, and as guilty as the rabbis I subsequently turned to for help and who looked the other way, who covered up for him.

According to The New York Times, the Florida Sun Sentinel, the New York Jewish Week (see Bibliography) and other newspapers in which I read reports about Rabbi Sheldon Zimmerman's transgressions, and according to people I spoke with about this case, he was accused by several women of sexually abusing them when he was rabbi at a Dallas synagogue, the one he went to after he left Central Synagogue in Manhattan. I had dinner with Shelly in Dallas when I went there for a professional conference. He met me in the lobby of my hotel, and we went to the restaurant there. He made no advances to me, did not ask to come up to my room, or do or say anything which appeared improper in any way. I was married to Jon (I thought happily, and did not feel, act, or appear 'vulnerable') at the time. This dinner meeting occurred before I learned about my rabbi/husband's sexual abuse of other women, more than two years before my rabbi/husband assaulted me and threatened to kill me if I told about his shocking secret 'double life.'

It now occurs to me that Shelly must have been abusing the accusing women during the time I met him in Dallas for dinner. When I read about this in the newspapers, I was in shock, incredulous. Was there no rabbi left for me to believe in, to trust, to respect, to accept as upholding the ethics of Judaism that he espouses, teaches, preaches about from the *Bimah*? I felt that the news about Shelly was a very heavy betrayal, like someone in my family had died, no, disappeared, no, never existed as I had thought of them. I cried at the sense of loss, of grief; a sense of loss not only of a man I had loved as a respected rabbi and friend, but a sense of loss and grief about ever being able to respect 'male-led,' 'male Judaism'[64] as we know it. No wonder so many Jews are not affiliated with synagogues, turn their backs on organized Judaism, are not 'Jewishly identified' Jews.

According to Judith Plaskow, until women as well as men "define Judaism.... there *is no Judaism* (italics hers) - there is only male Judaism - without the insights of both." According to Plaskow's reasoning, we have, tolerate, protect rabbis' sexual abuse of women because of the patriarchy of Judaism, because of patriarchal power in Judaism, because we have "male Judaism," not "human Judaism;" and, until Judaism is transformed to a universal Judaism that is both male and female, "with the insights of both," and with both having *equal power within all aspects of Judaism*, we can only "manipulate the rules of the system to alleviate" the abuse, the oppression of

---

[64]Judith Plaskow. Standing Again At Sinai San Francisco. Harper/Collins 1991.

women "without altering the assumptions from which that oppression (that abuse) arises." But, until Plaskow's vision becomes a reality, and I do not see this happening in the foreseeable future, we must do whatever we can to alleviate the abuse, to stop rabbis from sexually abusing women and teenagers. The purpose of this book is to aid in that goal as well as to help heal those who have already suffered from this abuse.

Rabbi Sheldon Zimmerman was suspended from the CCAR. He then resigned as president of Hebrew Union College. But he retained his title as "Rabbi." Students at Hebrew Union College were reported as being in shock, feeling "rudderless, abandoned," without a leader; as were former congregants. I still retain my connection to Central Synagogue. The current rabbi, Peter Rubenstein, sent a letter to congregants in December of 2000 about this news, saying that, ".... Rabbi Sheldon Zimmerman has been suspended from the Central Conference of American Rabbis.... for violation of the CCAR's Code of Ethics...." Rabbi Rubenstein went on to write that, "Since the Ethics Committee of the CCAR appropriately maintains silence about its deliberations, we cannot know about the events which led to Shelly's suspension.... there have been numerous rumors.... this news has caused an array of emotional response - anger, disappointment, confusion, bewilderment...."

The "silence" by the CCAR, the same silence they exhibit with regard to any case of rabbis' sexual misconduct is not "appropriate." This silence, in addition to creating rumors, confusion, and bewilderment contributes to the difficulty of putting an end to the dangerous, shocking problem of rabbis' sexual misconduct; and aids these rabbis in continuing their sexual misconduct. The CCAR, through its then executive vice president said only that the Ethics Committee had found Zimmerman guilty of violating a section of the ethics code, which the spokesman described as a "sexual boundary violation."

Not long after Rabbi Sheldon Zimmerman resigned as president of Hebrew Union College and was "suspended" for two years from the CCAR, he was given a post as an executive of a Jewish organization where I was told he "has access to college girls" whom he recommends for sponsored trips to Israel. This appointment caused controversy which was written about in the press. Zimmerman still has and is referred to by the title, "Rabbi," with its associated sacred mystique and power.

The Case of Rabbi Baruch Lanner

Rabbi Baruch Lanner had been the National Conference of Synagogue Youth (of the Orthodox Union) director of regions for many years. The editor of New York Jewish Week, Gary Rosenblatt, wrote a special report on the rabbi's alleged long-term abuse of teens - physical, emotional, psychological and sexual - and the failure of the OU to take decisive action over a period of three decades! Rabbi Lanner was finally forced to resign from his NCSY post. One can only imagine the horror experienced by Lanner's teen aged victims, some over a period of years. One also has to admire their strength in coming forward to expose this rabbi/molester/abuser so that he would not be able to continue to hurt others in NCSY. There were many letters to the editor of New York Jewish Week. Some vilified editor Gary Rosenblatt for his exposé, but most praised him for his research, the time he took to hear the stories of victims and the courage to publish his article "Stolen Innocence" on June 23, 2000.

People wrote that the OU's leadership was aware of Lanner's sexual abuse of teenagers for years and that the OU denied it, covered it up, or defended him on so many occasions that individual victims were discouraged from bringing complaints. An organization that professes to observe the *Torah*, that professes Judaic ethical values turned away from the anguished complaints of children about one of their rabbi's sexual abuse of them, and other shocking abusive behaviors toward them. Rosenblatt's courageous exposé resulted in a long overdue shakeup of the OU leadership, and an investigation of, in the words of Marcel Weber, chairman of OU, "The entire sorry episode" so that "nothing like this ever happens again." Rabbi Jerome Epstein wrote in an "Opinion" column in New York Jewish Week in July of 2000 "....not one person among the many who heard about (Rabbi Lanner's) improper behavior cared enough. Not enough to act, and not enough to put ourselves on the line." Rabbi Epstein continued that, "Many lives have been ruined.... Individual lives have been scarred permanently by emotional trauma.... we have come to tolerate the intolerable.... ignore situations in which we would appear to be acting in a judgmental manner. Nevertheless, as Jews, we have a responsibility to help shape the behaviors of others....When we are silent, we not only 'accept' deviant behavior, but ensure that it will be repeated. When people.... hurt others, we owe it to the victim and the perpetrator to say, "Stop!".... "Those who permitted Baruch Lanner to continue his allegedly hurtful behavior must share the responsibility for the damage he has done and for the ruin he has brought upon himself. We might have helped - but we didn't. We did not care enough."[65]

In June of 2001, one year later, Gary Rosenblatt wrote an extensive follow up article about the Lanner "scandal," reporting on whether or not anything had changed at the Orthodox Union and at its National Conference of Synagogue Youth. He reported that some things have changed, but in some ways, the status quo seems to have remained.

Rabbi Lanner was indicted in New Jersey on charges of criminal sexual assault. The trial is expected sometime in the year 2002. The chief executive of the OU stepped down and a new executive succeeded him. However, Rosenblatt reported that the chairman of a special commission appointed by the Orthodox Union to look into the charges against Lanner is concerned about whether the leadership of OU took the report seriously. For example, only a 54 page summary of the report was made 'public.' The 331 page private report named those lay and professional leaders held responsible for Rabbi Lanner's actions and was not even shared with the OU board. Many in the OU community were reported to express dismay that not one lay or professional leader of the OU was criticized publicly for the 'scandal.' In fact, the chief executive who did step down, and was cited in the report as having knowledge of Lanner's behavior received praise from OU officials, and it is believed he was given a generous compensation package, although even the members of the executive board reportedly were not told the details of the compensation he was paid.

This information indicates that the "old boys network" is alive and well within OU, that other rabbis who could be guilty of sexual abuse could still be protected by them. One board member was quoted as saying that the national organization of OU is run by a handful of men who have been in power for a long time, and that the men picked for

---

[65]Rabbi Jerome Epstein. "Guilty of Silence." The <u>New York Jewish Week</u>. July 2000.

key positions in the so-called reorganization were people who would not challenge the status quo. The one light in this darkness seems to come from a man who served on the commission and who is now a vice president of OU and chair of its new committee on structure and governance: New York attorney Allen Faigin. Rosenblatt wrote that Faigin told him he hopes to help open up the leadership by age and gender, as well as geographically. Perhaps the specter of legal suits by past victims against OU (along with the likelihood of continued scrutiny by courageous journalists like Rosenblatt) might spur them to bring about needed changes, not only with regard to protecting NCSY teens from sexual abuse by rabbis and making NCSY safe for teenagers, but also creating, adopting, and publishing a policy for dealing with *any* possible OU rabbis' sexual misconduct with any victims, whether teenagers or adult women.

Cases of Rabbis' Wives and Ex-wives Who Suffer(ed) Through Their Rabbi/Husbands' Sexual Abuse of Other Women

The large number of wives and ex-wives of rabbis who have spoken to me about their suffering because of their rabbi/husbands' abuse of other women is shocking. Because I cannot mention names here, I have disguised their identities and/or created composites of their stories. These wives are or were spouses of rabbis who are practicing rabbis in four denominations in Judaism: Conservative, Orthodox, Reconstructionist, and Reform, and in the Jewish Renewal movement.

Hilda called me early in my research. She heard about my work from someone in the spouse/network for Reform rabbis' wives. She told me that her rabbi/husband was a revered rabbi of the same synagogue for over 20 years She knew that he was a "philanderer." He made no secret of it, didn't even try to cover it up, sometimes bragged about his escapades to her. She thought, until she learned of my work, that she was the only one to have the misfortune to have married a rabbi who is guilty of such behavior. The only way she had found to cope with it was to maintain emotional distance from him, do her "wifely duties" such as cooking, cleaning, laundry, and never go to synagogue. She did not feel she had the emotional strength to face everyone there. More than that, she had grown to disrespect the congregants of the synagogue. She was sure that at least some congregants and board members had to know about his behavior, and, if this were indeed true, the fact that they did nothing about it, did nothing to help her, made her dislike them, feel betrayed by them as well as by her rabbi/husband.

The other way she "coped" was to "eat, and eat, and eat." She was so overweight she told me that she thought she was obese. She found it hard to get around anymore, and to perform even rudimentary physical tasks. She knew she should do something about this, but she did not feel motivated. She knew she was burying her sorrow, her anger at her husband, beneath the layers of fat which had accumulated on her body; that it was unhealthy for her. But the only solace she could find was in food, almost any kind of food. Also, she felt that the fat served as a kind of protection from the chance that her husband might ever want to approach her sexually. She could not bear the thought of this, since she knew he was unfaithful to her.

She felt hopeless to do anything about her situation. She had raised their children, who were now on their own, had never worked outside the home, only knew how to be a "housewife." Her husband seemed to want to go on the way they were. She did not believe he would ever want to stop his "philandering." They had lost touch with one another many years before. She was a virtual recluse. In fact, when she did try to reach out to another rabbi's wife and called her for support, telling her that her husband was "philandering," that rabbi's wife turned her back on her, saying that there was nothing she could do, and did not want her to call her again. However, she did tell her to call me, that I was a psychotherapist doing research for a book on rabbis' sexual misconduct and offered a pro bono session to wives, ex-wives, and victims of rabbis' sexual misconduct.

The first thing I did was to validate Hilda for feeling she could not go to synagogue; that she did not have to go. That was her husband's 'turf;' she had never felt a part of it, welcomed, respected there. I told her about Marcia Cohn Spiegel's work helping women to survive abuse by creating new rituals with old symbols, ceremonies and blessings.[66] I suggested she get Spiegel's article. In the meantime, I helped her to come to the decision to create a sacred space for herself,

---

[66]Marcia Cohn Spiegel, "Old Symbols, New Rituals: Adapting Traditional Symbols, Ceremonies and Blessings." <u>Neshama</u>. Winter, 1994, 6:#4.

one in which she could create a ceremony to bless herself, to feel herself as precious, a precious child of God, sacred; one in which she could begin through spiritual ceremony to feel a sense of self esteem, to reclaim her unique self and identity, to reclaim her power. One in which she could express her own "Jewishness," her own spirituality. And one in which she could begin to feel anger at her husband, to express it outwardly instead of turning it inward and burying it with food, and in folds of fat. I helped her to create an anger ceremony. Then, I helped her to begin to define what she wanted to do about her husband's abusiveness to her, whether she wanted to stay in this marriage, and if so, how - what would be a healthier way to do that; and if not, to begin to work on how she was going to continue her life independently. I also helped her to find a therapist in her area.

It turned out that the rabbi's wife to whom Hilda had turned and who turned her back on her was dealing with the sexual misconduct of her own rabbi/husband. **Rosalie** called me to speak about her rabbi/husband's "sleazy" activities. She told me she wanted to keep her adult children from knowing about his behavior. I told her that I believed that it was in the best interest of her children to know the truth; that to try to keep it from them was not only not in their best interest, but that they would find out anyway, and then might be angry with her for keeping them in the dark about their father's misconduct; and that to keep it from them was in fact protecting him and not the adult children. I advised her that the best course of action is to tell the truth, not to hide, especially from adult children.

When Rosalie had confronted her rabbi/husband about his sexual misconduct with other women, he "threw her out of the house and told lies about her to the community and to his rabbinic organization." He even told them that she was a lesbian. I pointed out that this was a way that her hiding the truth about her rabbi/husband had worked against her, protected him, and that to continue to try to hide the truth from her adult children might again work against her and protect him, instead of 'protecting' them. The immediate task was to help Rosalie find a place to live, set up a support system, and to find a way to support herself financially, since her rabbi/husband had found a way to cut her off, and turn her out without a cent.

Ruth called me as a result of an article I adapted and excerpted from this book which was published recently in the Jewish Journal of South Florida. She told me she had been married to her rabbi/husband for over 16 years. She said that for all those years they moved from city to city because the board of the synagogue where he was rabbi would find out about his sexual misconduct and would fire him and he would get another position at another congregation where they did not know about his sexual misconduct and start it all over again. She said she did not know what he was up to for all those years. I validated her that 'the wife is usually the last to know,' and that she is not alone.

Ruth confronted her rabbi/husband when she found out. His response was to walk out on her and their children - one was 11 years of age and one was 13 at the time. She said that the synagogue where he was then a rabbi turned their backs on her when she turned to them for help, and kept him on as rabbi. She had to find work to support herself and the children. Since her rabbi/husband/ perpetrator walked out on her and their children, she had not had anyone to talk to about what her rabbi/husband/perpetrator did, to support her, to validate her. She had no idea how extensive rabbis' sexual misconduct is. She said that for years she thought she was the only one, the only "*rebbitzen*" to have had the misfortune to marry a rabbi who was guilty of sexual misconduct with other women, many, many women, the only rabbi's wife to suffer from a rabbi/husband's transgressions and abuse.

Ruth felt very validated by my article. She wanted to know how she could help other women; how to help get rabbinical organizations to adopt open, clear, published policies for dealing with rabbis who are guilty of sexual misconduct, and especially for dealing effectively and fairly with those rabbi/perpetrators who abandon their wives, and whose wives and children suffer because of these rabbis'/husbands'/fathers' transgressions. She wanted to know how to get these rabbinic organizations to force these rabbis to make amends, or to be expelled from their rabbinic organizations and have the title "Rabbi" taken away from them. I told her about the steps in PART FIVE of this book and we discussed how she might continue her healing and become involved to help others.

I have too many other cases in my files of wives and ex-wives of rabbi/perpetrators of sexual misconduct to write about here. I can mention only a few of them. One especially shocking case is the case of a rabbi prominent in his movement who abandoned his wife and handicapped child when she confronted him after finding out that he had been unfaithful to her for many years. Other cases involve women who are either still married to their rabbi/perpetrator husbands and tolerate their abuse because they see "no way out," no way they could support themselves, survive financially if they were to leave, or whose husbands walked out on them and, in some cases, their children, when they found out and confronted them about their sexual misconduct. The many cases of rabbis having 'affairs' and then divorcing their wives attests to the urgency of education for rabbis not only about the importance of keeping boundaries, but also about self and identity, sexuality, and about integrity, about telling the truth to oneself and ones loved ones, and about ethical behavior.

The Case of Rabbi Jerrold Levy

I placed this case at the end of this part of the book because it is the only case I have information about concerning a rabbi who was arrested, pleaded guilty to, and was sentenced for "having sex with" a teen aged boy, "soliciting boys for sex via the Internet" and "throughout at least four states." After Rabbi Levy was arrested, he resigned from the synagogue, Temple Beth El in Boca Raton, Florida. I interviewed the senior rabbi of that synagogue about the case, and played the video for him of the WGRZ-TV/Buffalo news program on which I was interviewed about rabbis' sexual misconduct. I also interviewed other people in the Florida community about this case.

I learned that some people in the synagogue knew before they hired him that Rabbi Levy had been previously arrested in another state for soliciting sex in a public bathroom. But they did not do sufficient homework. Rabbi Levy reportedly told them that it was a case of "being in the wrong place at the wrong time during a sting operation." He said he had stopped in this bathroom only to use the facilities. The congregation believed him and hired him. It is my opinion that the congregation could have been spared the many months of anguish they suffered after Levy was arrested had they been informed about the truth about Rabbi Levy, and informed about the extent of and facts concerning rabbis' sexual misconduct that I write about in this book. Perhaps, then, they would have investigated further, not taken his word, and not hired this man as Rabbi of their Temple.

It took eight months (Rabbi Levy was incarcerated for those eight months) for the arrest of this rabbi to result in a sentence. Federal prosecutors called Rabbi Levy a "dangerous sex predator"[67] and asked for the maximum sentence, which could have been up to 60 years in prison because he pleaded guilty to two counts each of luring a minor over the Internet and distributing child pornography over the Web. Prosecutors stated that Rabbi Levy used his training as a rabbi to prey on "the young and confused." They called him a "skilled predator who uses his knowledge of human frailty to sexually abuse and exploit minor victims." They said that "just punishment requires that he spend the maximum time in prison where he can do no more harm." They also claimed that Rabbi Levy is "one of the most dangerous kind of sex offenders: a man who used the skills he developed on the job (as a rabbi) as a weapon to gain boys' confidence and seduce them."

According to Assistant U.S. Attorney Lothrop Morris, "In his capacity as associate rabbi of Temple Beth El in Boca Raton, Levy counseled many individuals in his congregation regarding their personal problems. He developed an ability to detect and understand people's vulnerabilities. Rather than use this ability to benefit society, Levy chose to use this ability to manipulate minors into engaging in prohibited sexual conduct.... His conduct is egregious and morally reprehensible.... the likelihood is that Levy would continue his ways once released."

Rabbi Jerrold Levy was not given the harshest sentence. In fact, instead of the up to 60 years this 59 year old rabbi could have faced, he was sentenced to only 6 ½ years in prison. People I interviewed believe that this light sentence resulted from a combination of factors, including the testimony of "character witnesses" who were Temple members. Perhaps had these Temple members been educated about sex addiction,[68] especially, in this case, about pedophilia, and also

---

[67]This case was extensively reported in the South Florida Sun-Sentinel, the Palm Beach Post, The Palm Beach Jewish News, and on the Web.

[68]Some experts believe that most 'sex addiction' is incurable, especially pedophilia. See, the works of Patrick Carnes, Ph.D., and Jerome D. Levin,

about rabbis' sexual misconduct, they would not have exhibited the outpouring of support for him that they did. As the judge said, "Levy was able to control his sexual impulses when he wanted to do so.... (he) has committed terrible acts."

Nevertheless, the judge imposed a sentence of only 6 ½ years which includes three years of probation. This means that Rabbi Levy may be out in less than three years, given that he has already served time in federal prison. During the sentence time, Rabbi Levy was ordered to undergo sexual offender treatment, can not hold a job that brings him into contact with children, can not go online without permission and can not have sexually explicit materials. Some Temple members were still unhappy with this sentence. They thought he should not have gone to prison at all.

Other Temple members were quoted, when the rabbi was initially arrested, as saying they had feelings of "disillusionment, shame, and breached trust." Still other members wondered aloud "why the temple's board, which knew that Rabbi Levy was arrested previously, hired him anyway." One member, reportedly serving as the Temple's lawyer, was quoted at that time as saying that, "This is not a common situation in the rabbinate." If he meant rabbis preying on boys, that seems to be true; if he meant rabbis guilty of sexual misconduct with teenagers and women, that it not true and indicates again the need for education of congregants (and even rabbis) about the facts and extent of rabbis' sexual misconduct.

Rabbi Merle Singer, the senior rabbi at Temple Beth El, was quoted at the time of Rabbi Levy's arrest that, ".... there is no simple salve to heal the wound caused by Levy's alleged actions and resulting media firestorm." Perhaps, had these victims (synagogue congregants and personnel, too, are victims of rabbis' sexual misconduct) of Rabbi Levy's abuse been educated to the facts about rabbis and sexual misconduct, there would have been no need for a "media firestorm." Meanwhile, we are fortunate to have "media firestorms." Those who have this information available to them will hopefully be alert so that other rabbis perpetrating sexual misconduct can be brought to justice, and so that rabbis who are at risk for this

---

Ph.D., for discussion of 'sex addiction,' and A.W. Richard Sipe for a discussion of pedophilia (listed in the Bibliography).

misconduct will be monitored, and those not yet hired who present such risks will not be hired as rabbis.

Rabbi Levy did seem to have some awareness at the sentencing of the abuse he has perpetrated. He was "tearful," and admitted that he "devastated his wife, children and congregation...." He detailed the painful difficulties he has experienced "by leading a double life." He was reported as actually turning "to his wife and their three grown children" who were sitting in the courtroom, and apologizing to them, and asking forgiveness from the Temple members who were in the courtroom. Rabbi Levy's daughter was quoted as saying she "thought the judge was fair in sentencing her father," and that it is her "hope he'll be able to get the help he needs." Certainly, Rabbi Levy's public apology and appearance of remorse is a good sign. Would that it would not take an arrest and sentencing for all rabbis guilty of sexual abuse of women and teenagers to exhibit remorse, publicly apologize, and start on the path to *Teshuvah*. We all hope that this is true, becomes true, for Rabbi Levy, that Rabbi Levy is on a path to *Teshuvah*, for the sake of Rabbi Levy, his family, the entire community.

The only other public apology this author knows of by a rabbi who was accused of sexual misconduct and abuse of women was that of Rabbi Kirschner, and he apologized to the press, not directly to those he hurt.

Susan Weidman Schneider, Editor-in-Chief, and Sarah Blustain, Associate Editor, of Lilith magazine recently wrote to the New York Times regarding "Sexual Abuse by Rabbis." "How *many* times will this story have to be told before those in positions of authority in Jewish institutions start to take responsibility for stopping religious leaders who violate ethical and legal boundaries and who hurt their followers?"[69] They went on to say, that, "Lilith, the independent Jewish women's magazine, exposed "The Paradoxical Legacy" of the late Rabbi Carlebach, known around the world for his neo-Chassidic spirituality, his charm and his music. Like (Baruch) Lanner's, Carlebach's alleged sexual misconduct was denied, ignored and

---

[69]"Sexual Abuse by Rabbis: A Letter to the New York Times." www.lilithmag.com/features/000724a.shtml.

covered up by his partisans. And like the Jewish Week's editor, (when he published the stories about Rabbi Lanner's alleged misdeeds) Lilith's staff was beseeched not to publish, for fear that the allegations brought against Carlebach would undo all the ostensible good he had done. The power and charisma of men like Lanner and Carlebach make it that much more difficult - and that much more important - to bring such allegations to light. The accusers in both cases felt violated twice: once by the sexual advances they say were made to them by a revered spiritual figure, and again by the silence that greeted them when they did come forward. And let us remember that in all the worry about "malicious gossip" and the hand-wringing about not making trouble for the rabbi, defensive members of these religious communities are missing the real point. If the allegations against Rabbi Lanner are proven true, he is not only in violation of ethics. He is in violation of the law." These rabbis and others like them must be exposed and stopped.

Let us hope that this book will help expose and stop rabbis' sexual abuse of teenagers and women so that the story will not have to be told "many more times."

PART THREE

Policies

Charlotte Schwab

Policies Concerning Rabbis' Sexual Misconduct: What Changes Are Needed

Maintaining sexual boundaries in the rabbinate requires effective policies, effective implementation of these policies, and the provision of a comprehensive, efficient structure to deal satisfactorily with allegations by a victim or other concerned party that a rabbi is guilty of sexual misconduct or abuse. This structure should not be characterized by secret and closed processes or hearings, but should be open to the concerned parties, and offer an atmosphere conducive to a rabbi and a complainant to disclose what we need to know to help all those involved.

We must not wait any longer in this litigious society for legal suits potentially harmful to the parties and even to the wider community before taking steps to support victims and weed out perpetrators. Where possible, offenders who are remorseful and cooperative should be helped by providing a realistic method of *Teshuvah.* According to Joseph Telushkin,[70] *Teshuvah,* or repentance, involves several stages: "The sinner must recognize his sin, feel sincere remorse, undo any damage he has done where possible, pacify the victim of his offense, and resolve never to commit the sin again." Rabbi Arthur Gross-Schaefer offers some specifics on what this process involves.[71] It would include: therapy by uninvolved, trained therapists; supervision by an uninvolved rabbinic mentor; acknowledging, naming the act or acts and validating the victims; confession; apologies to those wronged - the victims, the wife or ex-wife, the family, the synagogue, the community; restitution, including counseling costs for victims, and any other costs incurred by the victim(s) as a result of the abuse. Remember, as Rabbi Julie Spitzer stated, there is no healing for anyone involved in or affected by rabbis' sexual misconduct without justice.

---

[70]Joseph Telushkin. <u>Jewish Literacy</u>. New York. William Morrow And Company, Inc. 1991.

[71]Thanks to Rabbi Arthur Gross-Schaefer for a personal discussion of ideas on the subject of *teshuvah* and making amends. See also his papers, and others' papers listed in the Bibliography.

Rabbi Patricia Karlin-Neumann writes that, "sexual misconduct by a rabbi is not a private act. It needs a public response and a public responsibility."[72] She goes on to say that it is not always advisable to restore *avaryanim* to any religious standing. This possibility must be weighed after a carefully determined process. This process must take a good deal of time. Rabbi Karlin-Neumann states, "We must begin a discussion which will eliminate the present state of ambiguity: no clear process regarding options, no consensus about how we might respond to victims or offenders; and little recognition of how we struggle with our own passions." This ambiguity within denominations' rabbinic organizations is further exacerbated by the lack of communication among denominations.

In 1997, I was in California for four weeks interviewing involved parties about rabbis' sexual abuse. The people I interviewed included victims/survivors of rabbis' sexual abuse (I prefer the term victims/survivors, which helps these women to believe they can and will survive and move on with their lives), ex-wives of offending rabbis, other rabbis, and congregants or former congregants. I found that some people had left synagogues where there had been rabbi-offenders.

To help rectify these problems, in discussion with Rabbi Arthur Gross-Schaefer, I proposed the idea of convening a symposium in New York for rabbis, "Defining and Dealing With Rabbinic Sexual Misconduct." Rabbi Gross-Schaefer had organized and participated in a similar symposium in California. I attempted to assemble an interdenominational symposium for which I sought congregational rabbis representing the major denominations and the Jewish Renewal movement, as well as student-rabbi/participants who would be representatives of their seminaries. Speakers were to include both therapists and rabbis who were concerned with the problem of rabbis' sexual misconduct. I talked with the directors of *Elat Chayim*, a Jewish spiritual retreat center in the Catskill mountain area about holding the conference there.

---

[72]Patricia Karlin-Neumann. "Dealing With Rabbis Who Have Committed Acts of Sexual Misconduct." Unpublished manuscript.

Rabbis from California who had written about this problem and who had been educating other rabbis in their area including Rabbi Arthur Gross-Schaefer agreed to attend as speakers. I was not able to convince any male rabbis in New York to attend.

One of the female rabbis who supports my work told the Dean at the Jewish Theological Seminary, Rabbi Allan Kenski, about my work and my effort to convoke the symposium. He contacted me and in January, 1998, Rabbi Kenski brought me into the Seminary to give a lecture/seminar on rabbis' sexual misconduct. This rabbi/dean was very courageous. While some people supported him for doing this, especially the women students who had complained of sexual harassment by both male student-rabbis and male faculty, others opposed him. The students listened respectfully to my lecture. In fact, you could hear a pin drop. They participated in the seminar with great interest. Most were supportive of the need to learn about this problem; however, a few (males) questioned that this problem is "real," including a guest faculty member (a male) who was there to speak on another subject.

After the seminar, I was surrounded by female students who wanted my support for them to go to the dean in my presence and repeat their complaints about sexual harassment of them by certain male rabbinic students and male faculty members. I agreed to accompany them and, with my support, they reported the problems to the dean. He listened attentively and promised to take steps to rectify the problems. I recently spoke to Rabbi Kenski, and he informed me that the Jewish Theological Seminary adopted a sexual harassment policy. However, female students told me that these problems still exist at the seminary and that "not much has changed."

The attitude of lack of openness displayed by a rabbi/executive of the Rabbinical Assembly when he brought the draft of their "working policy" on sexual ethics for rabbis to a session prior to my presentation at the two day 'minimester' for discussion by those present, including this author, contributes to these problems still existing at the seminary and with the Rabbinical Assembly (about which, more below).

This rabbi/executive claimed that he wanted the opinions of those present about this "working policy," a discussion of this "working policy" by those present. Yet, he did not allow anyone present, even the student-rabbis, to retain a copy of this document so they could reflect on it, and contribute to it with thought and preparation, rather than "standing on one leg," as one student-rabbi complained we had been asked to do. He was very guarded about this "working policy," and took great care to ensure that not one copy was left behind, that he collected them all when he left. At this date, four years later, there is still no policy which has been adopted by the Rabbinical Assembly.

Ten years ago, when I started researching and working on this book, there was total lack of receptivity by the rabbinic organizations to a victim/survivor reporting a rabbi's transgression. Rabbis' transgressions were talked about by rabbis in a joking manner. I was present at several such occasions in the early and mid-eighties while I was married to my then rabbi/husband.

In the mid-nineties, when I lectured about sexual harassment to the UAHC "top rabbis and executives," the same atmosphere prevailed. There was no policy distributed to congregants for their knowledge so they might better avoid such transgressions. There was no action taken to stop any rabbi from his transgressions, according to people I spoke with. To my knowledge, there still is not, in any denomination. The worst thing that was done, and still is, in some cases, is that a rabbi is found a position in another city by the "old boys" in the rabbinic network. I know of several cases like this, including the one in which the student-rabbi was accused of molesting teen aged girls at his student-rabbi pulpit. This student-rabbi, although he was not ordained, was found a position as a rabbi in another state where they did not know of the accusations by several parents of what would be criminal acts. The "old boys" who found him this position were at the top of this denomination's rabbinic ladder. One of them was one of the rabbis whom I had asked to help with my rabbi/husband's transgressions. He was the rabbi who listened to me for a few minutes, then got up from behind his massive desk, and started walking toward the door, indicating my meeting with him was over. He said that my rabbi/husband being heavily involved in sexual misconduct and assaulting me when I found out and threatening to kill me if I told anyone what he was doing "did not involve" him.

It is imperative when dealing with rabbis' sexual abuse to be aware that the climate for victims who have reported *avaryanim* has been an unwelcoming, disbelieving one at best, and a hostile one at worst. Victims have been jeered, mistreated, and even ostracized by their synagogue communities. They have been blamed, treated as "trouble makers" or malcontents. Many of them have felt that they had to leave their synagogue and, in some cases, their communities. Some of them have felt that they had to leave their state, or the country. They have been asked why they are "making trouble" for the "beloved" rabbi, or, blamed and told they "created" the situation.

In her article, "Victims of Rabbinic Sex Abuse Suffer Pain of Communal Denial,"[73] Debra Nussbaum Cohen writes that, "People do not want to think that their rabbi is capable of sexual exploitation.... when exploitation does occur, the women who come forward often find themselves ostracized by their religious community.... on the rare occasions that they turn to their rabbi's professional associations or their movement's congregational organization, they say they are made to feel unwelcome. The result is often a conspiracy of silence that protects the perpetrators and leaves the victims feeling isolated and in pain, alienated from the very Jewish community to which they had turned for spiritual sustenance.... Congregants are often so deeply invested in keeping their rabbis on a pedestal that they are unwilling or unable to consider that they might do something so fundamentally offensive. And so they often deny it.... synagogue members will often stand up and ostracize the accuser. In some cases, the accusers have been called "liars" and "whores" - and worse...."

The synagogue in Cherry Hill, New Jersey, where the rabbi was arrested and jailed, and is awaiting retrial for allegedly hiring a hit man to murder his wife because she was a block to his ability to continue his nefarious actions, went through a similar experience. Many of the congregants did not want him to resign or to fire him when they found out about his sexual misconduct, not even when he was a suspect in the murder. He finally did resign, but there are many there who do not believe that he was/is guilty of any wrongdoing, let alone that he could be guilty of capital murder. If he is convicted, these people probably will still believe him innocent. It is the nature of the sacred aura which rabbis establish about themselves and which

---

[73] Debra Nussbaum Cohen, "Victims of Rabbinic Sex Abuse Suffer Pain of Communal Denial." JTA Daily News Bulletin (Jewish Telegraph Agency). September 19, 1996.

they are accorded. Many people see them as sacred, as holy, as beyond culpability, no matter what.[74]

In the case of the rabbi in California where the woman temple president was murdered by a hit man the morning after she left her husband to move in with the rabbi who reportedly had been having sex with her for some time (while she was living with her husband), the rabbi was never investigated as a possible suspect in her murder. Some people I interviewed think he is the guilty one to this day, even though the woman's husband was tried and convicted on what I was told was "hearsay" and "circumstantial evidence." Some people I interviewed in California told me that, "The rabbi was tired of (this woman)," that he was a "philanderer" and that "he could have arranged for her murder." They told me that, "The rabbi was known to have many sexual relationships with congregants and others." Michele Samit, who wrote about this case in her book, "No Sanctuary: The True Story of a Rabbi's Deadly Affair," described how she was vilified by members of the congregation for writing the book. Samit said she was harassed by congregants who supported the rabbi. They called her terrible names and asked her, "How could you have destroyed such a wonderful man." Debra Nussbaum Cohen reported that this rabbi denied that his relationship with the murdered temple president was an illicit affair. No doubt, he, himself, would not think he was/is guilty of sexual misconduct, of sexual exploitation.

There is a great deal of ignorance about what rabbinic sexual exploitation is, say those involved with the issue. Because of the anticipated reaction, victims of rabbinic sexual exploitation and harassment rarely come forward, experts say. Women who have experienced rabbinic exploitation often feel that they have a lot to lose if they come forward - their place in their synagogue communities, respect and success in their professional lives, and even in some cases, their marriages." Nussbaum Cohen reported that women who came forward to charge Rabbi Robert Kirschner of Temple Emanu-el in San Francisco with sexual exploitation were called "harlots and Jezebels," and that two complainants - students from Berkeley's Graduate Theological Union - who had obtained advance permission from the synagogue to come to the meeting and tell the congregation

---

[74]Gerald L. Zelizer, "Why Do Parishioners Stick by Clergy Who Commit Crimes?" USA Today. 5/24/99. p 27A.

about their experiences, said they were forced out of the building before they had a chance to speak.

Nussbaum Cohen reported that a congregant in another synagogue, Michael Hirsch, where the rabbi was known to be guilty of sexual misconduct (Rabbi Steven Jacobs) was so "outraged by his rabbi's behavior and his community's response, that he wrote to the head of the Reform rabbinical association's ethics committee charging Jacobs with violating the group's ethics code and demanding that it take up Jacobs' behavior. Rabbi Jeffrey Stiffman, then the head of the committee, wrote back to Hirsch that Jacobs had agreed "to uphold all provisions of our Code of Ethics," which requires rabbis "to adhere to an exemplary moral code" and "to avoid even the appearance of sexual misconduct." Hirsch responded to Stiffman with a letter saying that the action amounted to nothing more than a rabbinic consent decree for Jacobs to do it all over again. If there is a *shanda* (shame) here, it is not only in Jacobs' immoral conduct, but in your organization's complicity in covering it up." I interviewed Michael Hirsch. He related to me that he felt so strongly about the need to remove Rabbi Kirschner from his position at the Skirball that he picketed the institution. Michael Hirsch is a former investigative journalist and at the time he wrote this letter, was a television producer.

Nussbaum Cohen went on to write that Steven Jacobs, "remains the rabbi of Temple Kol Tikvah, the name adopted after it merged with another synagogue." And that, "Experts in clergy sexual abuse say the denial among congregants can be dangerous because a rabbi can go on harassing and exploiting many congregants for decades without any of them knowing that the others exist, forcing each of them to bear the suffering alone." She quoted Marie Fortune, a minister and founding director of the Seattle-based Center for the Prevention of Sexual and Domestic Violence who has run a seminar on rabbinic sexual misconduct at a regional meeting of Reform rabbis and for students at a Los Angeles rabbinical seminary and who has worked with more than 3,500 cases of clergy sexual misconduct in dozens of different religious denominations over a 15 year period as saying that ".... if a rabbi has sexually exploited one congregant, he almost always has exploited several.... "and that ".... there is long-term damage being done here we're going to have to be living with for years," and, "It doesn't have to be that bad if we respond better."

Nussbaum Cohen asserts that, ".... while the rabbinic perpetrators often move to another job within their movements or even stay in their pulpits after a slap on the wrist from their rabbinical organization, it appears that the victims often go away."

These rabbis have been supported by congregations and their rabbinic organizations at every turn and for every kind of transgression. This must stop. The belief that a rabbi can do no wrong is dangerous. It kept a rabbi out of jail for over five years who is now awaiting a retrial for allegedly committing capital murder by hiring a hit man to murder his wife, because, as some are saying, she found out about his sexual abuses of other women. (The first trial ended in a hung jury, reportedly nine for conviction.) It is important to offer validation, support, and help to victims of rabbinic sexual misconduct, be they wives of these rabbis, ex-wives, or victims/survivors of the abuse.

I, and other therapists working with victims of rabbis' sexual abuse find that victims of rabbis' sexual abuse are often more severely traumatized than victims of domestic violence, rape, and other violence perpetrated by non clergy. These victims/survivors need special help not only because of the aura of sacredness surrounding a rabbi who has abused them, but also because of the community's denial and mistreatment of them. For the past several years, I have been compiling a list of therapists around the country who help victims of rabbi sexual abuse. However, there are not enough therapists with knowledge about and with experience dealing with rabbis' sexual abuse. There are several web sites dealing with clergy abuse (of all religions). Some of them give resources for finding a therapist. They are listed in the Resources Appendix.

Because of the proliferation of newspaper articles on the subject of rabbi-perpetrators of sexual abuse, and because of the numbers of threatened or instituted legal suits[75] resulting from sexual harassment or abuse, and because of my and others' work in this area, the Reform

---

[75]I was invited to present the lecture/seminar for the Union of American Hebrew Congregations (UAHC) because, in the words of the then program chair, "We are experiencing many legal suits for sexual harassment by rabbis at congregations around the country, and we need to know what to do about it."

rabbinic organization (CCAR[76]), the Reconstructionist Rabbinical Association,[77] and the Rabbinical Assembly (Conservative) have worked on and, except in the latter case, produced and sent me a hard copy of a policy governing sexual ethics for rabbis. ALEPH: Alliance for Jewish Renewal would only send me an e-mail of their "Code of Ethics," claiming that, because their "brand of Jewish renewal is deeply informed by feminism and because ALEPH has a strong leadership for many years, we may be ahead of the curve on this issue." Yet, this e-mail and subsequent e-mails from their spokesperson revealed a defensive tone and stance. They would not give out any specific information.

A few years ago, someone in the UAHC (Union of American Hebrew Congregations), the congregational 'arm' of Reform Judaism, sent me a hard copy of a **"DRAFT UAHC SEXUAL HARASSMENT POLICY."** This draft finally appeared as **"Discrimination, Harassment and Offensive Conduct Policy of the UAHC"** on the Union of American Hebrew Congregations web site[78] in 2001. However none of the Reform congregants I questioned knew about this policy. The policy contains a "Disclaimer: This is the discrimination, harassment and offensive conduct policy that the UAHC uses. However for our synagogues' purposes, this should be treated as a sample policy for informational use only. This policy may not be suitable for your congregation nor the laws of the State in which the congregation exists. We strongly urge you to develop your own policy in cooperation with your congregation's legal counsel." People I questioned who were members of several Reform congregations knew nothing about such a policy in their own congregations, and told me that their synagogues were doing "nothing about educating congregants with regard to sexual harassment or sexual abuse by rabbis."

I quote from and discuss some aspects of these policies below, although I cannot go into great detail in this volume. I suggest that the

---

76"Code of Ethics for Rabbis." Central Conference of American Rabbis. Adopted in convention assembled, June, 1991, and as amended in 1993, 1998 and 2000.

77"Breach of Professional Trust: Sexual and Financial Ethics - Final Version June 1996." Reconstructionist Rabbinical Association.

78http://uahc.org/dhoc.shtml

171

reader try to obtain her/his own copy from the individual organizations. I say "try" because I and others have found it extremely difficult, if not impossible, to access the policies which do exist or any information about them. How these organizations can think that making it difficult to obtain copies of these policies will help anyone is a mystery.

Discrimination, Harassment and Offensive Conduct Policy of the UAHC

This policy is a "sample policy." I will not discuss it in detail here. The UAHC policy states, commendably, that they believe that "prevention is the best tool for the elimination of harassment." Educational sessions are an important tool for prevention. Yet, none of the congregants I questioned knew of any educational sessions about sexual harassment conducted by their synagogues. What is most important is that individual congregations must adopt a policy, distribute it to their congregants, and provide educational sessions for its congregants, employees and volunteers.

It tells us a great deal about the mind-set of the UAHC to read on their web site that the UAHC Congregational Insurance Program[79] advises that if a congregation's insurance policy "does not address all of the concerns raised" on their web site listing, including "Separate $1,000,000 limit for sexual misconduct claims" and "Umbrella Liability including excess insurance for Counseling and Teaching Services Liability and sexual misconduct," the congregation needs "to take a second look. Cutting corners on your insurance could be an expensive mistake!"

Rather than relying on insurance to handle sexual harassment and sexual misconduct by rabbis and others, I urge congregations to become informed about rabbis' sexual misconduct and to institute educational seminars about it. Let's hope that it won't take massive legal suits and massive payments of settlements before this happens. In addition, the seminaries must, "legitimize sexuality education as a necessary and efficacious part of seminary and theological school training for both personal enhancement and expedient performance of clergy roles. The goal of ongoing interaction among involved experts

---

[79]www.fcrystal.com/uahc "UAHC Congregational Insurance Program."

may lead to openly naming and articulating the pervasiveness of sexuality concerns for all theological study, as well as developing a conceptual scheme for theological education in which sexuality is a hub and institutional support is solid…. varying approaches, methods, and resources are needed for sexuality education of clergy of differing faiths beliefs, ethnicities, ages, personal backgrounds, and life situations."[80]

I asked several women Reform congregants to whom they would report an incident of sexual harassment in their synagogues. Their replies were all the same: they "did not know." One of these women went on to state that she would not "feel comfortable telling <u>anyone</u> in the congregation since the subject <u>has never even been brought up by any of the congregation's professionals.</u>"

CODE OF ETHICS FOR RABBIS, CENTRAL CONFERENCE OF AMERICAN RABBIS

The "Preamble" of the "Ethics Guidelines and Procedures For Responding to Allegations of Sexual Misconduct by CCAR Members" of the CCAR's "Code of Ethics for Rabbis" provides a reassuring first paragraph: "As rabbis, Jewish Leaders and pastoral guides we are commanded to exemplify holiness through our teachings and our lives. We bear the greatest responsibility for insuring that ethical and sexual boundaries are scrupulously respected in all our relationships with the men, women and young people who turn to us in trust. Sexual misconduct by rabbis is a sin against human beings; it is also a *Hillul Hashem*. It is the responsibility of the CCAR to uphold the sacred calling of the rabbinate by creating just and appropriate responses to sexual misconduct."[81]

One important point this paragraph and the subsequent paragraphs do not make clear is who "the men, women and young people" are that they are referring to "who turn to these rabbis in trust." Do these people include non congregants who turn to these rabbis "in trust" as rabbis? Do they include the non congregant who may consult them

---

[80]"Conclusions and Implications for Professional Sexuality Education of Clergy." <u>The Center for Sexuality and Religion</u>. Wayne, PA. 2002.

[81]<u>Central Conference of American Rabbis.</u> "Code of Ethics for Rabbis." p. 8.

"in trust" about the burial of a husband, as in the case of Elaine Soncini who consulted Rabbi Fred Neulander? Do they include students such as those who studied with Rabbi Kirschner, who may or may not even be Jewish, and trusted them as rabbis? These questions must be clarified in this policy.

The question of whether rabbis should "be trusted" to uphold ethical behavior with others besides their congregants and employees is a very important question which all policies regarding sexual conduct and misconduct by rabbis must adequately deal with. The paragraph on page nine of the CCAR Code does caution that, ".... any relationship which the rabbi feels compelled to keep totally clandestine or which raises doubts as to its ethical propriety or acceptance ought to give the rabbi serious pause and propel him/her, at the very least, to seek moral counsel. Among other considerations, rabbis are expected to honor the sanctity and fidelity of committed relationships, their own and those of others. Any sexual activity which betrays those relationships or leads others to betray like relationships constitutes an ethical violation."

I find that this policy fails not only in its lack of accessibility, but also in its lack of procedures and processes, including not making public, <u>at least to all congregations/congregants in its denomination,</u> when a rabbi has been investigated, reprimanded, censured, suspended, or expelled from the CCAR. To inform only the president of a congregation is not sufficient. All members must be informed.[82] When any of these four actions: "investigation, reprimand, censure, suspension" have been taken, the case should be made public so that these rabbis cannot go to congregations outside of the jurisdiction of the CCAR, those in other denominations of Judaism, or in other Jewish organizations or spiritual groups, obtain employment with the title "rabbi," and continue their sexual misconduct. To publish these actions in the <u>CCAR Newsletter</u> is not sufficient. The <u>CCAR Newsletter</u> is a newsletter for Reform rabbis. It is not made available to everyone concerned. To state as the CCAR Code of Ethics does on page 11, that "A rabbi under suspension may not seek or accept rabbinic employment or engage in the practice of the rabbinate in any institution, including, but to limited to congregations affiliated with the Union of American Hebrew Congregations or the World Union of

---

[82]See, for example, the <u>ISTI</u> Policy discussed below.

Progressive Judaism, or in institutions associated with the Reform movement (the Union of American Hebrew Congregations, the Hebrew Union College-Jewish Institute of Religion, and the Skirball Cultural Center)" puts trust in the rabbi who has violated a specific provision of the Code of Ethics to refrain from seeking a position as a rabbi in another denomination or Jewish organization, rather than informing congregations and other organizations of his[83] transgressions so they can protect themselves.

Certainly all congregants of the synagogue where he is employed must be told; congregants of other synagogues in his denomination must be told; congregants in synagogues of other denominations must be told. The Jewish community must know. Only then can we be sure we can protect our children, teenagers, sisters, wives, and mothers from (this) rabbi/perpetrator of sexual abuse. Usually, only when a rabbi's sexual misconduct is the subject of articles in the media do we hear about it. Rabbis might look to the example of the Pope John Paul II, who offered an apology recently[84] for sexual abuse by Roman Catholic clergy, saying it has caused the victims "great suffering and spiritual harm" and has damaged the church. The pontiff said the church is seeking "open and just procedures to respond to complaints in this area," and the Vatican has ordered a study of complaints of sexual abuse. While this report did not state that the pontiff named the names of those clergy it is investigating, it is a public statement, which was also published on the Internet. Naming names of clergy perpetrators of sexual abuse is an important step which must be taken by all religious organizations to help stop such abuse.

The "CCAR Code of Ethics for Rabbis," states that "The director of placement (of the CCAR) shall inform congregations considering the engagement of the rabbi of past complaints concerning the rabbi and of the rehabilitation that has been completed. This statement does not make clear who in the "congregations" should be informed. Again, what of those congregations in other denominations and other organizations where this rabbi may be seeking a position.

---

[83] I use male pronouns to refer to rabbi/perpetrators since male rabbis are the predominant perpetrators of sexual abuse.

[84] "Pope apologizes for clergy's sexual abuse." by Richard Boudreaux. The Palm Beach Post. Friday, November 23, 2001. p. 2A.

The Rabbinical Assembly

I was gratified to receive a letter in January, 2002, from Rabbi Allan Kensky, Dean of the Jewish Theological Seminary (of the Conservative denomination) that he has, "…. fond memories of (my) speaking to our students." It seems that as a result of my well-received lecture- seminar to them in 1998, and "after the exposés of recent years" they "recently held a "minimester" devoted to the question of the violation of sexual boundaries by rabbis. The three day program was received well by the student body."[85] He assured me that, "…. there is a well-developed sexual harassment policy now in place at JTS." He went on to write that, "There is also a policy on amorous relations which is in place. There were workshops with students and faculty (separate) to explain the workings of the (latter) policy. While the policy is per se public, it was intended for an internal audience." I was not able to obtain copies of either of these policies. Rabbi Kensky was also not able to provide me with the phantom Rabbinical Assembly policy regarding rabbis' sexual misconduct, because he does "not have a copy of it."

On December 27, 2001, I telephoned Rabbi Joel Meyers of the Rabbinical Assembly to ask him if they had adopted a written policy concerning rabbis' sexual misconduct. He told me, "We don't have a written policy. When an incident is brought to our attention we have a process in place. We don't have to write a policy to tell rabbis to behave themselves." I asked him what the process is. He said, "Everyone in this office is trained to refer 'issues' with rabbis to (him)." I asked him about the case in Buffalo. He said he was not free to talk about it. I told him that some of us have been waiting for this policy since we learned about it in January 1998 when he brought the "working policy" to the "minimester" at the Jewish Theological Seminary for discussion by the rabbinic students, faculty, and guest faculty present before I presented my lecture-seminar. (He did not choose to stay for my lecture-seminar.) I reminded him that at that time, he distributed the "working policy" (concerning sexual ethics for rabbis) to those of us at the "minimester," cautioning us that we must return it to him at the end of the discussion; we could not, "with no exceptions" keep a copy. I reminded him that he promised at that

---

[85]Letter to me from Rabbi Allan Kensky, January 16, 2002.

time that "within a few months we will have a written policy for distribution." On the telephone, December, 27, 2001, since there had never been any policy distributed, I asked him when we could expect this to happen. He said that, "Within a few months we will have a written policy." I pointed out to him that had been the promise for almost four years. His response to me was, "Sometimes women want to remain angry, want to exact vengeance, period, unless the rabbi is driven out of town, punished." I think this response speaks for itself. What woman would feel free and safe to report a rabbi's sexual abuse to Rabbi Meyers and believe that she would get a fair hearing, when this is his attitude?

On February 4, 2002, I spoke with Rabbi Bob Carroll of Edah, an Orthodox group which sponsored a "Jewish Town Hall" discussion on January 29, 2002, at the JCC in Manhattan on "Moral Offenses By Religious Leaders." Rabbi Joel Meyers was one of the panelists. He was quoted by a reporter who covered the event,[86] Joanne Palmer, as saying that, "…. the problem of rabbis who abuse their trust is not a common one. There are very few aberrant rabbis." Rabbi Meyers is clearly still in denial.

While it is encouraging that such a panel would be held at all, especially with interdenominational rabbis present,[87] and for the public, the danger is that such a panel could be construed as meaning that effective action is being taken by those in power over rabbinic conduct, and lead attendees to complacency. More helpful than Rabbi Meyers comments were those of Dr. Michelle Friedman, a panel member who is an assistant professor of clinical psychiatry at Mount Sinai Hospital in Manhattan and immediate past president of Drisha Institute for Women's Education, also in Manhattan. Dr. Friedman is Orthodox. Palmer quotes her as telling the audience that much of her work is "dealing with the fallout from (rabbis) crossing sexual boundaries, particularly in communities on the far right." She goes on to write that Dr. Friedman said that "People invest rabbis with enormous amounts of power. Crossing the boundaries that define

---

[86]Joanne Palmer. "Crimes and Misdemeanors: Panel addresses moral failures of religious leaders." Jewish Standard. February 1, 2002 p 8.

[87]Four years before, I attempted to convene a symposium with interdenominational rabbis on this subject. (I discuss this elsewhere in this book).

people in those relationships is an incestuous violation. It is necessarily predatory and exploitive." Palmer goes on to quote Friedman as saying that "the tendency to blame the victim, which is widespread, must be resisted. Often, victims don't feel free to say no;.... sometimes, particularly in communities on the far right, they don't even know they should. There is often a stigma attached to the victims, which makes them even less likely to come forward; compounding that problem is the reluctance people feel to attack popular, charismatic leaders." Friedman did "not see much hope for rehabilitating habitual (rabbi) offenders. There is very little treatment available, and they tend to move from community to community, with people in each place they leave glad to see their backs."

Gary Rosenblatt, the editor and publisher of New York's <u>Jewish Week</u> spoke in the question and answer period. "He said that he was inundated with stories about other abuses by other rabbis and Jewish educators" (after he broke the story about Rabbi Baruch Lanner, discussed in PART II). He said he chose not to run a "pervert of the week" column; but that "the temptation and - the copy- is real."

Rabbi Bob Carroll sent me the following comment with permission to quote it in this book. "There are cultural factors within the Orthodox Community which we need to face up to and confront if we are to deal effectively with this problem. (Rabbis' "crimes and moral failings.") There is a tendency, both on the part of some lay people and clergy, to perceive criticism of rabbinic malfeasance as an attack on rabbinic authority in general. In some cases, this has led to a reluctance to take whistle blowers seriously. This is not merely an issue of organizational process or governance; it calls for a re-examination of how we as a community relate to our institutions and leaders and to what degree we actively exercise 'ownership' of them."[88]

Rabbi Saul Berman, the founder of Edah, was quoted in the article by Palmer as saying at the Edah sponsored discussion, "A critically distinctive element of Jewish law and ethics is the duty of rescue. We must protect people's lives, their physical and emotional well-being, their property. We must act pre-emptively, in a way to prevent evil from being done. We must stop it from happening." Let us hope that

---

[88]Rabbi Bob Carroll of <u>Edah</u>. Via e-mail, February 4, 2002.

his statement does not prove to be only lip service. Let us hope that the rabbinical organizations and denominations will heed his call.

Another important step in achieving the end to rabbis' sexual abuse, in addition to adopting and enforcing effective policies and procedures for dealing with rabbinic sexual misconduct is educating seminary students and, possibly even more important, educating ordained rabbis about sexuality and sexual misconduct. Sally Conklin, Ph.D., writing about a seminary survey[89] of clergy students regarding their sexuality education, told of a woman who, along with three other women in her congregation were victims of clergy sexual abuse. This woman was "especially distressed by one seminary survey response." Namely, "Most of our students are over 40 years old and these sexuality issues are largely settled earlier in their lives." "Yeah, right," this woman victim of clergy sexual abuse sighed as she slumped into a chair and told (Dr. Conklin) her story. These issues are not "largely settled" early in rabbis' lives. They are largely unsettled, as is evidenced by the high numbers of cases of rabbis' sexual misconduct.

The Reconstructionist Rabbinical Association Policy

The Reconstructionist Rabbinical Association adopted a policy called "Breach of Professional Trust: Sexual and Financial Ethics" in June of 1996. I called their office on January 25, 2002 and spoke to their Executive Assistant, Linda Kaplan.[90] I asked her if there had been any changes to the policy since it was adopted. She said, "No. The policy remains the same." The RRA policy is strong in some ways, including its definition of "Unethical sexual activity," which states that, "It is unethical to engage in, or attempt to engage in, sexual activity with a minor, an unwilling adult, a married or partnered congregant, any person whom a rabbi is counseling or aiding in life cycle events, conversion, or other pastoral situation. **Such sexual relationships are unethical even if suggested or welcomed by the congregant. It is the responsibility of the rabbi**

---

[89]Sally Conklin, Ph.D. "CSR Seminary Survey Yields Robust Data." <u>CSR Connections</u>. Volume III Number 1. Autumn 2001.

[90]Telephone call to Reconstructionist Rabbinical Association. Church Road and Greenwood Ave. Wyncote, PA 19095, (215) 576-5210.

to maintain appropriate boundaries. (Emphasis theirs). Sexual activity may include intimate or unwanted physical contact as well as intercourse."

What is important about this statement is that it puts the responsibility for unethical sexual activity on the rabbi, where it should be, not on the congregant. I do object to the terminology of, "engaging in sexual activity." It is important to call this behavior "Misconduct" and "abuse." The phrase, "engaging in sexual activity" makes it sound mutual.

There are other issues that are not dealt with by this policy. What about rabbis 'engaging in sexual activity' with married persons who are not congregants? What about married rabbis 'engaging in sexual activity' with other women, whether or not the women are married? What about rabbis 'engaging in sexual activity' with students who are not congregants, and with those who may be of another faith? What about rabbis going to prostitutes? These are clearly unanswered.

This policy is strong in the specification of time periods for response to a complainant. However, this policy still protects perpetrators. The only way anything will be revealed is in response "to inquiries about allegations regarding a specific RRA member." Then, "The chairperson may reveal: a) that an investigation of the alleged violation is underway; b) that the investigation has been resolved but is confidential; or c) the member has been suspended or expelled. No other details are to be revealed." This provision protects the rabbi/perpetrators, not the victims.

Julie Wiener, a reporter for the JTA Daily News Bulletin wrote on Friday, December 15, 2000, that "Officials of the Reconstructionist Rabbinical Association would not disclose how many cases it has reviewed or what disciplinary action it took."[91] We need to know when a rabbi has perpetrated sexual abuse so that unsuspecting future victims can be protected. If these men are protected, if these perpetrators are kept confidential **unless we know to inquire about**

---

[91]Julie Weiner. "High-profile cases refocus attention on sexual misconduct." JTA Daily News Bulletin, December 15, 2000. Vol. 78, No. 235. Ms. Weiner also wrote in this article that, ".... the Orthodox (spokesperson) said they did not know of any cases of rabbinic sexual misconduct." Apparently, reports to them fall on deaf ears. Do they think Dr. Friedman, quoted above, is "making up" that she has so many cases?

them, how will unsuspecting potential future victims be protected? Also, to reveal the truth about perpetrators shows the good faith, the moral fiber, the spiritual strength of a rabbinical association, that that is their first and foremost objective; not to protect perpetrators.

Alliance for Jewish Renewal (ALEPH)

In late December, 2001, I wrote to Rabbi Daniel Siegel, Executive Director of the Alliance for Jewish Renewal to ask if there is a Jewish Renewal policy statement regarding sexual conduct (and misconduct) for their rabbis. I received an answer from Susan Saxe, the Chief Operating Officer of ALEPH. I subsequently asked her why Rabbi Daniel Siegel did not respond to me. Her response was that he is always "very busy." The e-mail correspondence we embarked on showed her to be defensive about answering this problem.

She wrote that "Jewish Renewal is a grassroots movement. ALEPH is only one organization within it. While we play some visible and crucial roles, we cannot and do not control the whole thing. In fact, there are many individuals, *havurot*, congregations and even organizations that also consider themselves 'Jewish renewal' that we don't consider renewal at all, some that we have next to nothing to do with and know very little about. People and groups pop up all the time that have been in existence for years before we even knew they existed."

I wrote Ms. Saxe that I had several cases involving male Jewish Renewal rabbis. I requested a list of the names of rabbis who are members of Jewish Renewal to determine that in fact these rabbis are members of this organization, but to date I have not received any such list. She did send via e-mail an ALEPH Code of Ethics, with the disclaimer that, "Since we are not a denomination, the standard of conduct in article 2 of the Code applies primarily to our events. Affiliated congregations and *havurot* are autonomous in governance and make their own rules." Ms. Saxe stated that, "If there is an incident, even a verbal one, the victim can go to any board member or senior staff person and expect a full investigation and resolution, usually on the spot." This sounds implausible, even ridiculous. (Rabbi Daniel Siegel was "too busy" even to answer my inquiry.) She went on to say that they have had a "handful of cases.... in my 11 years.... always male on female," including a "serious sexual predator who unfortunately slipped through our screening process. Very strong measures were taken and our process tightened...." and that.... "If the perpetrator just doesn't get it, we fire him, period." I asked the names of those fired. She refused to provide them. She did ask me for the names of those I know who told me they have been abused by Jewish Renewal rabbis. Of course, I refused to give her that information.

ALEPH: Alliance for Jewish Renewal Code of Ethics[92]

I print here only excerpts relevant to this book. "People in positions of leadership and/or authority at.... ALEPH sponsored gatherings (the word rabbi is not used) agree to abide by the following ethical guidelines:.... As ALEPH is committed to creating a community which is increasingly aware of the dynamics of power and potential abuses of power in spiritual community, we agree not to misuse our leadership role. This includes, but is not limited to refraining from beginning a sexual relationship with any participant in our class, group, workshop, prayer group or healing session during the period of the ALEPH sponsored (event)." Emphasis mine. What happens after the event? Is the person who was in a "position of authority" sanctioned by ALEPH at the event, including a rabbi, free to perpetrate sexual abuse after the event on an attendee? on anyone else?

The ALEPH Code of Ethics goes on to say that, "We at ALEPH are very aware that when we create intense spiritual community we are opening the door to opportunities both for great holiness and great danger. There is a thin line between spiritual energy and libido - the psychic space where one is open to ecstatic experience can also be a space where one is open to manipulation and exploitation...." It continues, "Single teachers who meet someone with whom there is a mutual attraction are advised to wait until the event is over, to end the student/teacher or rabbi/congregant relationship, and to start anew after a suitable waiting period.

.... Anyone who feels uncomfortable is welcome to bring their concerns directly to ALEPH.staff, board members, or spiritual leaders who will listen in confidence, take them seriously and respond....

---

[92]Received by e-mail from Susan Saxe, Executive Director. The e-mail address is: ALEPHAJR@aol.com

where intervention is called for, we try to do it in a way that is truly healing and supports every person involved in staying in community in a way that is healthy and safe."

There are serious questions about the adequacy of this policy. When an "event" is over, a rabbi does not stop being a rabbi, or lose his power. There is no specific statement, no definition of what taking a complainant "seriously" means, what this "truly healing" way is; no names of the persons to whom someone could report an abusive rabbi, what the specific process is for reporting or for dealing with the accused perpetrator.

The Code goes on to say, "On the rare occasions where intervention is called for...." How do they define "rare?" How do they know (before the fact?) that these "occasions" will be "rare?" According to my and others' information, the "occasions" where intervention is called for are not "rare." This attitude exhibits the dangerous denial I and others working in this field have found (including with regard to rabbi-perpetrators affiliated with Jewish Renewal).

Generally, the policies which do exist are a start, and only a start with regard to dealing with sexual abuse by rabbis. None of them are at all comprehensive enough. Much needs to be done to create an open climate for hearing and responding to women's and parents' reports as discussed above. There needs to be much clearer and more specific polices and processes for requiring admission of the transgression by the perpetrators, apologies directly to all affected parties, and procedures for making amends *(Teshuvah)* to victims by the rabbi-perpetrators. When a rabbi is found guilty as the result of an investigation by the rabbinic organization, the details of the investigation must be made public. When a rabbi resigns as the result of complaints and the investigation is thereby aborted, this also needs to be made public, along with details of the accusations, although never revealing the victims' names. The victims deserve protection, not the perpetrators. Resignation as a way of stopping investigation is tantamount to admitting guilt, and these rabbis should not be allowed to get away with this ploy to gain the advantage of avoiding the consequences of the truth, the details of the transgressions that led them to resign. They certainly should not be protected by being given positions conferring, retaining the title of rabbi, which allows them to continue their transgressions against unsuspecting potential victims.

Those giving these rabbis positions and 'looking the other way' are as guilty as these rabbis. The ones who need to be protected are the victims and their families, potential victims, and the congregation, the denomination, the community, not rabbi/perpetrators.

The entire veil of secrecy surrounding rabbi-perpetrators must be lifted. Further, there needs to be requirements for psychotherapy for the rabbi-perpetrators with a known expert in the field of clergy sexual abuse, who is not a rabbi, and who is not partial to rabbis, for as long a duration as the expert deems necessary. Only if and when this expert determines that the offender has acknowledged his misdeeds, apologized to all those he hurt, has been educated regarding sexuality, made *teshuvah*, and is recovered sufficiently for him to have a pulpit or other rabbinic position, or position carrying the title rabbi which brings him in close contact with teen aged girls and women, should he be allowed to do so.

For example, the rabbi in California, who resigned after, reportedly, many women accused him of sexual abuse was given a position at a Reform educational institution in Los Angeles. Some people were so outraged at this move, that they picketed the institution. Yet, he was retained in the position.

"Rabbi-mentors" are not adequate for supervision of a rabbi-perpetrator's recovery. They are too close to the issue. They are not trained as experts in clergy misconduct or in sex offender recovery programs. Perhaps when the transgressor is guilty of one offense at the lower end of the spectrum of offenses, this is adequate. It is not when there are multiple offenses, or when the offenses are at the higher end of the spectrum in seriousness. (I discuss definition of offenses in PART IV).

Rabbinic organizations must demonstrate that they are serious about acknowledging the gravity of rabbi offenders, and that they are serious about dealing with them effectively. They must create an atmosphere of openness, truth, integrity, caring toward the victims/survivors. They must show that they, themselves, are willing to come forward, to talk about this, to admit it, and stop hiding behind such excuses as it is *"loshen hora"* (gossip) to talk about this serious problem. Labeling someone who wants to talk about it as being guilty of *"loshen hora"* (gossip), again blames the victims/survivors. The truth must be told, welcomed, encouraged.

Because this is a difficult problem, one fraught with shame, fear, guilt does not excuse rabbis from facing the truth. In doing my research, I encountered many such excuses, such as, that I was "gossiping;" that this was better kept secret, hidden; that it is a *"Shande for the Yidn"* (shame for Jews); that, "What will the *goyim* (gentiles) think of us?" Even that it is "anti Semitic" to write about or even to talk about this problem. One feminist organization, of which I am a member, and which is directly concerned with preventing violence against women had scheduled me to speak about rabbis' sexual abuse of women and this book, even going so far as to publish the event in their own Newsletter. They canceled my talk when, after the forthcoming event appeared in a local newspaper, a woman called them and complained that it was "anti-Semitic" to have me speak. While this attitude reveals a lack of courage and integrity by an organization which exists to eliminate violence against women and advance the freedom of women, these attitudes are throwbacks to the fear emanating from persecution of Jews for centuries, including the Holocaust and the Russian Cossack pogroms of the early 20th Century. People I have questioned who express these attitudes state fears of an anti-Semitic resurgence in this country, citing such current events as synagogue attacks, and attacks on Jewish students on college campuses. My response to these fears is that only by honesty, openness, telling the truth, caring, and love will we combat any scourge, whether it be rabbis' sexual abuse of teenagers and women, or anti-Semitic attacks. Denying abuses of women and teenagers by our own rabbis within the institutions of the Jewish community will only foster attitudes of disrespect toward Judaism, Jewish institutions, and rabbis. By exhibiting the opposite attitude: openness, admission, telling the truth, coming forward, rabbis and institutions in the Jewish community will foster respect for rabbis and Jewish institutions.

Women in one small community reported to me that two rabbis there sexually abused them. They asked me to come out there to "do a healing" for the community. I proposed that they go together in a group to call on one of the rabbis they were accusing who is a venerated elder of a Jewish movement, and ask him to initiate admitting his transgressions, apologizing directly to those affected, and offering to make amends. I offered to be present with them to call on this rabbi. They thought about it at length, but concluded that they "did not have the courage" to undertake this step. This is a small

Jewish community and the women fear ostracization and further abuse by the community if they come forward. I believe that were this rabbi to come forward himself, because of his background and position, he could serve as a role model for other rabbis to come forward, to apologize, to make amends, and for rabbis of all denominations to take the steps needed to weed out those rabbi-offenders who can not/will not change; to clean up, if you will, the roster of rabbis in America. Were he to do this, he would set a precedent, and change the tendency to wait until rabbis are "investigated," or are dead, as in the case of Rabbi Shlomo Carlebach, for their sexual transgressions to be exposed.

When I was asked to contribute to the article <u>Lilith</u> magazine was preparing about Carlebach's alleged sexual misconduct, I refused, asking why they would not publish articles about living rabbis who have transgressed, who still transgress, rather than writing about a deceased rabbi, about cases which cannot be investigated formally because the accused rabbi is deceased. They chose not to write about living rabbis who are accused of sexual misconduct. I had the same experience with <u>Moment</u> magazine. I was told they would not publish anything "against" rabbis. An assistant editor there told me that a rabbi who was a regular contributor to the magazine had effectively "killed" the article I submitted to them which she, and possibly others there, wanted to see them publish. Further, in trying to find a publisher for this book, several large publishing houses told my agent that they "would not 'take on' the rabbinic establishment." Only if we 'take them on' can we bring about the necessary changes in Jewish organizations and denominations. Only then, can we create a climate of honesty, openness, integrity, caring, and love with regard to rabbis' sexual ethics and behavior.

The policies of denominations, of rabbinic organizations regarding rabbis' sexual conduct which do exist must be readily available to congregants, students, writers, the press, anyone who wants to learn about them. To keep them secret, to make them difficult to obtain when one requests a copy is to show fear, and/or that they have something to hide, and to foster disrespect, lack of trust, and even fear of these organizations. To be forthcoming and sharing and willing to talk about their policies and this problem in an open, honest, respectful, sharing manner would engender a climate of trust, would engender respect. Women must be able to trust the rabbinic establishment, to trust their synagogues, that they are safe, respected, honored by them. Being forthcoming about rabbis' sexual misconduct and about any policies these organizations have or are working on and/or developing open, effective policies and processes for dealing with rabbis' sexual misconduct and effective enforcement of these policies and processes would go a long way toward creating a climate of respect of rabbinic organizations and Jewish institutions. Stopping the covering up for rabbi perpetrators, and, certainly, not obtaining positions for them in other locations is also paramount.

There are other problems regarding implementation and enforcement of rabbinic policies governing sexual conduct of rabbis. One of the most difficult for rabbinic organizations and synagogues to grapple with is that rabbis, while they are usually placed in a position by their rabbinic organization, once they sign a contract, are employees of the synagogue. The rabbinic organization then loses any power over them with regard to removal from the position. For example, in one recent case, in Buffalo, New York, the rabbi of a synagogue (in this case, Conservative) was accused by several women of sexual transgressions. This rabbi was visited by the executive rabbi of the rabbinic organization in New York City who "handles" such complaints. He, reportedly, tried to persuade him to resign. He refused. He had a contract with the synagogue which I was told amounted to a half a million dollars over four years. The President of this synagogue called me in despair. He was concerned that the congregation, which was going to vote whether to keep him or fire him for cause was going to vote to keep him. I was told that the division in the congregation was approximately 60/40. Subsequently, I was told that approximately 60 percent voted to keep him and 40 percent voted to fire him. Those who wanted to keep him clearly did not understand the seriousness of the allegations. Many did not even believe them to be true. They talked about how he had "buried their parents, Bar and Bat Mitzvahed their children, married their daughters and sons, visited them when they were sick." They had placed him on a pedestal, which is common with congregants and rabbis and complicates the difficulties in bringing these men to justice. I was interviewed and filmed by WGRZ-TV Buffalo[93] about this case and

[93]Carol Kaplan and Rich Kellman, "A House Divided" WGRZ-TV Buffalo Aired in two parts, August, 1999.

about rabbis' sexual transgressions generally. The news anchor was interested in bringing out the truth about these cases and, while the hour's interview of me was cut to minutes, he did an excellent job with his partner of producing a two part program about this issue. I was given the video of the program and the permission to show it to educate concerned parties. The last I learned, this rabbi was still at the synagogue in his same capacity. This case points out one of the areas of rabbinic policy that needs to be changed. Congregations need to be educated about the problem of rabbinic sexual transgressions, about it seriousness, about its scope, and about how to handle it if it does occur. Changes need to be made in the process of hiring and firing rabbis. Since the rabbinic organizations are involved in placement, perhaps they, along with congregations, can adopt better screening policies, and they can adopt binding rules about monitoring these rabbis once they are placed, and dealing with them effectively if they transgress.

The synagogue in Cherry Hill, New Jersey, where the rabbi was arrested and jailed, and is awaiting re-trial for allegedly hiring a hit man to murder his wife, went through a similar experience. Many of the congregants did not want this rabbi to resign or to fire him when they found out about his sexual transgressions, or even when he was a suspect in the murder of his wife. He finally did resign, but there are many there who still do not believe that he was guilty of any sexual wrongdoing or that he could be guilty of capital murder. If he is tried and convicted, these people probably will still believe him innocent. It is the nature of the sacred aura which rabbis establish about themselves. Many people see them as sacred, as beyond culpability, no matter what. For a discussion of this point, see the article in USA Today, by Gerald L. Zelizer, "Why Do Parishioners Stick by Clergy Who Commit Crimes?" which is listed in the Bibliography.

In the case of the rabbi in California where the Temple president was murdered by a hit man the morning after she left her husband to move in with the rabbi who, reportedly, had been having sex with her for some time, the rabbi was never investigated as a possible suspect in her murder.[94] Some people I interviewed about this case, think this rabbi is guilty, even though the woman's husband was tried and

---

[94]This was discussed in a personal interview I had with Michele Samit, who wrote a book about this case. This book is listed in the Bibliography.

convicted on what I was told was "circumstantial evidence." Some of the people I interviewed told me that the "rabbi was tired" of her and saw no way of ending the relationship because she was so prominent in the synagogue. They believed he could have arranged for her murder. They told me further that this rabbi was known to have many sexual relationships with congregants and others.

Michele Samit, who wrote the book about this murder called, "No Sanctuary: The True Story of a Rabbi's Deadly Affair," was a former congregant. She was a columnist for a Los Angeles magazine for which she had also written an article about the murder. Samit told me that she was vilified, ostracized, and that she and her family ended up having to move to another town and another synagogue. Her son became a Bar Mitzvah at Masada in Israel shortly before I met with her in 1997. We had lunch on the terrace of the Loew's Santa Monica Hotel. In this beautiful setting, she told me the unbelievable, horrifying story that a congregant of this rabbi was at Masada, and that she ran up at her shouting, "If my 15 year old daughter has to learn about sex, I would rather it was with Rabbi Jacobs than anyone else!" Shocking! Yet, this is the attitude of many. They are accomplices or would-be accomplices in the rabbi's sexual transgressions, even with their own children! At last report, this rabbi is still in his pulpit.

Changing the policies of the rabbinic organizations and congregations to deal directly with these problems would greatly benefit victims/survivors, potential additional victims/survivors, families, synagogues, communities, denominations, and all Judaism. A 'by-product' benefit might be that more people, with an open, honest, atmosphere, might be willing to affiliate with synagogues who lament the low percentage of affiliated American Jews. Why would anyone want to affiliate with a synagogue which might harbor a sexual transgressor, at which there is an atmosphere of secrecy, even of upholding false 'gods.' The placing of rabbis on pedestals, acting toward them as if they are more than human, even 'sacred' is not to the benefit of congregations, of individuals, certainly not of women and teen aged girls. Rabbis are just men. Men with the same foibles as other men. But men with sacred power, which we are sadly learning, too many of them use in hurtful, abusive ways, and then, cover it up.

Abuse of power is the salient factor in rabbinic sexual abuse of women. Women and children have often been victims because of the

189

power differential between men and women in society as a whole. So-called 'domestic violence' or 'battered women' are terms that I want to see changed to indicate that men who abuse power are what we are talking about. Let's call this syndrome by an appropriate name, such as, "Battering Men," or "Violence Against Women."

There are organizations working to bring about this change in public consciousness and terminology who are helping victims/survivors, and working to change how batterers are dealt with. For example, my work is listed on the University of Minnesota Center Against Violence Against Women web site: MINCAVA.com. Too often, only women's organizations, feminist organizations and publications use these terms. The general media does not. This is because of the imbalance of power in society at large. Even though more than 50% of the population is women, more men hold positions of power in all institutions of society than women: in the media, in law, in government, in finance, in education, in religion, etc. Few women are found at the top echelons of these institutions. The practices of these institutions are still sexist. They do not protect women the way we must. We still have not passed the Equal Rights Amendment.

There are some who think that there is a "backlash" against women as a result of the feminist movement. Some women, though they believe in equal rights for women, equal opportunity for women, insist they are not feminists. Some cultural observers also decry what they see as a backward movement of women: toward playing into views of females as sexual objects - women are back to wearing shoes with stiletto heels, platform shoes, baring their navels, even breasts on the street, wearing clothes that make them appear all but nude - preventing them from moving with health and strength, and encouraging them to behave like sex objects.

Most men are usually bigger and stronger physically than most women. All of these factors when combined lead to men being awarded authority, their authority legitimized, and women usually being put in the position of being subordinate to them.[95] When men's authority is augmented by positions such as that of rabbi, to which is

---

[95]The scope of this book does not permit a more detailed discussion of this complex subject. The reader should see sources in the Bibliography for more extensive analyses.

added the element of the sacred, this position enjoys the ultimate in status, legitimacy, and power. (Remember, the rabbis involved in the two murder cases were either never investigated, or investigated only years after the murder. Even law enforcement officials, the police, district attorneys will not suspect a male with such legitimized authority. They see religious authority as above suspicion. I interviewed a law enforcement official involved in one of these cases, and he corroborated this attitude.)

Most women, who hold much less status and power than most men, and certainly much, much less than legitimized clergymen of status and authority, rabbis with pulpits who may be professors or deans at seminaries, or heads of Jewish organizations, are at a distinct disadvantage in the presence of these men. This power differential is not acknowledged, talked about, dealt with. It is the 'elephant in the living room' of rabbis' sexual abuse, just as rabbis' sexual abuse of women is the 'elephant in the living room' of Jewish denominations, organizations, congregations.

Rabbis are elevated, dominant. I am speaking of male rabbis. In those denominations where there is a female rabbi, she is an associate or assistant rabbi or rabbi of a small congregation, with few exceptions, and these associate and assistant female rabbis are not accorded the same power. I have cases in my files where these subordinate women rabbis have been abused by their senior rabbis. In our paternalistic, patriarchal, sexist society, this description applies to the system in Jewish organization, in Jewish 'community,' where even women rabbis are subordinate to male rabbis.[96]

While a woman rabbi, Janet Marder, is in line for the first time to be the next president of the Reform movement's Central Conference of American Rabbis, if this does happen, it will be the exception that proves the rule. There have been women Reform rabbis since 1972. If this does transpire, this means that it will have taken more than 30 years after women were allowed to become rabbis for a woman to hold a top position in this movement.

Women in both the Reform and Conservative movements are only beginning to achieve enough seniority to even be considered for top

---

[96]See Judith Plaskow's book, Standing Again At Sinai: Judaism From A Feminist Perspective Harper/SanFrancisco. 1991, for an excellent discussion of patriarchy in Judaism.

leadership positions, according to officials in these movements. But, 'seniority' can be a 'red herring.' 'Seniority' is often circumvented when those in positions of power desire to do so. This issue is more significant in the Conservative movement, which has only been ordaining women since 1986, and has a rigid placement system that requires a certain level of 'seniority' before a rabbi can assume the 'top' position in a large congregation. There are few women 'eligible' for these positions. Rabbi Francine Roston, of Congregation Beth Tikvah in New Milford, New Jersey, was quoted as saying that, "Many of us have had successes and troubles based on our gender."[97] Rabbi Rosten was also quoted in this article as saying that, "On occasion, women rabbis have also had to cope with sexual harassment from either professional colleagues or lay leaders."

Yes, some male senior rabbis sexually exploit subordinate female rabbis. One female rabbi who consulted me about the sexual exploitation, abuse, she suffered from the senior rabbi of their congregation was fearful of even seeing me, even talking to me. She feared if this were "found out," they "would find a way to fire her."

Policies of rabbinic organizations which persist in giving male rabbis 'top' positions must change. Women rabbis must be given some top posts at large, prestigious synagogues. Male rabbis must be given some posts as the assistants and associates to female senior rabbis. This change will go a long way toward equalizing power between men and women in the rabbinate and between male rabbis and women congregants. Changing the status of males as superior in the rabbinate will help to change the power differential between male rabbis and women so that they are not afforded the same opportunity for abuse.[98] Male rabbis recognizing and acknowledging the power

---

[97]See article by Ami Eden, Forward. October 19, 2001, "Barrier Falls As Women Set to Lead Key Bodies," for discussion of these points. The article title is misleading. It implies much more progress than is the case for women attaining 'top' positions.

[98]It will be interesting to see if senior female rabbis will be guilty of sexual abuse (of other women, of subordinates), when and if they finally become senior rabbis in any significant numbers, and if so, whether the estimated percentages or actual numbers will be anywhere near as high with female senior rabbis as they are with male rabbis. I doubt this because of complex factors, including female socialization and sexism in the wider society.

differential between male rabbis and female rabbis as well as between men and women, generally, is an important step.

When I conducted the lecture/seminar at the Union of American Hebrew Congregations for 65 rabbis and executives whom the program director told me comprised the "top" Reform rabbis and executives from North America, the head of the movement (at that time this was the late Rabbi Alex Schindler) was having an argument at a discussion roundtable with a female rabbi, the late Rabbi Julie Spitzer (of course, his subordinate). (I organized the group into tables for discussion, one table of all females, one table an equal number of males and females and the rest of the tables of all males, because of the much larger numbers of males in the group. There was only one table of all women and one table of men and women because of the substantially fewer women rabbis than men rabbis.) I circulated among the tables for questions and clarification. As I approached their table, Rabbi Julie Spitzer was saying, "No secretary would be able to tell you not to hug her, or hug her "that way." Didn't you pay close attention to the discussion of power by Dr. Schwab in her lecture?" "What do you mean?" the powerful, tall, strong, handsome, charismatic rabbi countered. "We are a 'family.' Any secretary in our organization knows she can speak to me frankly." I interjected, "Rabbi Spitzer is right." Not only could no secretary tell you not to do anything even when, or especially when it concerns how or that you touch or hug her, but also, no female rabbi could tell you this either. Both are subordinate to you. You hold the power over their positions, and power over them symbolically, physically. Your stature, and not just by your physical presence, but by your position, is dominant. *You dominate them.* I can tell you this because I am not your employee. I am a consultant. I do not risk my employment by telling you this. I do not stand in awe of you. I am here by your request to help you, to help your organization with a problem that you, your organization, denomination, your congregations have."

However, we are a long way off from the reality of a significant number of female senior rabbis in those denominations allowing women to be rabbis. In a personal conversation with Gary Schoener, Ph.D., who is an expert in treating clergy offenders, he told me he has only two cases of female rabbi perpetrators.

Not only the then head of this movement, but also the other male rabbis at this training <u>would not see</u> that sexual harassment is a problem in their movement.[99] As I approached all the male tables, the men were complaining that we were "making a mountain out of a molehill," that we were "making a Federal case out of small potatoes," and other such comments. They just would not see the problem in front of their noses. As I approached the all-womens' table, the women were complaining that the men "just would not see the problem (of rabbis' sexual misconduct) and asking "how long would this have to go on," "how bad will it have to get before they acknowledge it."We can ask that same question today, years after this lecture/seminar.

Rabbis have been, are still loath to see this power differential, let alone talk about it and deal with its repercussions. As long as rabbinic ethics committees operate in secrecy, it will be difficult to evaluate if any progress is being made toward rectifying this problem. Rabbi Shira Stern, who served as chair of the Reform movement's Women's Rabbinic Network was quoted as saying, that secrecy "by its very nature makes it difficult to evaluate" how fairly rabbinic sexual misconduct cases are handled.[100]

The Orthodox Union and Rabbinical Council of America

On the morning of January 25, 2002, I placed a telephone call to the Orthodox Union in New York City to see if anything had changed as a result of the Rabbi Lanner case (described in PART II of this book). I informed the receptionist who answered that this was a long distance call, and that I wanted information about whether the Orthodox Union or Rabbinical Council of America has a policy regarding rabbis' sexual misconduct. The call was given to a man who sounded angry from the minute he answered, and became angrier by the minute. I repeated to him that I was calling to ask if the Orthodox Union or the Rabbinical Council of America has a policy

---

[99]"Sexual Harassment. Some see it. Some won't." Eliza G.C. Collins and Timothy Blodgett. <u>Harvard Business Review</u>. March-April 1981

[100]Julie Weiner. "High-profile cases refocus attention on sexual misconduct." <u>JTA Daily News Bulletin</u>. December 15, 2000. Vol. 78. No. 235

regarding sexual misconduct by their rabbis. He said, "I do not know what that means." Then, he snapped, "Any behavior that is contrary to *halacha* is not permitted." I asked what that meant. He said, abruptly, angrier, "Any behavior contrary to Jewish law or civil law is not permitted." I asked how a woman who has a complaint would proceed. He said, angrily, curtly, "Send me a letter; I presume your name will be on it," assuming I have a complaint. I asked, "What is your name?" He barked, "Rabbi Steven Dworken." I asked him to spell it. He did, curtly. I asked the address and he said, still snapping, "305 Seventh Avenue." I asked the zip, another snap, "10001."

I asked, "What will be done with the letter? Is there any written down procedure? Who will be involved? How will you handle it?" He said, tersely, still sounding very angry, "We'll see! This is an internal matter! *Shabbat shalom!*" He sounded almost as if he were spitting the latter words out. The words, which mean have a peaceful *Shabbat*, and his tone were in entire contradiction. I could only shudder at what a woman who might call about having been abused by a rabbi would do at such a hostile response, and I could imagine her fear, and her tears. I can also only imagine the treatment any complaint by a woman about sexual abuse by one of their rabbis would receive.

What can I say about Rabbi Dworken's response? To say that the climate of the Orthodox Union/Rabbinical Council of America would probably not be supportive, let alone, kind or helpful to a woman calling about being abused by a rabbi seems hugely understated. The response I received was not amicable. It is hard for me to think of this organization as a spiritual Jewish organization when it is obviously not welcoming or friendly to a woman calling about information regarding whether they have a policy concerning their rabbis' sexual misconduct, as evidenced by the behavior of Rabbi Dworken.

Equally as important as the rabbinical organizations and denominations adopting effective policies regarding sexual misconduct by rabbis is enforcement of these policies - even retroactively when the accused rabbi is still in a position as rabbi. Because the experts seem to be in agreement that when a rabbi has seriously transgressed, has abused teenagers and women, especially more than once, and especially at the "high end" of the scale (see PART IV for definitions of transgressions), that he is unlikely to stop, to be able to make *teshuvah*, this step is paramount.

Richard M. Joel, who is a lawyer, is international director of Hillel, and is Orthodox, was a panelist on the "Moral Offenses by Religious Leaders" discussed above. Joel acknowledged that sometimes these perpetrators can repent, can even make *teshuvah.* But, he stated that "*teshuvah* is not the issue. The community does not owe them a second chance.... The tendency in the world of Jewish communal professionals is to focus on the professional rather that the community the professional serves. Therefore, when a professional is accused of acting inappropriately, his or her colleagues tend to circle the wagons to protect their colleague. Such behavior is wrong." He went on to say that, ".... the Talmudic scholar Adin Steinsaltz once reassured (me) on this subject, saying, 'Truth is the shield of the Torah'." Joel talked about those who knew about Rabbi Lanner and looked the other way. ".... We must not allow such behavior.... It's all up to us.... "[101] Are rabbis who know about colleagues who are abusers listening?[102] Are rabbi/policy-makers regarding rabbis' sexual misconduct listening? Are rabbinic ethics committees listening?

THE INTERFAITH SEXUAL TRAUMA INSTITUTE

The Interfaith Sexual Trauma Institute (Rabbi Marcia Zimmerman sits on their board) posts a policy called "Recommendations for the Prevention of Clergy Sexual Misconduct" on its web site.[103]

The ISTI policy states that, "At minimum, congregational healing and prevention of abuse of leadership trust within faith communities and systems require:

1. a regularly updated policy document that explicitly sets professional standards and behavioral expectations and that includes a

---

[101]Palmer. Op. Cit.

[102]The rabbis and leaders at Temple Emanu-El in Manhattan are not listening as evidenced by their response to the accusations that their Cantor, Howard Nevison, is guilty of sexual molestation, and faces extradition and criminal charges. See Debra Nussbaum Cohen. "Temple Emanu-El Hunkers Down: Congregation's Leaders Not Answering Questions About Cantor's Case." New York: The Jewish Week. March 8, 2002.

[103]www.csbsju.edu/isti adopted June 6, 2000 at the ISTI National Conference. Roman Paur is Executive Director of ISTI. Rabbi Marcia Zimmerman is on the Board, as is Rev. Nils Friberg.

structure of supervision and accountability at all levels of ministry service in pastoral and educational settings, as well as a code of professional ethics in ministry leadership. This readily available, widely disseminated public document (emphasis mine), is to include procedures for:

    (a) reporting allegations of misconduct
    (b) follow-up processes of impartial investigation and conclusion
    (c) support for the victim and the victim's family and loved ones
    (d) appropriate assistance by a person selected by the victim and
    (e) help for the congregation.

2. education programs for ordained and lay leaders of faith communities that promote a sound and affirming understanding of sexuality and the ability to assist congregants and peers who seek help in the development of sexual and spiritual health.

3. an ongoing education program mandated for ordained and lay leaders about boundaries that focuses on relational integrity, professional propriety, and responsible self-care in ministry leadership. Such a program is to include legal consequences of misconduct, issues of gender, power and leadership, and transference/counter transference.

4. a continuing education program for congregations to identify and promote health, reduce risk, and increase safety in faith communities. This program is to include procedures for pastoral supervision and reporting and accountability. It should also alert the faithful to inappropriate pastoral leadership behaviors.

5. a written procedure for reporting and acting on allegations of ministry misconduct and communicating appropriate information within the congregation. This written procedure establishes a system-wide norm of appropriate disclosure following disciplinary action. (emphasis mine) It is essential that this document safeguards internal accountability about reporting practices and underscores the safety needs of the victim including an impartial advocate who physically accompanies the victim as appropriate.

6. support for victims and their families and loved ones that models affirmation, even when they are no longer members of the congregation. Victims require immediate and direct communication with appropriate judicatory levels of leadership within faith tradition. Victims need continuing advocacy to assist the victim-disclosure process at every juncture, explicit pastoral affirmation, financial

support, and other resources of their congregations. They require ongoing assistance in reclaiming their sense of personal safety and well-being. The goal is a restoration of trust, congregational inclusion, and education about victimization to reduce risk.

7. a policy that an offender be removed, consistent with due process and written procedures, when there has been an authoritative determination that an offense occurred. Structural safeguards are to be implemented <u>to protect all current and future congregants from further abuse by the offender in any faith community. The policy should seek means of identifying offenders even when they leave the faith community.</u> (emphasis mine).

8. ongoing, careful analysis of each case of sexual misconduct in ministry leadership in order to increase learning and reduce systemic and personal causes of misconduct and to strengthen confidence in the tradition of the religion and its ministry. <u>Denominations and the therapeutic community are encouraged to make available files on clergy sexual misconduct for research and monitoring.</u>" (emphasis mine).[104]

Judith Plaskow writes that post biblical rabbinic legislation was written to regulate, to control women's sexuality, and implied "danger to men of women's sexual attractiveness." The rationale of the legislation "was always to protect men from the temptations posed by women." [105] Now, we need 'rabbinic legislation' to control rabbis' sexual misconduct in order to protect teenagers and women.

The rabbinic and congregational organizations listed in this chapter would do well to consult the ISTI policy and the policies of other faith based communities listed in the Resources section of this book for assistance in changing the policies that do exist and developing effective policies where there are none regarding rabbis' sexual misconduct. The policies they develop should govern cantors, educational personnel, and employees of these organizations as well

---

[104]I thank Dr. Nils C. Friberg, a member of the board of ISTI for sending me this policy, as well as for a list of web sites of other faith based communities that deal with and/or describe their policies and procedures regarding clergy sexual misconduct. I also thank Dr. Friberg for extensive discussion about much of this book.

[105]Plaskow. <u>Op. Cit</u>. pp. 176-177.

as rabbis. The trouble I and others have had obtaining those policies that do exist should not continue. They must be readily available to all those concerned. Rabbis must stop being afraid to confront their shortcomings, tell the truth, and adopt openness. Rabbinic governing authorities must stop "laundering" rabbis. With or without their consent and participation, their sexual abuse problem will/has come out of the closet.[106] 'If not now, when?'

---

[106]Julie Wiener. "No Longer Taboo: For Years, the Orthodox Community Has Hidden It. Now, a Confluence of Factors is Making Their Sexual Abuse Problem Come Out of the Closet." Jewish Telegraph Agency 1/22/02. Reported on the web: www.jewsweek.com/society/080/htm

Charlotte Schwab

PART FOUR

Definitions Of Abuse

The Kinds Of Personalities Which Can Lead To Rabbis Becoming Sexual Predators

Some Suggestions For Prevention

Charlotte Schwab

Some experts estimate that between 18 and 39% of Jewish clergy are involved in sexual harassment, sexual exploitation, and/or sexual misconduct - the same percentage as non Jewish clergy.[107] All denominations are involved. The large number of cases I, alone, have in my files bears out this estimate.

Simpkinson states that, "The problem of sexual misconduct by spiritual authorities.... is vast.... News articles detailing accusations and lawsuits against Catholic priests...unleashed a flood of revelations concerning sexual misconduct not only by Catholic priests but by spiritual authorities in virtually every religion.... reports of years-old as well as current sexual improprieties have surfaced...."

While there is no hard data precisely measuring the numbers of spiritual authorities who are guilty of sexual abuse, largely because spiritual authorities cover-up for these abusers, despite the lack of official figures, as Simpkinson goes on to state, ".... most professionals agree that the problem is far-reaching not only in Catholic, Protestant, and Jewish congregations, but in Buddhist sanghas and Hindu ashrams as well. Abuse by spiritual leaders is nondenominational, and the dynamics between clergy and parishioners, between gurus and devotees, between spiritual teachers and students, bear striking resemblance to one another."

The problem is much more widespread than most people, even professionals realize. In study after study, the percentages are shocking. Here are just a few examples:

1.) 23% of evangelical ministers admitted they had been "sexually inappropriate" with someone other than a spouse in a study published in 1988. Since all of those surveyed did not respond, and since not all probably "admitted" their misconduct, the actual figure is most likely much higher.

107Telephone conversation with the Rev. Marie M. Fortune, Director of the Center for the Prevention of Sexual and Domestic Violence, Seattle, Washington. See also such articles as, "Sex Abuse by Clerics - a Crisis of Many Faiths: While Sexual Misconduct has Rocked Many Religions, Leaders of Some Have Acted Far More Quickly Than Others." Teresa Watanabe. Los Angeles Times. March 25, 2002; "Soul Betrayal: Sexual Abuse by Spiritual Leaders Violates Trust, Devastates Lives, and Tears Communities Apart. No Denomination or Tradition is Immune." Anne A. Simpkinson. Common Boundary. Nov/Dec 1996.

2.) 70% of the respondents in a study published in a 1993 pastoral journal said they knew of pastors who had had sexual contact with a congregant.

3.) A.W. Richard Sipe, a former Roman Catholic priest and current Baltimore, Maryland psychotherapist, estimates that nearly 50% of Catholic priests break their vow of celibacy; that sexual abuse of minors is only art of the problem; that four times as many priests abuse adult women.

4.) In a 1990 church sponsored study (United Methodist), 41.8% of the clergywomen surveyed reported unwanted sexual behavior by a colleague or pastor; 17% of laywomen reported that their own pastors had sexually harassed them.

5.) There are no studies that have been done by Jewish denominations. All we have are newspaper reports, and now, this book.

Rabbis' sexual misconduct affects not only the victim and the rabbi/offender and their families, but also, the synagogue, the immediate community, the denomination, and some say, all Jewish people, and the entire non-Jewish community. Over the last several years, there has been a good deal of media publicity about rabbis' sexual misconduct cases. There have been a number of (known) legal suits related to rabbis' sexual misconduct. There have been rabbis who have resigned their pulpits, or most recently, a rabbi who resigned as the head of a major seminary. These communities are trying to heal. I have been asked by communities to help them to heal. The late Rabbi Julie R. Spitzer wrote that, "The congregation suffers in ways that are generally overlooked, and rarely acknowledged and treated."[108]

Keep in mind that, utilizing the estimate of 18 to 39% of rabbis' being guilty of some kind of sexual misconduct, the majority of rabbis - between 61 and 82% are estimated not to be offenders. Still, these percentages mean that a large number of rabbis probably are offenders. Often multiple victims are involved. In one case, 40 women, reportedly, came forward to accuse one rabbi of abusing them all. Some of these victims were students, some congregants, some were even non-Jewish students in a theology class taught by this rabbi. This rabbi was finally forced to resign. Yet, he was given a

---

[108]Rabbi Julie R. Spitzer, "Response." <u>CCAR Journal</u>. Spring 1993.

position in another city where he is said to "have access to college age women."

Most often, these rabbis remain in their pulpits and thereby can continue their abuse, as there are few effective procedures for dealing with them. Or, they are given pulpits or positions in other communities where they are not known. Rabbi Debra Orenstein, a Conservative rabbi was quoted in an article as saying that, "There's a desire to reshuffle people, to keep it quiet and move them to a new community where they succumb to the same temptations."[109] This policy puts more teen aged girls and women at risk of abuse by these rabbi/predators. Learning about rabbis who might be most likely to become perpetrators is of great concern to rabbinic schools, congregations, denominations, and the entire Jewish community.

First, it is important to look at definitions of sexual abuse.

DEFINITIONS OF SEXUAL ABUSE

For our purposes, we will look at four terms:

      1. Sexual Harassment
      2. Sexual Exploitation
      3. Sexual Abuse
      4. Sexual Misconduct.

While definitions are important, it is important to point out that a Harvard Business Review study found that the biggest issue is not defining sexual harassment, but *"recognizing it when it occurs."*[110] Here are some descriptions which will, hopefully, help you to recognize it. Keep in mind that there is some overlap among all four terms.

109"Rabbinic Sexual Misconduct is Rarely Taken Seriously." Debra Nussbaum Cohen. Jewish Bulletin of Northern California. October 26, 1996, p 2.

110"Sexual Harassment.... Some See it.... Some Won't." Eliza G.C. Collins and Timothy Blodgett. Harvard Business Review. March-April, 1981.

Keep in mind that the order of the definitions as stated above does not imply any gradation of seriousness. Gary Schoener, a clinical psychologist in Minneapolis who specializes in treating clergy who have engaged in sexual boundary violations as well as their victims, talks about how sometimes what seems like a "mild" verbal sexual harassment by a rabbi can be as difficult for the survivor of this harassment to overcome as physical sexual abuse.[111]

1. Sexual harassment

Sexual harassment is a legal term defined by the U.S. Equal Employment Opportunity Commission. It includes sexual comments or jokes; creation of a gender hostile atmosphere; voyeuristic inquiries; pressuring for dates; unwanted touch, hugs, kissing; unwelcome sexual advances; requests for sexual favors; and other verbal or physical conduct of a sexual nature with an employee.

Other varieties of sexual harassment include surreptitious touch during a hug, hugging too closely, sexist statements - those that convey insulting, belittling, or degrading attitudes toward women; statements like, "Are you a women's libber? You need to learn to be intimate. Let me show you" - the so-called Henry Ward Beecher syndrome.[112]

For our purposes the above described perpetrations are considered sexual harassment when congregants, students, and counselees of rabbis are the victims. Some experts on this subject include members of other congregations than that of the rabbi/perpetrator, or even of other denominations, or even the Jewish community. I include members of the non-Jewish community whom a rabbi/perpetrator harasses under the cloak of his rabbinic title.

2. Sexual exploitation

Sexual exploitation involves more forceful sexual advances: requests for dates, to "see you alone;" forceful touching, feeling, grabbing; "romantic" and/or sexual involvement; sexual intercourse; oral rape; genital rape. This may take place in or outside the rabbi's

---

111Gary Schoener, Ph.D. Personal Conversation.

112Marie M. Fortune Is Nothing Sacred? Harper/SanFrancisco, 1989.

office or the synagogue. The victim may be an adult who is single or married, and who is an employee, a congregant, a member of another congregation, a member of another denomination, a student, or a non-Jewish woman. The victim may be a minor. In the case of a minor, criminal charges may be brought.

The rabbi may be married or single. If the rabbi is married, sexual involvement with any other woman, whether she is single or married, or whether she is an employee, congregant, member of another congregation, denomination, or a non-Jewish woman is not only sexual exploitation, but is sexual misconduct. Some consider sexual involvement with anyone by rabbis who are not married to be sexual "transgressions."

3. Sexual abuse

Some experts define the first two terms as sexual abuse. In other words, whenever one person dominates or exploits another by means of sexual suggestion or action, *that* is sexual abuse. Unwelcome sexual behaviors are intended to degrade, humiliate, control, hurt, and otherwise take advantage of another. Coercion, secrecy, and betrayal often play a part in sexual abuse. Sexual harassment, exploitation, and abuse are never consensual, but involve a power differential between two people. The person perceived by himself or the other as having more power or authority is the offender or perpetrator. The person perceived as having less power or authority is the victim. This can involve persons of any age and any gender pairing, although as previously said, most cases involve a male rabbi and female victim.

Some think this may change as more women become rabbis. However, in this author's opinion, this will probably not change much because in our sexist society, and in the sexist Jewish community, as explained and discussed by Judith Plaskow,[113] most men have power over most women. For example, some women rabbis have reported being harassed by male congregants as well as by male senior rabbis.

---

[113]Judith Plaskow. Standing Again At Sinai: Judaism From A Feminist Perspective. San Francisco. Harper/Collins. 1991. p. 89. Plaskow's book provides a good insight into patriarchy in Judaism, which is still widespread, and good insight into patriarchy as a foundational cause of rabbinic sexual misconduct.

Women student rabbis, that is, rabbinic students with student pulpits, have been reported being harassed by the congregational rabbi as well as by male congregants. Women rabbinic students have reported being harassed by male student rabbis as well as by faculty rabbis. Judith Plaskow states that, "Until we understand and change the ways in which Judaism as a system supports the subordination of Jewish women as a subsystem within the Jewish people, genuine equality of women and men is impossible."

Consensual sexual activity can only take place in a context of mutuality, of choice, full knowledge, equal power, and without coercion, fear, or "awe" - "sacred trust." When one person is a professional and the other is not, especially when one is a rabbi, a *kli kodesh*, a vessel of holiness, who is looked up to as keeping a sacred trust, there can never be consensual sex. In fact, rabbis have rules regarding limits of sexual involvement - the 10 commandments, *halachot* about fidelity and monogamy, and in some <u>recent</u> precedents, policies published by rabbinic and synagogue organizations.

4. Sexual misconduct

Sexual misconduct by rabbis has been defined as some or all of the above behaviors. Certainly, every rabbi has an ethical and moral obligation not to have sex or sexual contact outside of marriage; or, if single, at least not with a congregant, student, staff member, or subordinate colleague.

It is **always** the rabbi's responsibility to keep sexual boundaries **no matter what**. Even if the woman "comes on" to him, goes so far as to raise her skirt to show thong underwear, or any other obvious effort at involving him in sexual contact, it is **his responsibility** to protect her and himself, and maintain sexual boundaries. If she needs therapeutic help, it is his ethical responsibility to do what he can to see that she gets it.

Any of the above with children or teenagers is a criminal offense. At the date of this writing, in at least twenty states, any of the above with anyone who could be considered a counselee is illegal. All of this information raises many questions about sexuality for all rabbis, whether single, married, divorced, widowed, and whether heterosexual or gay. One gay female rabbi I spoke with who attended a seminar I gave told me she was not willing to say that it is sexual misconduct when a married rabbi has sex with women who are not his congregants because this raises issues about the "private" sex life of not only married rabbis, but also, gay rabbis. Two heterosexual male rabbis told me they were not willing to say it is sexual misconduct when a married male rabbi has sex with other women who are not his congregants, or even when he frequents prostitutes!

How and why does sexual abuse by rabbis happen? First, let's look at the following question. Why are adult women, single, married, divorced, or widowed, susceptible to rabbis' sexual misconduct, to abuse? There are complex factors. We will look at a few here. Often, these clergy are charismatic; they give impassioned sermons about God, ethics, morality, family, social justice; they take a seemingly sincere personal interest in women, especially the ones they "target;" they provide a warmth often lacking in these women's lives. They hug them, have the ability to make an emotional connection, albeit spurious; they have knowledge of the women's personal lives and access to their homes; they visit them when they are in hospital.

Rabbis are trusted by women with the most important and intimate aspects of their lives, such as, *Brit*, baby namings, *Bar and Bat Mitzvah*, marriages, visiting the sick, burials, consoling the bereaved, and often counsel women about many aspects of their lives. They know which women are vulnerable, and these women become the "targets" of these rabbi/perpetrators. Women I have talked with or counseled have said that they "looked up to (this) rabbi" (the rabbi who abused them) "worshipped him," even "thought he was like God," and would "do anything he wanted." Only later did they feel shame and fear, and shaken in their religious beliefs, in some cases leaving their synagogue, denomination, community, or even Judaism, and when possible, moving thousands of miles away.

Women are also susceptible to rabbis' sexual misconduct because women in our society are often in vulnerable situations. I will give some examples here. Many women have financial difficulties.[114] For the most part, women, even today, earn less than their male counterparts in almost all lines of work. Divorce leaves women living

---

[114]Charlotte Schwab, Ph.D. External Causes of Depression in Women. A paper presented to the American Psychological Association. New Orleans. 1989.

on a fraction of what their ex-husbands live on, often with children to support. They are in unhappy marriages with no way out that they can see, especially if they have children at home. They are single parents with all the difficulties inherent in that situation. They are single and lonely, divorced and lonely - more women than men never marry, or remain single after divorce. They are widowed and lonely - most men die earlier than women, now an average of about seven years.

Many women whom these rabbis target for abuse have been prior victims of domestic or sexual violence, either in their family of origin, or by their husbands, or both. A shocking number and percentage of Jewish women are physically and/or sexually abused. Marcia Cohn Spiegel writes that, "Abused Women do not Make Choices."[115] Certainly, they can not make choices while they are being abused, while they are in an abusive marriage or relationship. It is shocking to learn about the high numbers of all women who are victims of abuse in our society. Jewish women are no exception.[116]

Children and teen aged girls are susceptible to rabbis' sexual abuse because they are often alone with the rabbi who may be training them in a private office for their Bat Mitzvah.[117] It is especially heinous when rabbis prey upon children and teenagers. Judy Klitsner, who teaches Bible at the Pardes Institute of Jewish Studies and lives in Jerusalem, was a victim of (Rabbi) Baruch Lanner in 1974, when she was 16. She wrote an article for New York Jewish Week[118] about

---

[115]Marcia Cohn Spiegel. "Abused Women Do Not Make Choices." Genesis. Spring 1989. pp. 34, 35.

[116]UJA-Federation of NY. Family Violence Resource Directory. 1997. Available from UJA Federation social service agencies.

[117]Cantors, too, often train teen aged girls for Bat Mitzvah. While I have cases in my files of (male) cantors sexually abusing girls and women, this book is about (male) rabbis. The estimates that apply for cantors and sexual abuse may be lower than the estimates for rabbis and sexual abuse. Cantors, for the most part, do not have, and are not perceived as having as much power as rabbis. The fact remains, however, that they are in "sacred positions."

[118]"Preventing Future Lanner Cases: One Suggestion to Safeguard Our Children - A Monitoring Committee of Religious Leaders and Professionals in Psychological Services." Judy Klitsner. New York Jewish Week. March 15, 2002.

this case. She writes that, "If in my day I knew about a dozen of his victims, how many were there in the intervening 28 years? If in my day hundreds of people knew on some level that Baruch Lanner was a dangerous man, how many must have known over all these years?"

Rabbis who prey upon women and girls know which ones are vulnerable and how to set up situations where they can perpetrate this abuse.

It is important for all rabbis to be aware of their own sexuality. All human beings have sexual feelings. Rabbis are no exception. Even though rabbis are often looked up to, often, idolized and revered, thought of as sacred, they are only men. Rabbis must learn to acknowledge sexual feelings to themselves, be aware, and know what to do and what not to do. Feelings are one thing: to act on them, quite another. Because of the intimacy in relationships offered to rabbis by many of their women congregants or counselees, a rabbi must ask himself such questions as, "Would I do or say the same thing if my wife, significant other, rabbinic mentor, or the national press were watching?" Would I be able to answer, "*Hineni*" (here I am) when God asks, "*Aiecha?*" (Where are you?) "Would I have to be answered to if the same behavior were directed to my mother, sister, daughter, wife?"

Other questions to ask oneself as a rabbi are: "How do I approach physical contact?" "Do I ask, "May I give you a hug?" And, if the answer is "Yes," "What kind of hug do I give?"[119] "How close do I sit to someone? Where do I meet with her? Do I leave the door open if we meet in my office?" Some rabbis have installed a window between their office and the secretary's office. These are serious questions and have no easy answers. A congregant may want privacy to speak with her rabbi. What is the best way to handle each situation?

A rabbi must be aware that the intimacy afforded him is often a very intense experience that affects both the *yetzer har-tov* and the *yetzer ha-ra*, the good and the evil inclination, and, if not contained, can blur boundaries for the rabbi and others.[120]

Judith Plaskow discusses how rabbinic legislation regarding sexuality was all geared to controlling women, to controlling

---

[119]Kathleen Keating. The Hug Therapy Book. ComCare Publication. Minnesota. 1983.

[120]Thanks to Rabbi Judd Levingston for discussion of this concept.

women's sexuality, and to protecting men from temptations posed by women.[121] Now, we need rabbinic policies to protect women from male rabbinic sexual predators. Equally important is education for prospective rabbis and ordained rabbis regarding sexuality. Rabbis could begin by studying both Plaskow's definition of sexuality and her "theology of sexuality."[122]

Rabbis must learn with regard to sexuality "to insist that the norms of mutuality, respect for difference, and joint empowerment.... apply."[123] Plaskow sees sexuality as the expression by humans where we can be closest to God. She refers to the "Song of Songs" as the model because "it unifies sensuality, spirituality, and profound mutuality, and may offer us the finest Jewish vision of what our sexual relationships can be...." Plaskow believes that ".... mutuality is most fully possible in the context of an ongoing, <u>committed</u> relationship in which sexual expression is one dimension of a shared life." (Emphasis mine.) This is also my belief, which I share with my own clients.

Nils C. Friberg and Mark R. Laaser have written a guidebook for church and theological seminary leaders to help them orient candidates for ministry to the issue of sexuality and ministry and for the prevention of sexual misconduct by clergy.[124] They discuss the characteristics of clergy sexual misconduct, the personal etiology of clergy sexual misconduct, assessing candidates for the ministry, environmental factors, victims and vulnerability. They pose solutions, including a healthy sexuality model, cognitive education, field education.

Rabbinic organizations and congregations would benefit from looking at this important pioneering work to help them formulate effective policies for prevention of rabbinic sexual misconduct. There are also excellent sources for dealing with clergy sexual misconduct

---

[121]Plaskow. <u>Op.Cit</u>. Chapter 5.

[122]<u>Ibid.</u>, especially pp. 205-210.

[123]<u>Ibid</u>. p. 206.

[124]Nils C. Friberg and Mark R. Laaser. <u>Before the Fall</u>. Collegeville, Minnesota. The Liturgical Press. 1998.

published by ISTI, the Interfaith Sexual Trauma Institute, available on the World Wide Web.[125]

Rabbis do their best work when they and others feel safe due to clear and maintained boundaries. Rabbi Arthur Gross-Schaefer states that, "There is no such thing as a 'consenting adult' in issues of rabbinic sexual misconduct." He lists behaviors that blur boundaries when rabbis are working with staff members, congregants, counselees, students.[126] These behaviors include: sitting close; hand or body touching; meeting too long, too frequently; meeting in inappropriate places; going on to other discussion besides the planned subject of the meeting; giving special treatment, such as time, gifts, excessive phone calls; using alcohol or drugs; sharing intimate information, especially "secrets."

Factors that blur boundaries for individual rabbis include: having marital problems; being in a crisis; being lonely; being attracted because of the woman's intelligence, kindness, humor, beauty, wealth, position, energy, or other factor; the woman's implied or expressed sexual desire. Even if the congregant, staff member, counsellee, or student initiates the sexualization of the relationship, it is **always** the rabbi's responsibility to maintain the boundaries of the professional relationship - **no matter what**.

All of the women I have counseled told me that the rabbi initiated the sexual contact. I believe them. If a rabbi feels attracted to a woman with whom it is inappropriate for him to act on these feelings, he must handle this attraction himself, get help from a colleague or a mentor, or get counseling if necessary. He must do whatever it takes to prevent any misconduct on his part. It is the rabbi's duty to protect the vulnerable from harm. To paraphrase Reb Nachman of Bratslav, it is your duty, "to seek (their) benefit for the welfare of the house of God." Further, as it says in *Pirke Avot*,[127] *chesed (*kindness*)* is utmost.

---

[125]The e-mail for ISTI: isti@csbsju.edu. The web site address is: www.csbsju.edu/isti

[126] Rabbi Arthur Gross-Schaefer, personal conversation. Also see his published and unpublished writings, some of which are listed in the Bibliography of this book.

[127]*Pirke Avot* (Sayings of the Fathers). Translated by the Very Rev. Dr. Joseph H. Hertz, Chief Rabbi of the British Empire. New York. Behrman House, Inc. 1945.

Leila Gal Berner, a Reconstructionist rabbi and expert on Jewish ethics has stated that rabbis have to guard against "the hubris that comes with the moral authority that people give (rabbis)" and that some rabbis, "allow (themselves) to fall into a sense of self-importance" and then, "moral lapses can happen." They can even tell themselves that, "no one would believe I would do such a thing,"[128] and feel a kind of license to transgress. Conversely, it states in *Pirke Avot*, "It is essential for rabbis to cultivate humility."

THE KINDS OF PERSONALITIES WHICH CAN LEAD TO RABBIS BECOMING SEXUAL PREDATORS

Let's look at those rabbis most susceptible to acting on these feelings inappropriately. Schoener identifies six types of clergy who violate sexual boundaries.[129] He does not find these types mutually exclusive, nor does he necessarily sort offenders into them. His purpose in creating these categories is to describe a variety of reasons for offenses from the perspective of offender pathology. Situational factors, policies of the organization, whether there is effective screening and assessment of prospective rabbinical students, effective education regarding sexuality, effective training, supervision, effective screening of ordained rabbis who move to a new pulpit or position, and other factors, may all play a role in whether clergy violate sexual boundaries. I will give a simplified presentation of Schoener's typology here. For his in-depth discussion, see his publications listed in the Bibliography.

The six types of clergy who violate sexual boundaries, as identified by Schoener are:

1. Psychotic and Severe Borderlines, Including Manics, Drug users, or those with Neurological Problems.
2. Sociopaths and Severe Narcissistic Character Disorders.
3. Impulse Control Disorders.

---

[128]As quoted by Debra Nussbaum Cohen, <u>Jewish Telegraph Agency</u>, New York. 12/19/97. Cohen wrote a series of articles about rabbis and sexual misconduct for the <u>JTA</u> in 1996/97.

[129]Gary Schoener, Ph.D. Personal conversation. Schoener's typology can be found in, "Assessment, Rehabilitation and Supervision of Clergy who Have Engaged in Sexual Boundary Violations," an unpublished paper, 1996.

4. Severely Neurotic and/or Socially Isolated.
5. Mildly Neurotic and Situational Breakdown in Otherwise Healthy Person
6. Uninformed/Naive

The more serious pathologies (the first four) seem to apply when the case involves a rabbi and many victims, a rabbi and prostitutes, or a rabbi and the so-called heavier sexual abuses, which would be categories two and three in the definitions; namely, sexual exploitation, and sexual abuse. In the case of my rabbi/husband, the chief psychiatrist who was treating him when he signed himself into the hospital to get out of arraignment, said that he was a "manic," a "sociopath," and a "sex addict." That description of my ex-husband/rabbi fits all of the first three types identified by Schoener; namely, "Psychotic and Severe Borderlines, including Manics, Drug Users, or those with Neurological Problems; Sociopaths and Severe Narcissistic Character Disorders; and Impulse Control Disorders."

According to Jerome D. Levin, Ph.D., "Although there are sex addicts who are sociopaths - those who are totally unprincipled and do not have any sort of moral restraints at all -.... this accounts for only 20 percent of the sex addict population.... most addicts do not lack consciences.... they express guilt for their addictive behavior, and feel badly about themselves, which in turn leads them to further engage in their behavior in an attempt to try to feel good about themselves. So, in effect addicts continue spinning in the vicious cycle of addiction not because they lack consciences but because they do have consciences telling them that their behavior is wrong. In this way, addicts actually become trapped in their addiction by their guilt. Unless they come to terms with the underlying forces beneath their addictions, they have no hope of reorganizing and reclaiming their lives. This means that my rabbi/husband, and other rabbi/sex addicts know that what they are doing is wrong, but they are caught in a trap (of their own making)."

Levin states that "outbursts of rage and temper tantrums," are not uncommon with sex addicts, as are "feelings of grandiosity and entitlement," and the "belief that they are above the rules that govern everyone else. Because of this belief, such individuals are prone to lying and justifying their actions with self-righteous rationalizations.... They are certain they can do anything and get away with it." That was the case with my rabbi/husband who threatened that he could kill me and get away with it. Some believe that Rabbi Fred Neulander who is accused of hiring a hitman to kill his wife also believed this. Levin states that, "Denial, repression, and distortion are standard defenses of addicts."

Levin makes clear that such individuals, although "surrounded by people," often feel "utterly lonely." This was true of my rabbi/husband, and is true of many rabbis who are "surrounded by people." Levin explains that, ".... unless one has the skills to connect with people on a personal level, one feels completely alone even though one is constantly in the midst of people."

Levin discusses how having a successful older brother can sometimes lead younger brothers to develop addictions. This was the case with my rabbi/husband, who had two successful older brothers, and who expressed his feelings of worthlessness. The dichotomy of feelings of worthlessness and grandiosity, arrogance, and entitlement all exist side by side in addicts.

Levin explains that, "All addicts suffer from a condition called emotional arrest. Emotional arrest is the inability to emotionally mature. It occurs naturally as addictions progress and take over all aspects of the addict's life."

Rabbis are simultaneously idolized, and yet, not loved for their "real" selves. In the case of sex addicts, who are "wounded, hurt, angry, and shamed," they look for love in the form of approval from crowds and supporters: for rabbis, from congregants. Rabbis receive adoration; they are put on sacred pedestals. Yet, it is conditional. They must please their congregants, or at least the Board of the synagogue, to remain in their positions. For sex addicted rabbis, the constant need for approval and fear of abandonment (by a congregation) is devastating and propels them to continue the impulsivity and compulsivity of their addiction.

Most people think that the sociopathic predator is the most prevalent clergy perpetrator. On the contrary. The work of John C. Gonsiorek, Ph.D., in the area of typing exploitative professionals, although based primarily on cases involving mental-health providers, is applicable to clergy. He found that "reasonable well-trained, responsible individuals" who are undergoing a stressful time are at greatest risk of violating boundaries. He also found that, almost without exception, these perpetrators have only one victim, are remorseful, and usually confess to authorities. Gonsiorek also found perpetrators who are severely neurotic and whose problems are more long-standing and significant. For these clergy perpetrators, work tends to be the sole source for filling their personal needs, and transgressions by individuals in this group tend to recur every few years or so. They are self-punitive rather than motivated to change. Prognosis is mixed; rehabilitation may or may not be feasible.

Other categories of predators identified by Gonsiorek include the impulsive, character-disordered perpetrator whose main problem with impulse control can lead not only to sexual boundary violations but to criminal activities as well: sex offenders who are clinically diagnosed as pedophiles or ephebophiles (those who abuse teenagers); the medically disabled who have impaired judgment and poor behavior control (those with bipolar disorder, manics fall into this category); and naive individuals who lack training and experience.

Rabbis who abuse a single victim and are then remorseful are usually those who fit Gonsiorek's last category, and Schoener's types five and six above: "Mildly Neurotic and Situational Breakdown in Otherwise Healthy Person," and "Uninformed/Naive." Situational factors and timing often play a major role in this type of abuse. In situations where a married rabbi has a long term illicit sexual relationship with one woman (often a congregant, and often a married congregant), lack of education about sexuality and relationships, and lack of support, especially support by colleagues, all play an important role.

SOME SUGGESTIONS FOR PREVENTION

What can you as a rabbi do to maintain boundaries? First, inform yourself. If you are reading this book, it is a good start. Create a network of peers and mentors whom you trust and respect. Tend to your own personal life outside the synagogue and form trusting relationships beyond those in your congregation, denomination. Maintain a personal spiritual life beyond what is work-related. Be aware and respond to your own warning signs of burnout: sleep disorder; fatigue; depression; an increase in your own, significant other's or family's problems; overwork to avoid going home; not taking vacation days, weeks; not including significant other, spouse or family in plans; keeping secrets; dreaming or fantasizing about colleagues, congregants, or other inappropriate people.[130]

Rachel Adler, a theologian and ethicist who has written extensively about the inclusion of women in Judaism wrote a comprehensive article for the CCAR Journal[131] about sexual exploitation in pastoral counseling. While the article specifically focused on clergy counselors, she discusses rabbinic sexual misconduct generally as well. Adler believes that "some personal therapy should be required for all rabbis." She states that "A congregant bill of rights would make rabbi-congregant relations safer by clearly articulating standards, rules, appropriate expectations, and a complaint process. Through their national organizations, congregants and rabbis could draft the document cooperatively. Congregants could receive a copy when they join the congregations and, again, at first appointments for counseling or other individual attention."

Adler objects to placing maximum stress upon the complainant for any grievance procedure regarding rabbis' sexual misconduct, and that the procedure should be specific in delineation of response to a complainant, acknowledging the risk that a victim of a rabbis' abuse takes in coming forward at all. Adler also objects to any "closed" system for dealing with rabbi/perpetrators. She cautions that if the process offers little satisfaction to a sexually exploited complainant, such as offering neither apology by the perpetrator, amends, reparations to help finance any therapy the complainant may require in order to recover, nor compensation for injury it is "small wonder that if civil litigation is feasible, complainants will prefer it."

Adler closes her article with a discussion of the meaning of rabbinical standards. "The standards for service articulated by rabbinical associations, and the treatment they accord those who complain of injustice or injury at the hands of their members, display how the obligations of social justice and *tikkun olam*, which are incumbent upon all Jews, are fulfilled in the organizational behavior of the teachers of Judaism." She goes on to say that, "Sexual boundaries make covenant possible.... The opportunity to reformulate

---

130Thanks to Rabbi Arthur Gross-Schaefer for the content of this section.

131Rachel Adler. "A Stumbling Block Before the Blind: Sexual Exploitation in Pastoral Counseling." <u>CCAR Journal</u>. Spring 1993.

standards of practice, policies and procedures is a chance for rabbis and congregations to make *tikkun* in their own domain."

Prevention of rabbis' sexual misconduct is a far better course for synagogues to take than to go through the pain of the aftermath when a rabbi goes astray. Rabbi Gary Mazo wrote a book, "the first insider account of the scandal that rocked South Jersey (and Congregation M'kor Shalom in Cherry Hill, New Jersey, where Rabbi Fred Neulander was accused of hiring a hitman to murder his wife, and is currently awaiting retrial - the first trial ended with a hung jury) with tales of adultery, betrayal and murder."[132] Mazor stated that he wrote the book, "to show how the embattled congregation, bound by ties of faith and community, overcame adversity."[133]

Rabbi Jeffrey K. Salkin in his "Response" to Adler's article[134] writes, "There's an elephant in the living room and no one wants to speak about it. That is how most of us have dealt with the issue of sexual exploitation by rabbis. We whisper about it, we gossip about it, but rarely, if at all, have we publicly analyzed this difficult and growing issue." He goes on to say that Adler's article is a "shofar blast of warning. She issues a challenge that we ignore at our own peril." Salkin continues ".... Rabbinical sexual impropriety is one of the more demoralizing factors of the contemporary rabbinate. Each new case elicits groans and head-shaking. Each new incident damages both a career and a congregation. It can take years for a congregation to recover from such profound betrayal. Each new incident damages the credibility of the rabbinate...."

Since there has been little progress with instituting effective policies and processes for dealing with rabbis' sexual misconduct since Adler's article and Salkin's response in any of the denominations, I propose that this book is a further "shofar blast of warning which is ignored at (rabbis') own peril."

---

[132] Rabbi Gary Mazo. And the Flames Did Not Consume Us: A Rabbi's Journey Through Communal Crisis. California. Rising Star Press. 2001

[133] Jim Walsh. "Book on Neulander Case Covers More than Crime." Courier Post Online. January 28, 2001.

[134] Rabbi Jeffrey K. Salkin. "Response." CCAR Journal. Winter 1993.

The late Rabbi Julie R. Spitzer in her response to Adler's article[135] wrote from the perspective of what she learned at the Center for the Prevention of Sexual and Domestic Violence.[136] To quote Rabbi Spitzer, "…. rabbis are not vulnerable when it comes to such role violations. Vulnerability implies that we lack power in relationship to our congregants. Rather, it is our congregants who are almost always vulnerable, particularly when they come to us at some time of disequilibrium in their lives. We are at risk for violating the boundaries of our role. We are most at risk when we are not meeting our personal, social, sexual, physical and psychological needs. Working in isolation, without even peer supervision or comment, suffering silently and stoically through our own personal life crises, working too long without any real time away on a regular basis, all increase our risk. They do not make us vulnerable. And *the responsibility for protecting the relationship always rests with the rabbi*." (emphasis hers).

Concluding, Rabbi Spitzer wrote, "In order for justice to be served, we must end the secrecy that surrounds such abuse, acknowledge the violation, and hear the victim…. At one retreat held by the Center (for the Prevention of Sexual and Domestic Violence) for victims of clergy sexual abuse, a question was informally posed to the group: What was the cost of the abuse to you, in measurable terms? The eleven victims wrote their answers down, and they were added up. The total? Fifty-five years, and $278,000. Denominations around the country are becoming increasingly embroiled in lawsuits relating to such misconduct. There are many moral arguments that are certainly compelling us to take a long hard look at this issue and how it is handled. But if those aren't enough, the dollars are a most compelling argument, too. If not now, when?"

Other aspects of maintaining sexual boundaries include what Rabbi Martin S. Lawson has called the "Duty of A Rabbi to Disclose Knowledge of Sexual Misconduct of a Colleague."[137] This "duty" has now become more than a moral, spiritual, or ethical duty because of

---

[135]Rabbi Julie R. Spitzer. Op.Cit.

[136]Center for the Prevention of Sexual and Domestic Violence. "Clergy Misconduct: Sexual Abuse in the Ministerial Relationship. Trainer's Manual." Seattle: CPSDV, 1992.

[137]Rabbi Martin S. Lawson. Unpublished manuscript.

the increase in legal suits and extensive newspaper coverage of rabbis' sexual transgressions and the danger this means to Judaism.

When I first began this research, there was practically nothing being written anywhere about rabbis' sexual misconduct. It was not even acknowledged. Now, it seems that we are bombarded by news reports in the general press as well as the Jewish press. I have a massive file of newspaper articles about rabbinic sexual transgressions. In addition, in the first several years of the existence of the World Wide Web, there was nothing to be found about it; gradually, the numbers of listings increased until now, there is a plethora of information. My work on this problem was listed on one web site in the beginning. Now, I keep learning of new web sites on which my work is listed. At last count, there are seven that I know about, including MINCAVA.com, AdvocateWeb, and Marcia Cohn Spiegel's Bibliography of Sources on Sexual and Domestic Violence in the Jewish Community.[138] There are now many other web sites concerned with clergy sexual abuse. There are even sites on the World Wide Web listing attorneys offering legal representation for sexual harassment and abuse.[139]

Rabbi Jack H. Bloom writes in an article that, "Rabbis and lay people must work together so that rabbis are able to know, believe, and say: "I may not be much, *and yet* I'm a symbol of the divine (emphasis mine) and I'm here with you - by the power vested in me."[140]

Bloom acknowledges that rabbis are a symbol of the divine, that they hold, are given power. Bloom writes that rabbis are expected to be symbolic exemplars and yet they do not, often, live up to this expectation. Therefore, Bloom argues for removing rabbis from their pedestals, for changing the deification of rabbis so that they are perceived as the human beings they are, by utilizing didactic and experiential instruction, workshops, lectures, whatever is needed so that rabbis can be perceived as *both* a symbolic exemplar *and* a human being. It seems to this author that this is an extremely difficult,

---

[138]See the Resources section in this book for these and other sources.

[139]One example: Herbert D. Friedman, Esq. Home page channel 11.com.users/therapy/

[140]Jack H. Bloom, Ph.D., Rabbi, "By The Power Vested in Me: Symbolic Exemplarhood and the Pulpit Rabbi." Conservative Judaism. Summer, 1998

if possible task, and that it will take many years to accomplish, if, in fact, denominations even set out to do this. In the meantime, rabbis <u>are</u> deified, <u>and</u> they have enormous power.

More practical, immediate safeguards must be put in place such as those discussed in this book, particularly in PART III, and in the references listed. In the words of Rabbi Julie R. Spitzer, "In order for justice to be served, <u>we must end the secrecy</u> (emphasis mine) that surrounds such abuse, acknowledge the violation and hear the victim."[141] "If not now, when?"

---

[141]Rabbi Julie R. Spitzer. <u>Op. Cit</u>.

PART FIVE

Seven Steps For Recovery

Charlotte Schwab

As discussed in PART III of this book, the shocking facts are that the organizations governing rabbis' sexual and other ethical behavior have either no policies to define or deal with rabbis' sexual misconduct or, at best, they have ineffective policies. Nor do these organizations often even censure or, when necessary, remove these rabbis from their posts. Only because, thankfully, newspapers around the country have been putting forth some information on cases of rabbis' sexual abuse, and on the prevalence of these cases, and because of threatened or actual lawsuits against synagogues have some clergy governing groups become willing to look at this serious problem.

When women have had the courage to come forward and report a rabbi's sexual abuse they, themselves, have been blamed, disbelieved, accused of being "troublemakers," "hysterics," "mentally disturbed," "seeking revenge," "making it up," and even ostracized or banned from their religious communities.

There is considerable risk to women coming forward to report a rabbi's sexual misconduct or abuse. Because of this, why would any woman risk reporting a rabbi's sexual misconduct or abuse if she is "making it up," when she knows how she will be treated. Why would she take this risk if she initiated the sexual "experience," and if the "experience" was truly mutual, egalitarian.[142]

I have never found in my work with women victims/survivors of rabbis' sexual abuse that even one of them could be suspected of being the initiator of sexual contact with the rabbi, or of "making it up," or "seeking revenge." I have found them all to be believable. In the case of teenagers, we do not question that sexual contact with a rabbi is never mutual or egalitarian, although teenagers, too, have been accused of "making it up," of being "troublemakers."

Why are adult women susceptible to rabbis' sexual misconduct and abuse? There are a number of factors. These rabbis are often charismatic. They preach impassioned sermons about God, ethics, morality, family, social justice. Women believe these rabbis adhere to, believe, practice what they preach. Women admire these rabbis. They look up to them; put them on a "sacred" pedestal, grant them a "sacred" trust. They literally look up to them when they preach from a

---

[142]We have discussed previously in this book the definition of a mutual, egalitarian sexual experience.

physically elevated *bimah* or pulpit. These rabbi/perpetrators often take a seemingly sincere personal interest in their "marks" or "targets" for sexual abuse. They may hug them, show them special warmth, interest in their lives, have an ability to make emotional connection with them, albeit spurious, and for their own evil intentions. Rabbis, of course, have knowledge of women's personal lives. They know which women recently buried a parent, a husband, or, tragically, even a child, because they officiate at the funerals. They know which women have medical problems, and they visit them in the hospital. They may know which women are in a "troubled" or abusive marriage, or which women are recently divorced or divorced for a long time and lonely; or who are widowed and lonely; or single and lonely. They often counsel such women. They know which women are single parents and are struggling, financially and otherwise. In other words, these rabbi perpetrators know which women are vulnerable and which women to target. Rabbis are trusted by women with the most important and intimate aspects of their lives, including *Bar* and *Bat Mitzvah*, marriages, baby namings, *brit milah*, visiting the sick, funerals, burials, consoling the bereaved. These rabbis have access to women's homes and can visit them there when they are alone.

Children and teenagers are susceptible to rabbis' sexual abuse because they are often alone with the rabbi, student-rabbi, or cantor who may be training them for *Bar* and *Bat Mitzvah*. Rabbis who prey upon girls, teenagers, and women know how to set up situations where they can perpetrate this abuse.

Women I have talked with and counseled said they "looked up to (this) rabbi," "worshipped him," even thought "he was like God," and "would do anything he wanted." Only later did they feel shame and fear, and shaken in their religious beliefs, in some cases even leaving their denomination, or even their religion, their communities, or states. Another reason why women are susceptible to rabbis' sexual abuse is that many women are raised to love a father figure at whatever cost, to be passive, dependent, and submissive to a father and father figure, especially to a "sacred" father figure, a "holy" father figure. Patriarchal society sets women up to be abused, especially by the ultimate father figure, in this case a rabbi.

Some women who contacted me years after the abuse, whatever the nature or severity of the abuse, whether it was verbal sexual harassment, emotional sexual harassment, or oral rape, told me how/that it had "ruined" their lives; that they "could not get over it." It is as if they suffer from a severe post traumatic stress syndrome.

What can women do? First, unless you are absolutely positive of your rabbi's trustworthiness do not leave your child or teenager unattended with him. I have outlined seven steps for aid in recovery from rabbis' sexual abuse and to help put a stop to rabbis sexually abusing teenagers and women, and to bring about positive change with regard to these rabbis.

Step I TELL THE TRUTH

It is paramount to tell the truth <u>to yourself</u> and <u>to others where appropriate</u> about what this rabbi did to you. <u>Name</u> what happened as <u>abuse</u>. Stop doubting yourself. Do not blame yourself. Understanding and believing that this was not your fault, that what this rabbi did was abuse is the first step.[143] Rabbis are entrusted to keep their sexual feelings outside of their contact with congregants. Rabbis are expected not to commit adultery, which they preach is wrong. Prohibition of adultery is an integral part of their religion.[144] Rabbis are responsible for whatever sexual misconduct they perpetrate, not the women they victimize.[145]

Do not suffer in silence. To do so erodes your beliefs, values, and thereby your self-esteem, and also enables this rabbi to continue his misconduct and to victimize others. Silence also erodes the religion

---

[143]All seven steps overlap. You may go back and forth among them, especially to this one. You may have to work on this step over and over before you come to know the truth: that you are not to blame; that this was/is rabbi-sexual-abuse.

[144]The view of adultery as "wrong" does seem to vary by individual rabbi within a particular denomination. One woman Reform rabbi told me that she could not censure adultery, especially because this "got into whether lesbians and gays could have sexual relationships outside of marriage since homosexual marriage is not recognized."

[145]Charlotte Schwab, Ph.D. "Maintaining Proper Sexual Boundaries in the Rabbinate: Rabbis' Sexual Misconduct." A lecture/seminar presented to the <u>Jewish Theological Seminary</u>. New York. January 19, 1998. See also Rabbi Arthur Gross-Schaefer's papers listed in the Bibliography.

you hold sacred. Believe in yourself. This may be especially hard to do because the rabbi may have told you such things as "God wants us to do this." "I am healing you by doing this." "You must keep this secret to protect yourself." "If you tell, I will deny it, and you will be the one to be blamed." "No one will believe you. I am the rabbi and they will believe me." Unfortunately, the latter is most often the case. Congregants want to believe in the rabbi. They may cling to their idealized view of him and their wish that he is the person they believe him to be, want him to be. They may be cruel to you. They are wrong.

It is frightening, difficult to come forward. You may feel devalued, suffer a loss of self esteem, a loss of your sense of dignity, feel lost, hurt and abandoned, that you will be cast out, adrift, isolated, alone. You need to know that there are some people who understand and who are sorry for the suffering this rabbi has caused you. A letter I received from a woman in January, 2002, said simply, "I am suffering a long time." In silence. Alone, unsupported. Afraid even to tell her husband, who is ill with a disability. Breaking this silence, finding others who support you, knowing that I and others grieve with you over this breach of sacred trust you have suffered which threatens your connection to God, to life, to feeling loved, is a start on the road to healing. You must feel, acknowledge, and express your sense of violation, of being devalued, of loss, of grief and sadness. To learn and to come to know that you will be able to heal yourself, it is important to reach out to others you can trust to validate you, listen to you, support you.

It is also imperative to acknowledge, be validated for, and to be supported to express your anger. You have every right to be angry. It is imperative to find constructive ways to express your sadness, grief, sense of loss, and anger. Seek out a counselor, preferably a woman who has experience helping women who have been abused, either sexually, by battering, or emotionally. Ask her to help you find, or to organize, a support group of women who have been sexually abused by clergy. Getting heard, validated, and supported by as many people as possible who have "been there," who understand, is a very important first step. If there is no support group in your area, start one.

There are people you can trust. There are some counselors and therapists who, by now, have some experience dealing with rabbis' or other clergy sexual abuse, counselors who will not overstep their boundaries, who will not take advantage of you. Be careful to choose a counselor or therapist who is right for you.[146] "All therapies are based on value systems. Existing therapies and therapists usually are reluctant to acknowledge this fact. Most therapies claim to be based on scientifically established truth.... They reflect and reinforce dominant societal values which are sexist, racist, ageist and elitist."[147] "12 Steppers" may be able to help you find a therapist. Women in groups for victims of "domestic violence" may be able to help. Women's centers, rape crisis centers, or women's shelters are good resources.

Check out the therapist's background. Make sure she has experience counseling sexual abuse victims. Ask what techniques she uses, her understanding of forgiveness. (The concept of "forgiveness" is discussed here later.) Ask how much she charges per session, whether she is comfortable and knowledgeable about your religion, your denomination, and that of the rabbi/ perpetrator. Make sure she knows and believes that sex between an adult woman and rabbi is not consensual when the woman is not his wife. A good counselor/therapist is very important in the healing process of a victim/survivor of a rabbi's sexual abuse.

Trust yourself and feelings of comfort when choosing a counselor/therapist to help you with your healing. You have the right to ask any questions you want and to believe that the therapist/counselor is open, honest, supportive, and knowledgeable about this kind of abuse. Be good to yourself. Put yourself first. This may not be, probably is not something you are used to doing. Many women have been conditioned to put others first, to take care of others' needs before their own. You need to practice being good to yourself, putting yourself first. Set goals to be good to yourself and schedule ways to do this into your day. Make such lists as, "What Makes Me Feel Good," "Things I Like to Do," and choose and schedule at least one of these each day. Things on your list can include such things as seeing a movie, taking a walk on the beach,

---

146 See Irene Javors and Charlotte Schwab, Ph.D. "Choosing a Therapist" in A Woman's Guide to Therapy by Susan Stanford Friedman, Linda Gams, Nancy Gottlieb, Cindy Nesselson. Englewood Cliffs, NJ. Prentice Hall.1979. pp.. 118-121, for help in choosing a therapist.
147Ibid.

getting a massage, volunteering to help someone else in some way, or participating in a larger effort at *Tikkun Olam*, such as joining in a walk to raise money for a health cause.

Learn healing processes and techniques you can perform alone or with support, such as: "Conscious, Connected Breathing" tm. [148] This technique can be done lying down on a couch or bed, or in a bathtub, hot tub, or pool, which can serve as a *mikveh* for healing and cleansing. You can create healing rituals either alone, with a friend or friends, or with your counselor/therapist which are connected to your Jewish Experience. Marcia Cohn Spiegel has written about how Jewish women can heal themselves from domestic violence.[149] Her suggestions can be utilized for healing from rabbis' sexual abuse as well. Some examples you may want to use: cleansing in a moving body of water so the sea can bring your pain to God; writing the name of the perpetrator on a piece of paper and stomping on it with your shoe; burning anything you have about him ("burning the *chometz* of his abuse"); establishing, delineating a sacred space[150] in your home in which to perform the rituals, songs, and prayers you create.

You may want to use or adapt prayers from Judaic sources for your healing process. If you find it hard to pray since this rabbi's abuse, you might start with the prayer adapted from Nachman of Bratzlav, "Help me to Pray."[151]

Psalm 139, especially as adapted by Rabbi Marcia Prager, "Blessing the Body,"[152] could be used to remind yourself that you are the creation of God, you are holy, you are precious, and that God performs both the miracle of (your) creation and (your) healing.

---

[148]A trademarked process developed by Dr. Charlotte Schwab, described in a lecture-workshop presented at the New Life Expo. New York, 1996. Available on audio tape from this author.

[149]Marcia Cohn Spiegel. "Spirituality for Survival: Jewish Women Healing Themselves." Journal of Feminist Studies in Religion. Fall. 1996. 12 (2) pp. 121-137.

[150]Marcia Cohn Spiegel, "Old Symbols, New Rituals." Neshama. Winter. 1994. (6) #4.

[151]Siddur Sim Shalom for Shabbat and Festivals. New York. The Rabbinical Assembly. May, 2000. p. 353.

[152]"Shabbat Morning Siddur," complied and edited by Rabbi Marcia Prager. P'nai Or Religious Fellowship. page 2.

If you were abused in your home by this rabbi, you may want to re-consecrate your home as a *mishkan*, a tabernacle, a sanctuary, a holy place, a sacred space where God dwells with you. To do this you may want to perform a cleansing ceremony for your home. Burning sage is considered by some to provide cleansing. You can create prayers for the cleansing of your home, for re-consecrating your home. The Jewish people created a *mishkan*, a portable sanctuary in the wilderness. You might want to create a separate holy space in your home to observe your prayers and rituals. You might use dried flowers, ribbons, a *tallit*, or special beautiful cloths and candles to specify the space.[153] The *Mah Tovu* prayer is a good choice to consecrate your sacred space, your *mishkan*. The translation by Burt Jacobson, quoted in Rabbi Marcia Prager's service, "We Create Sacred Space"[154] is a beautiful option.

If you find it hard to believe that God cares about you or this abuse would not have happened to you, Rabbi Harold Kushner's, "One thing I ask of God,"[155] might be reassuring to you.

It is very important, because it is a powerful healing technique, for you to create your own prayers and rituals for healing from this abuse. A good source for creating prayers and rituals to help you feel like you can recover yourself as a woman of wisdom so that this will never happen to you again, so that you can heal yourself, and even help to heal others is the video, "Timbrels and Torahs: Celebrating Women's Wisdom."[156] While this is a video "documenting *Simchat Hochmah* - a new rite of passage marking the journey from mid life to the elder years," the ceremonies celebrating the wisdom that Savina Teubal, Marcia Cohn Spiegel, and Miriam Chaya (a.k.a. Harriet Fields) have gained from their lives can be easily adapted for ceremonies to heal from sexual abuse by rabbis. Debbie Friedman sings many of her songs on the video, including *"Mi Shebearach,"* a song taken from the *misheberach*, a prayer of healing which is

---

153See Marcia Cohn Spiegel, Op. Cit for more ideas.

154Ibid. p. 1.

155Siddur Sim Shalom. Op. Cit. p. 357.

156Miriam Chaya and Judith Montell. "Timbrels and Torahs: Celebrating Women's Wisdom." Available to order on the World Wide Web, or by writing to: P.O. Box 8094 Berkeley CA 94707, or e-mail: Mirchaya@aol.com.

customarily said when the *Torah* is read. Debbie Friedman wrote this song for Marcia Cohn Spiegel's ceremony on this video. This song was sung for the first time for this ceremony.

Acts of burning, tearing, cleaning, casting out, breaking, stamping, cleansing, moving all exist in Jewish ritual.[157] These rituals can all be adapted to cleanse, heal the pain, sorrow, and anger of a rabbi's sexual abuse. Other good Judaic sources for creating healing prayers and ritual include Penina V. Adelman's, Miriam's Well: Rituals for Jewish Women Around the Year; Marcia Lee Falk's, The Book of Blessings: A Feminist Jewish Reconstruction of Prayer.

Jewish Healing Centers connected with the Jewish Family Service organization helps Jews who are seeking to heal from any kind of loss or abuse. I took a training course with the National Center for Jewish Healing in Manhattan, and broached the idea for them to create healing groups for women who have suffered rabbis' sexual abuse. They were receptive to the idea. Ask a Jewish Family Service agency or Jewish Healing Center in your area to institute a healing group.[158]

Another important element in your healing is to learn to laugh again. Norman Cousins wrote a book about using laughter to heal from a life threatening illness.[159] Schedule "laugh times" in your days until you are able to laugh again spontaneously. Utilize anything that might help you, such as audio tapes and videotapes of comedians; film comedies, with comedians such as Rita Rudner, Mel Brooks and Carl Reiner; television situation comedies like "All in the Family;" whatever might make you laugh. Spend time playing with a baby, which is a good way to begin to smile and laugh again. After the nightmare experience with my rabbi/husband, I thought, like the title of the song, "I'll Never Smile Again," made popular by Frank Sinatra, that I would never smile again, let alone, laugh. These techniques helped me to smile, laugh again.

At first, playing audio tapes of songs that bring out sadness, and help you to cry and express the grief you feel is helpful. This is important to do in the beginning when you need to express and let go

---

[157]Marcia Cohn Spiegel. Op. Cit. gives a good description of how to do this.

[158]See for example http://www.jfsatlantic.org/healing.html

[159]Norman Cousins. Anatomy of an Illness as Perceived by the Patient. New York. W.W. Norton. 1979.

of the grief. But, it is very important to move past this stage, not to get stuck in grief, or hurt. It is important to move on, by expressing these feelings, to anger, then to laughter and to healing, and dealing constructively with what the rabbi/perpetrator did to you.

Your body believes every word you say.[160] You do not want to store the grief and hurt in your body. You must move beyond grief to anger, and then to laughter, and onward to *Tikkun Olam*. Contact such resources as Dr. Joel Goodman's The Humor Project to help you with this goal. Dr. Goodman maintains a bookstore for laughing aids, and publishes "Laughing Matters" magazine.

Tap into additional sources that are good healing techniques for you, whether they be Biofeedback, music therapy, Reiki, massage, aerobics, swimming, or other physical exercise, whatever you find that works for you, and schedule them into your days.

Step II BIBLIOTHERAPY

Read everything you can about cases of rabbis' (and other clergy) sexual misconduct and abuse - newspaper, journal, and magazine articles, books, court cases. I list this as a separate step because reading and informing yourself about the facts of rabbis' sexual abuse is very important for not believing you are in some way responsible for the rabbi abusing you, that he probably abused others; and for learning and believing that he is the guilty party, not you. Use the bibliography in this book, and go to web sites listed in the Resources section of this book such as Advocate Web and ISTI (Interfaith Sexual Trauma Institute) for additional sources.

Step III TALK, SHARE

Talk and share with other women who have been victimized by rabbis' sexual misconduct - on the telephone, in person, or by e-mail. Go to workshops and seminars on this problem, even if they are given by other religions. This is another way to obtain information. Sharing with others is a powerful tool for healing. Just one victim/survivor/friend, or one victim/survivor support group can be

---

[160]Barbara Hoberman Levine. Your Body Believes Every Word You Say. Fairfield, CT. Wordswork Press. 2000.

extremely helpful in both general and specific ways. When you hear other women's stories, you don't feel so alone, singled out, as if you are the only one who is/was sexually abused by a rabbi or other clergyman, as if there is something wrong with you.[161] It is easier to hear about another woman's victimization and realize the injustice, the wrongdoing of the clergyman, than to confront your own situation. Hearing about other women's abuse helps you to face and understand what the clergyman, the rabbi did to you, and that you are not to blame, you are not the guilty party. Women's centers, rape crisis centers, 12 Step Programs, such as Alanon, or women's shelters are good resources.

Step IV BECOME SELF - DEPENDENT AND SECURE.

PROTECT YOURSELF AND YOUR CHILDREN.

All women need to protect themselves and their children. There may be further risk to you and your children because of what this rabbi did to you. Whether you are a rabbi's wife, who suffered through your rabbi/husband's transgressions with other women (and often, when this is the case, his verbal, emotional, and physical abuse of you as well), or a victim of a rabbi's sexual abuse, take whatever steps needed to protect yourself and your children physically, legally, financially, and otherwise. Work with your counselor/therapist and women's support group on the knowledge and skills you need to become self dependent and more secure so that you won't believe you are stuck and stay in a destructive way of life.

Often, other women will blame, disbelieve, and ostracize a woman who reports a rabbi's abuse, even when she is the rabbi's wife, supporting the rabbi, no matter what. Women blaming other women victims instead of rabbis is often the case when they are women who appear to be in solid, happy marriages, appear not to have strife in their lives, and may not be vulnerable to the rabbi's

---

161"Restorative Justice for All: Speaking Truth to Power: The Victim/Survivor of Clergy Sexual Misconduct." http://www.uua.org/cde/csm/survivor.html. Some non-Jewish religions are much further along in acknowledging and dealing with clergy sexual abuse of teenagers and women. This is a helpful web site.

sexual misconduct. Other vulnerable women, who may or may not have been abused by this rabbi may also blame the victim instead of the rabbi. Many victimized women are surprised to learn of other women who are being or were sexually abused by the same rabbi; yet they will defend him and deny his abuse of them. It is important to know this and seek the support of women who will believe you and join in supporting you and taking whatever action you decide to take, whether they themselves have been victims of this rabbi or not. You may possibly obtain the support of another rabbi. There are some rabbis around the country, male and female, who are supporting women with these efforts and, in some cases even risking their employment and status with their rabbinic organization's governing authorities by pressuring them to take action. Be sure you check out any rabbi who claims to want to help you by asking for references of other women s/he helped, or articles s/he may have written about this problem.

Work with your therapist to learn your options and how to make choices and set and achieve goals that are positive and life enhancing in the six major life areas: physical/health, family/home, spiritual/ethical, career/financial, social/cultural, mental/educational.[162]

Learn the skills for assertiveness and begin to practice them in all six major life areas. Women are conditioned to be passive. Passive, passive/aggressive or aggressive behaviors are not productive of positive results in relationships. Before being able to learn assertiveness, it is important to learn and know your basic needs, wants, and rights. Learn how to be "centered," to attain a level of energized relaxation. Utilize breathing techniques. Discard dysfunctional, automatic thoughts based on negative beliefs.[163] You are "reinventing your life." Learn that you deserve love,[164] not abuse.

---

[162]Charlotte Schwab, Ph.D. "Achieving Positive Self Identity and Self Defined Success." Ask Women Magazine. copyright C. Schwab. 1994 - 2002. (Reprints available from the author. This article outlines a ten step program for setting and achieving goals in all six major life areas.)

[163]Jeffrey E. Young, Ph.D. and Janet S. Klosko, Ph.D. Reinventing you life: How to Break Free From Negative Life Patterns. New York. Dutton. 1993.

[164]Sondra Ray. I Deserve Love. Berkeley, CA. Celestial Arts. 1976.

Learn the techniques of positive visualization and affirmation.[165] Learn communication and negotiation techniques, such as VECAM tm, and GENDER NEGOTIATIONS tm, two processes created and trademarked by this author.[166] A helpful chart, modified by Patricia Jakubowski-Spector from the original by Alberti & Emmons, for learning assertiveness is "A Comparison of Non-Assertive, Assertive, and Aggressive Behavior."[167]

Another chart which is helpful is "A Comparative Analysis of Some Costs and Benefits of Traditional And Feminist Values."[168] This chart, and the book in which it is found, will help you to change beliefs, thoughts, attitudes and behaviors which have kept you stuck in traditional values, such as: reliance on a male provider for sustenance and status, living through others and for others (men and children), putting a ban on assertion and power strivings, emphasizing physical beauty and erotic qualities. These beliefs, thoughts, attitudes, and behaviors to which women are traditionally conditioned are accompanied by the following costs: subordination to men, lack of autonomy, lack of training and skills, phobias, anxiety, depression (especially if there is no one left to care for), loss of personal identity, emotional dependency, feelings of powerlessness, dependency on fair play from others, no opportunity to develop confidence and determination, constricted personal development, crisis in aging, and frequent feelings of inferiority, which are stimulated by unrealistic cultural and stereotypic standards of beauty and sexuality.

By learning alternative values, such as psychological and economic autonomy, having the skills to provide for yourself even if choosing not to do so, self-determination, control over your life,

---

[165] Ibid. Also see Adelaide Bry. Visualization: Directing the Movies of Your Mind. New York. Harper and Row. 1978.

[166] Charlotte Schwab, Ph.D. Op. Cit. See also, Charlotte Schwab, Ph.D. "On the Job Negotiating Skills Lay Groundwork for Project Success." Contract magazine. September 1982. pp. 184, 185.

[167] Robert E. Alberti & Michael L. Emmons. Your Perfect Right: A Guide to Assertive Behavior. San Luis Obispo, California: Impact. 2nd edition, 1974.

[168] Edna I. Rawlings, Ph.D. and Dianne K. Carter, Ph.D. Psychotherapy for Women: Treatment Toward Equality. Springfield, Illinois. Charles C. Thomas. 1977. pp. 68, 69.

development of a full range of interpersonal skills and personal power, pride in having a healthy, strong body, and emphasis on natural appearance, you will gain benefits such as possessing your own social and professional status, development of your own competencies and skills, not being dependent on the benevolence of men, development of your own fully-functioning identity, freedom to give to others by choice rather than by expectation, attendance to your own needs before the needs of others, having more to give to others since more of your own needs are met, greater satisfaction from personal and professional relationships, a sense of control over your own life, self respect.[169]

Consider and confront the possible ongoing risks to you, when you decide to report this rabbi/perpetrator, and find help to deal with them, whether it be from your counselor/therapist, a lawyer, or other source. Obtain an advocate to be there for you, to listen to you, support you, and also to promote justice for you.[170] Healing for victims/survivors of rabbis' sexual abuse is a long and difficult process. An advocate can aid you in many of the steps of this process, including becoming self reliant and pursuing justice and amends, including possible financial amends for what you suffered. While there are no guarantees that you will obtain justice, let alone receive compensation financially for what was done to you, and it is a risky and difficult process, many professionals, including this author, believe that telling the truth and taking action is the way to healing and possible restitution, as well as preventing possible harm to others. Some organizations, such as the Coalition for Family Justice, have trained advocates.

An advocate may help you in the following ways: listening - in a believing and nonjudgmental manner; supporting; problem-solving; locating other supports; locating the denomination's policy regarding sexual abuse by rabbis (if there is one); suggesting options; helping you to write down the abusive experience; attending meetings or investigatory hearings with you; clarifying goals; speaking out on

---

[169]Ibid. This section was adapted from Table 3-11, pp. 68 and 69.

[170]"Restorative Justice for All: The Advocate." http://www.uua.org/cde/csm/advocate.html. The material regarding advocacy and in the source cited was all adapted from Heather Block, "Advocacy Training Manual," Mennonite Central Committee Canada, 1996.

your behalf when you may not be able to speak for yourself; modeling appropriate boundaries; documenting; locating information.[171]

It is important to realize that an advocate is not a counselor/therapist, nor is she a lawyer. She should not make decisions for you, but help you to make them. It is important to outline clear boundaries for the advocate. Any advocate whose help you enlist should have specific skills, training, preparation and personal qualities. These include knowledge of sexual abuse by a clergyman and its effects; good listening, problem solving and communication skills; and the ability to provide an objective perspective. She should be in touch with her own feelings and able to process them. She should be of the same gender and race as the victim.[172] Your advocate should probably not be a clergy person in the same denomination.

Step V WRITE LETTERS

With the support of your counselor/therapist and other women supporters, write to the rabbinical governing authorities of the denomination involved about the rabbi who sexually abused you, and to the news media, as well as to other rabbis around the country who are supportive of women who have been abused by rabbis and are trying to bring about change. This writer knows of a few such rabbis. Some of them are cited in the Footnotes and Bibliography of this volume. Because most clergy, most rabbis who are guilty of sexual misconduct often prey on more than one woman, you might be able to find others to write the letters with you. There is strength in numbers. Further, the rabbinical governing authorities may have other letters about this rabbi, and more letters may push them to stop ignoring the problem and do something about it. The more women who write letters to rabbinic governing authorities and to other rabbis, and to the media reporting rabbis' sexual misconduct, the more likely these governing authorities will have to take action to rid the rabbinate of these predators, screen more carefully those they ordain, and create methods to monitor rabbis. Gary Rosenblatt, editor of <u>New York Jewish Week</u> was instrumental, with his coverage about Rabbi Baruch

---

[171]<u>Ibid</u>. p. 2.
[172]<u>Ibid</u>. p. 3.

Lanner, in bringing about an investigation of that rabbi's then-alleged sexual misconduct. Rosenblatt's coverage generated a shakeup in the leadership of Lanner's specific rabbinic organization as well as within the denomination.

Write "snail mail" letters, e-mail letters, letters to editors. Write to Jewish newspapers in your area and around the country and to secular newspapers. Reporters and editors who have written articles cited in this book about rabbis' sexual misconduct are a good place to start. Taking action related to the rabbi sexual abuse you suffered will help you to heal and become strong. Taking action is empowering and helps women to establish a more secure position in their lives.

Step VI Lawsuits

Obtain information about legal suits against rabbis who have been accused of sexual misconduct. Most records of court proceedings are usually open to the public. Only when a legal suit was filed against a prominent rabbi who was thought to be in line for the position of director of the large denomination with which he was affiliated was he finally forced to resign his post as senior rabbi of a very large synagogue; and only after five years did he release a public apology for his sexual misconduct. The rabbinic governing authority of his denomination finally put him on suspension, although it was only for two years and he was given another post where he has contact with college-age women. As of this writing, he has yet to apologize to the women he victimized, a step which could be of healing benefit to all, and which could set an example for other rabbis to follow and for rabbinic governing authorities, who, themselves owe many women apologies.

Learning about legal suits against rabbis for their sexual misconduct is empowering for victims of rabbis. It is especially important if you are considering reporting the rabbi who abused you, and filing a lawsuit against him and the synagogue.

Step VII Confronting the rabbi/perpetrator;

Reporting the rabbi/perpetrator; Filing a complaint against him.

This three-part step is the most difficult emotionally for a woman to face who has been abused by a rabbi. It is a very powerful step in the healing process and possibly the most liberating for a victim/survivor of a rabbi's sexual abuse. If you choose to confront the rabbi directly, do not do it alone. Be sure at least one other person who supports you, such as your advocate, is present.

Ask yourself before the meeting what you hope to gain from the confrontation and what you might lose.[173] Know your purpose and motives for the meeting. Ask yourself if you are strong enough to tolerate the pressure of such a meeting. One of the women I counseled, who was orally raped by a rabbi in his study at the synagogue, did confront him many years later. She said that telling him he was an "abuser," a "perpetrator," finally freed her from the "horror" she had carried for more than ten years.

You may choose to ask this rabbi/perpetrator to acknowledge that he was abusive, and for an apology to you, to the congregation, and for any amends that are reasonable. Judaism believes in amends, in *Teshuvah*. It is an important step for him, for the congregation, for the denomination, for Judaism, for the general public, and for you, your family, and any other women he may have exploited. The amends you ask for may include financial help for therapy and whatever else you may need to heal what he did to you, to heal your life.

Be sure, if you choose to pursue this step, that you feel strong enough for any invective, any anger, or name calling that this rabbi/perpetrator may spew out at you. Be sure your support system is as strong as his, including the numbers of people present to support you. One of the women I counseled, set up a confrontational meeting with the rabbi/perpetrator, traveled many miles to see him, arrived at the designated meeting place with her advocates, and, although he had agreed to be there, the rabbi/perpetrator did not show up. She was

---

173Thanks to "Restorative Justice for All: Speaking Truth to Power - The Victim/Survivor of Clergy Sexual Misconduct," http://www.uua.org/cde/csm/survivor.html, which helped me to develop this step.

able to talk with his advocate (a rabbi) and felt a sense of release, of closure, of freedom, by telling his advocate directly, to his face, that this rabbi had been abusive, was a perpetrator of abuse.

If you decide not to confront the rabbi/perpetrator, know your reasons. Be sure this decision is not because you feel guilt or shame, or that you feel in any way responsible for the abuse he perpetrated, or that you want to "protect" him or the congregation. If you can get past these feelings, past avoidance and denial, past feeling in any way responsible or to blame, past any feelings that you have something of which to be ashamed, and you choose to confront him, you may break unhealthy patterns and gain from this courageous step in immeasurable ways.

This decision is very difficult. It is a personal decision which, either way, will have a deep impact on you and your life. Be sure you talk over this step with your advocate, counselor/therapist, women's support group and any other trusted support people, including your spouse, provided he is supportive.

The next important, difficult decision is whether to report this rabbi/perpetrator to the denomination's rabbinic governing body. They decide whether to consider your report, whether to investigate the report, and whether it will result in censure, suspension, or other action. They may not respond to your report. Given this author's knowledge of how these bodies respond, or, more accurately, don't respond, your report may not result in any action at all by the rabbinic governing body. They may not return your follow-up telephone calls, may not answer your follow-up letters, may, if they do take your calls, call you names, such as, "crazy," "hysterical," "vengeful," a "complainer." They may say things like, "you need a psychiatrist." They may not acknowledge you as a congregant if you are one. They may blame you for "whatever happened." They may say, "if anything did happen, you must have caused it." Yet, they may refer to the rabbi/ perpetrator as "the rabbi," not a "defendant in a formal complaint" you are making.

It is very important to be prepared that they may not keep your name confidential, but may keep his name confidential. This process can be very frightening. Just as when rape victims report a rape, they are often 'raped' again by the process, victims of rabbis' sexual abuse often become a victim of a possible backlash against them, a hostile response, a system hostile to the victims, and feel abused all over again. Your support system is essential to pursue this process. You may find a rabbi in the denomination's rabbinic organization who might be willing to help you. This will make the process somewhat easier. However, you must be sure of this person. A good idea is to have your advocate speak with him/her. He/she would be straddling a precarious fence to come to your aid if this is not the protocol of the organization.

Yet, with all these caveats, this is an important step to take. At the very least, you will have reported this rabbi/perpetrator. If you are the first to report him, the denomination's rabbinic organization will be put on notice. If you are not the first, they may well then take action. This step is important for your statement of belief in your denomination and it is important to the denomination. Taking this step makes the statement that you believe the denomination is capable of "justice, mercy, and walking humbly with God," a basic belief in Judaism, and that they adhere to the higher standard they profess. It says that your love of your religion, of Judaism is stronger than the rabbi/perpetrator's, stronger than any stonewalling you may receive from rabbinic authorities; and that you refuse to be silent, to disappear; that you have the courage to hold your religion, this denomination, to the higher standard they profess.

A word about "forgiveness." Many "new age" type so-called healing methodologies preach that unless we forgive we will not be able to heal; we will "store" the anger in our bodies, and even cause illness to ourselves. I do not agree with them. I have found in my more than twenty-five years as a psychotherapist, that when I validated a woman's need not to forgive, and supported her that this was a valid course to take in her healing process, as long as she had expressed her hurt, her grief, her sense of loss, and her anger, she was able to move on. She was thus able to heal herself more quickly than those who were trapped in the belief of the need to forgive their abuser. I believe a victim/survivor of a rabbi's sexual abuse must forgive <u>herself</u> for any thoughts of self blame. It is not necessary or even healthy for a woman to forgive a rabbi/perpetrator of sexual abuse. Only God can forgive him, and then, only after he has made *Teshuvah*.

Marcia Cohn Spiegel has collected sources from the *Mishnah*, and from Moses Maimonides which she provided to me for this book.[174] These sources validate the requirement of *Teshuvah* by a rabbi who has "transgressed," and validate the right, even the importance of not forgiving by the victim/survivor, at least until *Teshuvah* has been made by the perpetrator (to her satisfaction).

Women are socialized to and expected to be forgiving. Women often apologize when they know they are not at fault, causing a loss to themselves of self esteem, self respect, and self empowerment. Equally important, when women apologize to a perpetrator of wrongdoing, they reinforce his belief in his right to abuse. Women are conditioned to be peacemakers, to be "the bigger person," to maintain the relationship even at their own expense. Rabbi Susan Schnur writes that, "…. the place where we reach some resolution in our hearts in relation to the betrayal and are no longer ruminatively obsessed with the hurt or injustice, or actively under its omnivorous pall, may NOT be 'forgiveness' at all, but rather indifference or detachment or unforgiving reconciliation…." (with ourselves and the abuse). "…. It is not, that is, that forgiveness is the bottom line, but rather that emotional resolution is. That is the real achievement and hard-won freedom."[175]

Rabbi Schnur goes on to say that "…. not forgiving can be a precondition for moving on into a reconstructed emotional life, especially, say, if your betrayer has impaired your sense of self, or mistreated you when you were young, or were particularly vulnerable."[176] Rabbi Schnur continues, "…. Judaism's liturgy and theology need to support women in our work towards responsible not forgiving, when that's appropriate, so that we can come to believe that the world, indeed, won't explode as a result…. of our not being the placating one. For many of us, not forgiving is more difficult than

---

174Marcia Cohn Spiegel. Unpublished collection; includes "discussion from the *Talmud* on repentance and atonement: Yoma 85b-88a; excerpts from Maimonides' <u>Mishneh Torah</u> edited by Philip Birnbaum: <u>Book One: Knowledge: Repentance</u>; "Baba Kamma on not forgiving personal injury."

175Rabbi Susan Schnur. "Beyond Forgiveness: Women, Can We Emancipate Ourselves From a Model Meant for Men?" <u>Lilith</u>. Fall, 2001. p. 16.

176<u>Ibid</u>. p. 18

forgiving, and having Judaism support us in our authentic journey towards emotional resolution would be a deeply religious experience."[177]

What can you expect by following these seven steps? You will never be the innocent teenager or woman you were before the abuse. You probably won't ever forget the abuse. You will, hopefully, eventually get to a place where the abusive experience is not a repeated, frightening flashback, a constant "reoccurrence." You will, hopefully, come to a place where you will be able to integrate the experience into your life in a way in which it will not keep you frozen. You will, ultimately, experience emotional health, physical health, spiritual health, centeredness, a sense of freedom, empowerment, a new and powerful sense of self and identity, self esteem, self-acceptance, and self reliance.

Having suffered a rabbi's sexual abuse gives you a depth and compassion that you probably did not have before. This is usually true of all suffering and loss, provided one works through the experience and grows beyond it. By following this "Seven Step Healing Program," you will probably become a resource for others who have suffered or will suffer a rabbi's (or other clergyman's) abuse. You may become an advocate yourself, or a counselor/therapist. You may write a book.

---

[177]Ibid. p. 45.

GLOSSARY[178]

Avaryanim, h. Transgressors.

Bar/Bat Mitzvah, B'nai Mitzvah (pl.). Son, daughter, children of the commandment. These terms also mean a ceremony marking the attainment of age (13 for boys and 12 for girls) and becoming obligated to fulfill Jewish laws; when one can be counted in the *minyan.*

Basherte, y. Fated. Often refers to the person fated to become a life partner.

Bimah, h. Podium on which the rabbi stands to lead services at the synagogue.

Bris, y. *Brit,* h. Covenant of circumcision. Ritual male circumcision eight days after a Jewish baby boy's birth.

Cantor. A trained professional singer who sings the liturgy, prayers, at a service, and often has other duties, such as training children for *B'nai Mitzvah.*

Chai, h. Life.

Chavurah, h. Prayer or study group.

Cheder, h. (See also *Talmud Torah.*) Hebrew School. Jewish elementary and secondary school; children attend after the secular school day is over (excluding Friday) and also on Sunday.

Chesed, h. Kindness.

178Hebrew and Yiddish words often have multiple spellings in English transliteration. Hebrew words are indicated by the letter h and Yiddish words by the letter y.

Chometz, h. Something not eaten during Passover. "Unwanted, needing to be cleaned out."

Chupah, h. Wedding canopy.

Daven, y. Pray.

D'var Torah, h. Any talk or teaching one gives on *Torah*.

El Molay Rachamim, h. Exalted, compassionate God. A prayer said in memory of the dead.

Frum, y. Religious, observant, orthodox.

Goy, y, h. Non-Jew. Also means nation.

Halacha, h. *Halachot* (pl). Jewish law(s). Legal postbiblical Jewish literature, religion, and morals. "The proper way" for observant Jews.

Hashem, h. God.

Hasidim, h. A Jewish religious movement that arose in 18th Century Eastern Europe.

Havdalah, h. Separation. Ceremony at the conclusion of *SHABBAT* and festivals, indicating the separation between the holy and the mundane, observed with candles, spices, and wine.

Havurah, h. (Also, spelled *Chavurah*, or *Chaverah*.) Study, or prayer groups.

Kabballah, h. Jewish mysticism.

Kaddish, h. A memorial prayer of sanctification.

Mikveh, y. Body of running water used for ritual cleansing.

Minyan, h. A quorum of ten Jews required for significant parts of religious service, only recently beginning to include women in some denominations.

Mishebeirach, h. A prayer recited to petition God for recovery.

Mishnah. Rabbinical collection of *Halachot* (laws) compiled in the third century.

Mitzvah, Mitzvot, h. commandment(s), good deed(s).

Oneg, h, y. Pleasure. A reception after *SHABBAT* services.

Rabbi. The chief religious official of a synagogue who performs ritualistic, educational, and other functions as a spiritual leader of a congregation.

Rebbe, y. A rabbi of a Hasidic group who inherits the position.

Rebbitzin, y. Wife of a rabbi. There is no comparable word for husband of a rabbi.

SHABBAT, h. The Jewish Sabbath, observed Friday at sundown to Saturday, sundown.

Shalom bayit, h. Peace in the home.

Shanda, Shonde, y. shame.

Shiksa, y. Non-Jewish woman.

Shimoneh Esrai, h. Eighteen blessings. A prayer recited at SHABBAT services.

Sh'ma, h. The 3,000 year old prayer which is Judaism's core belief: the belief in monotheism. "Hear Oh, Israel, Our God is One."

Shtetl, y. A small village or town of Eastern Europe where Jews were ghettoized, forced to live.

Shul, y. Synagogue, house of prayer.

Succah, h. A temporary dwelling large enough for a family to eat and live in which pious Jews construct on the holiday of *Succoth*, symbolizing the booths or tents in which the Jewish people lived during their forty years of wandering in the desert. (Leviticus, 23:42-43.)

Succoth, h. A Jewish holiday celebrating the harvest in the land of Israel.

Tallit, h. Ritual fringed prayer shawl.

Talmud, h. Study or learning. Two thousand year old compendium of oral law, philosophy, and legends that comprise the central body of Jewish teachings and guidance for Jewish life.

Talmud Torah, h. Hebrew School. Students attend classes after the secular school day (excluding Friday) and on Sunday. Also, study of *Torah*.

Teshuvah, h. Repentance, return to Jewish thought and practice. Jewish tradition teaches that Teshuvah consists of several stages: the sinner must recognize his sin, feel sincere remorse, undo any damage he has done and pacify the victim(s) of his offense(s), and resolve never to commit the sin again. *Teshuvah* literally means 'return,' a return to God after going through the process of repentance.

Tikkun olam, h. Healing the world, the ethical bettering, perfecting of the world. Jewish people have a responsibility to help repair or heal the world. Judaism believes that the purpose of Jewish existence is nothing less than "to perfect the world under the rule of God." This belief is reiterated in a important prayer that is recited on *SHABBAT*.

Torah, h. Literally, the parchment scroll that contains the handwritten Five Books of Moses; in the broadest sense, all of Jewish law and teachings.

Tzedakah, h. Charity, justice, righteousness. Performing deeds of justice is considered the most important obligation of a Jew. The *Torah* instructs that Jews give ten percent of their earnings to the poor, to charity, every third year (Deuteronomy 26:12) and, additionally, a percentage of their income annually (Leviticus 19: 9-10.)

Yetzer har-tov, h. Literally, "the good inclination." God created us with a good and an evil inclination. God created us with choice to pursue our good inclination, life, *chai*, or our evil inclination.

Yahrtzeit, y. Anniversary of someone's death. One attends synagogue for evening, morning, and afternoon services to say the *Kaddish* prayer on a relative's *Yahrtzeit*. A twenty-four hour candle is lit at home. A burning light is connected with the idea of immortality, perhaps as suggested in Proverbs 20: 27, "The spirit of humans is the candle of God...."

Yetzer ha-ra, h. Literally, "the evil inclination."

Yiddish, y. Jewish. A language of Eastern European Jews, written in Hebrew letters.

Charlotte Schwab

RESOURCES

Web Sites

1. http://members.aol.com/vickipolin/page 26. html

2. www.advocateweb.org

3. www.MINCAVA.umn.edu

4. http://users.aol.com/Agunah/bib-jdv.htm

5. http://www.csbsju.edu/isti/Treatment%20Programs.html

Education and Treatment Programs for Women and Men

Adult Survivors of Child Abuse (ASCA). A Psychological Recovery Program for adult survivors of physical, sexual and emotional child abuse. The Morris Center.
Telephone: (415) 564-6002

ANACAPA by the Sea. 224 E. Clara St. Port Hueneme, CA 93041. Telephone: (805) 488-6424. Contact Person: Mark R. Laaser

Center for Abuse Recovery Empowerment. The Psychiatric Institute of Washington, D.C. 4228 Wisconsin Avenue, NW. Washington, D.C. 20016. Telephone: (800) 369-2273. Contact Person: Barry M. Cohen

Center for the Prevention of Sexual and Domestic Violence. (An Interreligious, Educational Resource.) 936 North 34th Street, Suite 200, Seattle, WA 98103. Telephone: (206) 634-1903. Contact Person: Rev. Dr. Marie M. Fortune

Family and Children's Services of Central Maryland. 204 West Lanvale Street. Baltimore, MD 21217. Contact Person: Stanley A. Levi.

Interfaith Sexual Trauma Institute (ISTI). An interreligious, educational resource. Saint John's Abbey and University. Collegeville, MN 56321. Telephone: (320) 363-3994. Contact Person: Rabbi Marcia Zimmerman.

Jewish Family Counseling and Psychotherapy Service (ask them for referrals to their agencies around the country, to their KOLOT agencies, and to their Jewish Healing Center agencies.) 211 W. 56 Street. NY NY 10019. Telephone: (212) 245-9130.

Jewish Women International. Assists victims of abuse with education, advocacy, and action.
http:www.jewishwomen.org/batterer.htm
jwinfor@jewishwomen.org e-mail:jwi@jwi.org Telephone: (202) 857-1300.

Pia's Place. Extended Care for Women. 615 Hillside Avenue. Prescott, AZ 86301. Contact Person: Pat Phillips.

Sexual Recovery Program At Birchwood Centers, Inc. 9531 West 78th Street, #350. Eden Prairie, MN 55344. Telephone: (612) 944-2842. Contact Persons: Patrick Carnes, Mark Laaser, Glenn Pickering.

Sexual Abuse Treatment Center. 4623 Falls Road. Baltimore, MD 21209. Telephone: (410) 366-1980. Contact Person: Laura Covington.

The Awareness Center. P.O. Box 578-328, Chicago, IL 60657. Telephone: (773) 297-8854. Contact Person: Victoria Polin, MA, ATR, LCPC - Director.

University of Minnesota Program in Human Sexuality. Department of Family Practice & Community Health. Medical School. 1300 South Second Street. Minneapolis, MN. Telephone: (612) 625-1500. Contact Person: S. Margretta Dwyer.

University of Tennessee at Martin. Counseling and Career Services. 213 University Center. Martin, TN 38238. Contact: Jennifer Y. Levy, Ph. D. Works with victims of abuse. Telephone: (901) 587-7720.

Walk-In Counseling Center. 2421 Chicago Ave. S., Minneapolis, MN 55404. Telephone: (612) 870-0565. Contact Person: Dr. Gary Richard Schoener.

Womanspace Services and Programs. 1800 Brunswick Avenue. Lawrenceville, NJ 08648. Telephone: (609) 394-2532.

Individuals and Therapists who offer help to victims of abuse:

1. Rabbi Sue Levy Elwell (215) 563-8183 ext. 20.

2. Rabbi Claire Green (Coalition Against Domestic Violence of Delaware Valley. 852 Red Wing Lane Huntingdon Valley, PA 19006-2114. Telephone: (215) 938-1833.

3. Dr. Charlotte Schwab (works with both women victims of clergy and wives and ex-wives of clergy.) E-mail: char01@earthlink.net

4. Dr. Gary Schoener (works with both clergy/perpetrators and victims.) E-mail: GRSchoener@aol.com

5. Jan Singer, MSW (works with victims of clergy.) Santa Barbara, CA Telephone: (805) 687-0814

6. Marcia Cohn Spiegel (helps victims of clergy and domestic violence). E-mail: MCSpiegel@aol.com

7. Debra Warwick-Sabino. California Center for Pastoral Counseling. 2200 L Street, Sacramento, CA 95816. Telephone: (916) 484-4137. E-mail: DWSabino@GV.net

Hot Lines

1. National Domestic Violence Hotline (800) 799-SAFE

2. National Organization for Victim Assistance (800) TRY-NOVA

3. National Victims Center (800) FYI-CALL

12 Step Programs

Al-Anon is a 12 step program for partners, family members and friends of addicts. You may find support there. Look in your town's telephone directory for Alcoholics Anonymous and ask them how to contact Al-Anon. They may also have a **CODA** (Co-dependents Anonymous) group which you can attend if you are having a hard time letting go of a rabbi/husband or ex-husband/rabbi who was/is a sexual abuser of other women.

Sex and Love Addicts Anonymous **(SAA)** is a 12 step program. You may find help there if your rabbi/husband or ex-husband/rabbi was/is a sexual abuser of other women.

Bibliography

Adelman, Penina V. *Miriam's Well: Rituals for Jewish Women Around the Year.* New York: Biblio Press. 1986.

Bisbing, Steven B., Jorgenson, Linda Mabus, & Sutherland, Pamela K. *Sexual Abuse by Professionals: A Legal Guide.* Charlottesville, Virginia: The Michie Company Law Publishers.

Bloom, Claire. *Leaving A Doll's House: A Memoir.* New York: Little, Brown and Company. 1996.

Brownmiller, Susan. *Against Our Will: Men, Women and Rape.* New York: Bantam Books. 1976.

Bry, Adelaide. *Visualization: Directing the Movies of Your Mind to Improve Your Health, Expand your Mind, and Achieve Your Life Goals.* New York: Barnes & Noble Books, A Division of Harper & Row. 1978.

Carnes, Patrick Ph.D. *The Sexual Addiction.* Minneapolis, Minnesota: CompCare Publications, 1983.

Carnes, P.J. *Don't Call It Love: Recovery from Sexual Addiction.* New York: Bantam Books, 1991.

Cooper-White, Pamela. *The Cry of Tamar: Violence Against Women and the Church's Response.* Minneapolis, MN: Fortress Press. 1995.

Fedders, Charlotte and Elliott, Laura. *Shattered Dreams: A True Story.* New York: Bantam Doubleday Dell Publishing Group, 1988.

Flinders, Carol Lee. *At the Root of This Longing: Reconciling a Spiritual Hunger and a Feminist Thirst.* San Francisco: HarperSanFrancisco, A Division of HarperCollins. 1998.

Fortune, Marie M. *Sexual Violence: The Unmentionable Sin. An Ethical and Pastoral Perspective.* Cleveland: The Pilgrim Press. 1983.

Fortune, Marie M. *Is Nothing Sacred?* New York, New York: Harper Collins Publishers, 1992.

Freeman, Tzvi. *Bringing Heaven Down to Earth.* Holbrook, MA: Adams Media. 1999.

Friberg, Nils C. and Laaser, Mark R. *Before the Fall: Preventing Pastoral Sexual Abuse.* Collegeville, MN: The Liturgical Press. 1998.

Friedman, Susan Stanford. With Gams, Linda, Gottlieb, Nancy, and Nesselson, Cindy. *A Woman's Guide to Therapy: A Complete Consumer's Guide to Therapy for Women; What it Can do for you; What it costs; and How to Avoid the Destructive Therapist.* Englewood Cliffs, NJ: Prentice-Hall, Inc. 1979.

Gabbard, G. *Sexual Exploitation in Professional Relationships.* Washington, D.C.: American Psychiatric Press, 1989.

Gardner, Lisa. *The Perfect Husband: What Would You Do If the Man of Your Dreams Hides the Soul of A Killer?* New York: Bantam Books. 1998.

Gonsiorek, John C. *Breach of Trust: Sexual Exploitation by Health Care Professionals and Clergy.* Thousand Oaks, CA: Sage Publications 1992.

Grenz, Stanley J. and Bell, Roy D. *Betrayal of Trust: Sexual Misconduct in the Pastorate.* Downers Grove, IL: InterVarsity Press. 1995

Hopkins, Nancy Myer and Laaser, Mark R., Editors. *Restoring the Soul of a Church: Healing Congregations Wounded by Clergy Sexual Misconduct.* Collegeville, MN: Liturgical Press. 1995.

Hopkins, Nancy Myer. *The Congregational Response to Clergy Betrayals of Trust.* Collegeville, MN: The Liturgical Press. 1998.

Horst, Elisabeth. *Recovering the Lost Self: Shame - Healing for Victims of Clergy Sexual Abuse.* Collegeville, MN: ISTI and The Liturgical Press. 1998.

Kemmelman, Harry. *The Day the Rabbi Resigned: A Rabbi Small Mystery.* New York: Fawcett Crest. 1992.

Kushner, Harold S. *When Bad Things Happen to Good People.* New York: Avon Books. 1981.

Lebacqz, Karen & Barton, Ronald G. *Sex in the Parish.* Louisville, Kentucky: Westminster/JohnKnox Press, 1991.

Levin, Jerome D. *The Clinton Syndrome*: *The President and the Self-Destructive Nature of Sexual Addiction.* Rocklin, CA: Forum, Prima Publishing. 1998.

Loftus, John Allan, S.J. *Understanding Sexual Misconduct by Clergy: A Handbook for Ministers.* Washington, D.C.: The Pastoral Press. 1994.

Mandel, Bob. *Open Heart Therapy.* Berkeley, CA: Celestial Arts. 1984.

Matas, Carol. *The Primrose Path.* Winnipeg: Bain & Cox. 1995.

Peck, M. Scott. *People of the Lie: The Hope for Healing Human Evil.* New York: Simon & Schuster, Inc. 1983.

Peterson, M.R. *At Personal Risk: Boundary Violations in Professional-Client Relationships.* New York: W. W. Norton, 1992.

Poling, J.N. *The Abuse of Power: A Theological Problem.* Nashville, Tennessee: Abingdon Press, 1991.

Poling, Nancy Werking. Ed. *Victim to Survivor: Women Recovering from Clergy Sexual Abuse.* Cleveland: United Church Press. 1999.

Ray, Sondra. *Loving Relationships.* Berkeley, CA. Celestial Arts. 1980.

Rush. Florence. *The Best Kept Secret: Sexual Abuse of Children.* New York: McGraw-Hill Book Company. 1980.

Rutter, Peter. *Sex in the Forbidden Zone: When Men in Power - Therapists, Doctors, Clergy, Teachers, and Others - Betray Women's Trust.* New York: Ballantine Books, 1991.

Rutter, Peter. *Sex, Power, & Boundaries: Understanding & Preventing Sexual Harassment.* New York. Bantam Books. 1996.

Samit, Michele. *No Sanctuary The True Story of a Rabbi's Deadly Affair.* New York: Carol Publishing Group, 1993.

Schneider, Jennifer P., M.D. *Back From Betrayal.* New York: A Hazelden Recovery Book. Ballantine Books. 1988.

Schoener, Gary R. and Milgrom, Jeanette Hofstee. *Responding to Clients Who Have Been Sexually Exploited by Counselors, Therapists, and Clergy.* Sexual Assault and Abuse: A Handbook for Clergy and Religious Professionals. Pellauer, Mary D., Chester, Barbara, and Boyajian, Jane A., editors. San Francisco. Harper & Row. 1987.

Schwab, Charlotte. *MI-COVE: A Study of Political Behavior in Community Building.* Doctoral Dissertation. New York University. 1973. Available from University Microfilms International. Ann Arbor, Michigan. 1979.

Shupe, Anson. Ed. *Wolves Within the Fold: Religious Leadership and Abuses of Power.* New Brunswick, NJ: Rutgers University Press. 1998.

Siegel, Rachel Josefowitz and Cole, Ellen, editors. *Celebrating the Lives of Jewish Women: Patterns in a Feminist Sampler.* New York. Haworth Press. 1997.

Siegel, Rachel Josefowitz, Cole, Ellen, and Steinberg-Oren, Susan, eds. *Jewish Mothers Tell Their Stories: Acts of Love and Courage.* New York: Haworth Press; 2000

Silverman, Toby. *Murder In Bed Pan Alley.* Salt Lake City, Utah: Northwest Publishing Inc. 1995.

Sipe, A. W. Richard. *Sex, Priests, and Power: Anatomy of a Crisis.* New York: Brunner/Mazel. 1995.

Spitzer, Julie Ringold, Rabbi. *When Love is Not Enough: Spousal Abuse in Rabbinic And Contemporary Judaism.* New York. Women of Reform Judaism, The Federation of Temple Sisterhoods. 1995.

Walker, Lenore. "Jewish Battered Women: *Shalom Bayit* or a *Shonde?*" in Siegel, Rachel Josefowitz and Cole, Ellen, editors. *Celebrating the Lives of Jewish Women: Patterns in a Feminist Sampler.* New York. Haworth Press. 1997.

See also the Bibliographies in books listed here as well as others' Bibliographies, such as:

AdvocateWeb HOPE Bookstore. *Sexual Exploitation Victim/Survivor Book Resources.* http://www.advocateweb.com/hope/books.htm

Center for the Prevention of Sexual and Domestic Violence: An interreligious, educational resource. Books, articles, videos, training programs. http://www.cpsdv.org

ISTI (Interfaith Sexual Trauma Institute) *Bibliography.* http://www.csbsju.edu/isti/information_about_isti.html

Spiegel, Marcia Cohn. *Bibliography of Sources on Sexual & Domestic Violence in the Jewish Community.* MINCAVA.com (Go to Bibliographies).

Newspaper Articles[179]

2002

March 25, 2002. *Sex Abuse by Clerics - A Crisis of Many Faiths. Clerics: While Sexual Misconduct Has Rocked Many Religions, Leaders of Some Have Acted Far More Quickly Than Others.* Los Angeles Times. Teresa Watanabe.

March 1, 2002. *Emanu-El Criticized Over Cantor Case.* Jewish Week (New York). Cohen, Debra Nussbaum and Greenberg, Eric J.

February 20, 2002. *Cantor Charged with Sex Abuse Freed from Jail.* The Philadelphia Inquirer. Vigoda, Ralph and Stroh, Mark.

January 22, 2002. *No Longer Taboo: For Years the Orthodox Community Has Hidden It. Now, a Confluence of Factors is Making Their Sexual Abuse Problem Come Out of the Closet.* http://www.jewsweek.com/society/080.htm

2001

December 29, 2001. *Rabbi Gets 6 ½ Years in Teen Sex Conviction.* Sun Sentinel. Franceschina, Peter.

December 29, 2001. *Rabbi Gets 6 ½ Years for Youth Sex Crimes.* The Palm Beach Post. Pacenti, John.

December 21, 2001. *Rabbi Spared Harshest Sentence.* Sun Sentinel. Burnstein, Jon.

December 12, 2001. *Prosecutors: Give Rabbi Maximum: Levy Called a Dangerous Sex Predator.* Sun Sentinel. Franceschina, Peter.

---

[179]These articles were selected from a full file drawer of articles about rabbis' sexual misconduct.

November 15, 2001. *Officials: Most Jurors Wanted to Convict Rabbi.* Courier-Post Online. Winkler, Renee.

October 16, 2001. *Sexual Misconduct by Rabbis: We Need to Know. Victims of Rabbi Sexual Predators Suffer Psychologically from the Abuse, Often for the Rest of Their Lives.* Jewish Journal. (Florida). Schwab, Charlotte.

August 24, 2001. *Getting Our Houses in Order.* Jewish News of Greater Phoenix. Eckstein, Flo.

July 6, 2001. *Boca Rabbi's Trial Postponed.* The Palm Beach Jewish News.

June 22, 2001. *The OU, A Year Later: How Much Has Changed.* Jewish Week (New York). Rosenblatt, Gary.

May 15, 2001. *Boca Rabbi Arrested on Child Porn Charges: Change to Federal Jurisdiction Bumps Possible Jail Time from 5 to 15 Years.* Sun Sentinel. Krause, Kevin.

May 2001. *Testimony of Rabbi's Child to be Used.* Courier-Post Online. http://www.southjerseynews.com/issues/may/m050201g.htm.

April 28, 2001. *Feds Look Into Ex-Rabbi's Sex Case: Internet Images Could Violate Child Porn.* Sun Sentinel. Krause, Kevin.

April 15, 2001. *Community Tries to Heal After Charge: Rabbi Accused of Soliciting Sex with Boy.* Sun Sentinel. Dozier, Marian.

April 10, 2001. *Rabbi Resigns Temple Position: Meeting Tonight to Help Members, Children.* The Sun Sentinel. Krause, Kevin.

April 9, 2001. *Rabbi Told Synagogue About '84 Sex Arrest: Attorney Says Levy's Work Allayed Concern.* The Sun Sentinel. Hahn, Brad.

April 7, 2001. *Arrest Stuns Temple Members.* The Sun Sentinel. Krause, Kevin and Brochu, Nicole Sterghos.

April 7, 2001. *Father Acted to Save Son - And Others.* The Sun Sentinel. Othon, Nancy L.

April 7, 2001. *Member: "He's Like Your Father.* The Sun Sentinel. Pensa, Patty.

April 5, 2001. *Months After HUC Resignation, Zimmerman Hired by Birthright.* http://www. Jta org/story.asp?story=7424. Wiener, Julie.

April 4, 2001. *Boca Rabbi Charged in Solicitation. The Sun Sentinel.* Krause, Kevin.

March 16, 2001. *Lanner Indicted on Sex Abuse Charges: Two Former Students at Deal, N.J., Yeshiva Provided Key Testimony.* Jewish Week. (New York). Rosenblatt, Gary.

January 28, 2001. *Book on Neulander Case Covers More Than Crime.* Courier-Post Online. Walsh, Jim.

2000
December 29, 2000. *Report Slams O.U.'s 'Failure' in Lanner Abuse Scandal.* Forward. Klein, Amy.

December 27, 2000. *Orthodox Unit Details Accusations That New Jersey Rabbi Abused Teenagers.* New York Times. Jacobs, Andrew.

December 15, 2000. *High Profile Cases Refocus Attention on Sexual Misconduct.* JTA Daily News Bulletin. Wiener, Julie.

December 15, 2000. *Sexual Boundaries for Rabbis: Zimmerman Case Puts Spotlight on How Movements Monitor Ethics.* Jewish Week (New York). Cohen, Debra Nussbaum.

December 12, 2000. *Cantor Charged in Prostitution Ring.* Palm Beach Jewish Journal. Silverman, Ruth.

December 8, 2000. *HUC Head Resigns; Sexual Misconduct Cited: Rabbi Sheldon Zimmerman Guilty of 'Sexual Boundary Violation'*

Following Yearlong Probe by Reform Movement; Campus in Shock. Jewish Week (New York). Ain, Stewart.

December 6, 2000. *Respected Reform Leader Resigns Amid Sexual Misconduct Charges.* JTA Daily News Bulletin. Wiener, Julie.

August 22, 2000. *Thou Shalt Not Kill Or Commit Adultery: Cheating N.J. Rabbi Charged in Wife's Slay.* New York Post. Fearon, Peter.

1999
May 24, 1999. *Why Do Parishioners Stick by Clergy Who Commit Crimes?* USA Today. Zelizer, Gerald.

January 16, 1999. *Fighting Clergy Sexual Abuse.* Omaha World-Herald. McCord, Julia.

1998
September 11, 1998. *N.J's Rabbi Neulander Charged with Arranging Wife's '94 Killing.* The Philadelphia Inquirer. Phillips, Nancy and Jennings, John Way.

1997
December 26, 1997. *Former Petaluma Rabbi Gets 3 Years for Molesting a Child.* Jewish Bulletin of Northern California. Caplane, Ronnie.

October 7, 1997. *Rabbi Wanted Wife Dead, Panel Told.* Philadelphia Online.
http://www.phillynews.com/inquirer/97/Oct/07/front_page/RABI07.ht
m.

April 30, 1997. *Rabbi Molesting Girl has Three Years to Regret.* National Jewish Post & Opinion.

February 21, 1997. *Petaluma Rabbi Pleads No Contest to Charges of Sexual Misconduct.* Jewish Bulletin of Northern California. Caplane, Ronnie.

1996

December 19, 1996. *Victims of Rabbinic Sexual Exploitation Suffer Pain of Communal Denial.* MW Jewish News. Cohen-Nussbaum, Debra.

December 19, 1996. *Spector of Impropriety — Rabbis Worry About Closing Doors.* Metrowest Jewish News. pages 17 & 22. Klebanoff, Abbe.

December 6, 1996. *When Rabbis Go Astray: Sexual Misconduct is a Problem. How Seriously Does the Jewish Community Take Rabbinic Sexual Misconduct.* Jewish Week (New York). Cohen-Nussbaum, Debra.

November 2, 1996. *Apology Offered in Sex Scandal.* Los Angeles Times. B4

November 1, 1996. *Few Local Safeguards to Prevent Indiscretions.* Cleveland Jewish News. Light, Nina.

November 1, 1996. *"Conspiracy of Silence" Fuels Rabbis' Sexual Misdeeds.* Jewish Bulletin of Northern California. Cohen, Debra Nussbaum.

October 26, 1996. *Second in a Series: Rabbinic Sexual Misconduct is Rarely Taken Seriously.* Jewish Telegraphic Agency. Cohen, Debra Nussbaum.

October 18-24, 1996. *Rabbinic Misconduct: Sexual Exploitation by Some Spiritual Leaders Raises the Question - Are There Really Rules or is it an Old Boys' Network?* The Jewish Journal of Greater Los Angeles. Cohen, Debra Nussbaum.

October 18, 1996. Loving Rabbis *Why Can't a Spiritual Leader Date a Congregant?* Jewish Sentinel. Cohen, Debra Nussbaum.

October 18, 1996. *Rabbinic Sexual Misconduct - Breaching a Sacred Trust.* Jewish Bulletin of Northern California. Cohen, Debra Nussbaum.

October 11, 1996. *When Rabbis Overstep Their Bounds: Facing the Reality of Sexual Exploitation in Shul.* Forward (New York). Cohen, Debra Nussbaum.

September 25, 1996. *The Dilemma for Single Rabbis: To Date or Not to Date Members.* JTA Daily News Bulletin. Cohen, Debra Nussbaum.

September 23, 1996. *Rabbi Forced to Leave Pulpit Finds Place at Reform Center.* Jewish Telegraphic Agency Daily News Bulletin. Cohen, Debra Nussbaum.

September 20, 1996. *Critics Push for Stricter Codes for Handling Sexual Misconduct.* JTA Daily News Bulletin. Cohen, Debra Nussbaum.

September 19, 1996. *Victims of Rabbinic Sex Abuse Suffer Pain of Communal Denial.* Jewish Telegraphic Agency Daily News Bulletin. Cohen, Debra Nussbaum.

September 18, 1996. *Rabbinic Sexual Exploitation: Leaders Breach a Sacred Trust.* JTA Daily News. Cohen, Debra Nussbaum.

September 4, 1996. *Polygraph Indicates 'Deception' by Rabbi. His Lawyer Discounted the Results Because of the Rabbi's Medication.* The Philadelphia Inquirer. Phillips, Nancy.

May 30, 1996. *Sexual Abuse in the Synagogue: Board of Rabbis Hosts Conference for Rabbis and Cantors on Preventing Sexual Abuse in Religious Contexts.* Jewish Exponent. Silverstein, Marilyn.

May 16, 1996. *Breaking the Silence. Board of Rabbis Conference to Explore Issue of Sexual abuse.* Jewish Exponent. Silverstein, Marilyn.

April 11, 1996. *Citing Marital Infidelities, Reform Rabbis Take Action Against Neulander.* Jewish Exponent. Silverstein, Marilyn.

April 3, 1996. *Panel Suspends Rabbi for Trysts With 2 Women.* The Philadelphia Inquirer. Phillips, Nancy.

January 19, 1996. *Rabbis Draw Up Ethics of Nonmarital Sex.* New York Times. Steinfels, Peter.

January 19, 1996. *Teenager Confronts Rabbi at Molestation Sentencing Hearing* Los Angeles Times. Boxall, Bettina.

1995
November 26, 1995. *Tribute Celebrates Life of Carol Neulander. Music was Commissioned in Honor of the Cherry Hill Woman. Her Family Remains Divided by Her Murder.* The Philadelphia Inquirer. Phillips, Nancy.

October 1995. *A Death In The Family.* Philadelphia. Saline, Carol.

September 12, 1995. *Rabbi Facing Discipline Over Two Romantic Entanglements. The Central Conference of American Rabbis is Studying Complaints Against Rabbi Fred J. Neulander.* The Philadelphia Inquirer. Phillips, Nancy.

August 31, 1995. *After Losing Wife and Job, Rabbi Emerges as Slaying Suspect.* The Washington Post. Goldberg, Debbie.

August 26, 1995. *Officer in Cherry Hill Death Probe Forced Out: He Was Dating Elaine Soncini. The Chief Doesn't Believe The Case of the Rabbi's Wife was Tainted.* The Philadelphia Inquirer. Sanginiti, Terri & Phillips, Nancy.

August 22, 1995. *DJ Apologizes for Affair with Rabbi. Elaine Soncini Called Her Affair with Rabbi Neulander A "Mistake." Police are Probing his Wife's Death.* The Philadelphia Inquirer. Phillips, Nancy.

August 20, 1995. *Radio DJ Helps Police Investigate Rabbi: WPEN'S Elaine Soncini Says They Were Lovers Until His Wife was Beaten to Death.* The Philadelphia Inquirer. Phillips, Nancy.

August 18, 1995. *Cherry Hill Rabbi Denies Role in His Wife's Killing: Rabbi Neulander Said that He Had No Knowledge of a Hit Man who Prosecutors Say He Hired to Kill His Spouse.* The Philadelphia Inquirer. Phillips, Nancy.

August 17, 1995. *Rabbi's Wife was Hit Target, Say Police. A Disguised Killer May Have Been Hired by Carol Neulander's Husband. He Denies any Involvement.* The Philadelphia Inquirer. Phillips, Nancy.

June 16, 1995. *Focus on Crimes Involving Religious Jews Sparks Debate.* Jewish Bulletin of Northern California. Cohen, Debra Nussbaum.

June 14, 1995. *Rabbi Aide Indicted in Molestation.* Los Angeles Times. Boxall, Bettina.

June 3, 1995. *Accused Rabbi Will Stayed Jailed for Weekend.* Los Angeles Times. Boxall, Bettina.

March 24, 1995. *Counselor Steps In to Comfort N.J. Synagogue in Pain.* Jewish Exponent. Silverstein, Marilyn.

March 3, 1995. *Synagogue in Anguish as Cherry Hill Rabbi Resigns, Members Struggle with Their Grief and Anger.* Jewish Exponent. Silverstein, Marilyn.

February 28, 1995. *Mystery Grows in Death of Rabbi's Wife.* The New York Times. Peterson, Iver.

February 27, 1995. *N.J. Rabbi Resigns, Alluding to Lapses. Rabbi Neulander Gave No Details, And Denied Any Involvement In His Wife's Slaying.* The Philadelphia Inquirer. Phillips, Nancy.

February 25, 1995. *Death of Rabbi's Wife a Puzzle. She is Killed in Cherry Hill Nov. 1. After Scores of Interviews, No Weapon, No Sure Motive.* The Philadelphia Inquirer. Phillips, Nancy & Jennings, John Way.

February 24, 1995. *Rabbi On Leave in Aftermath of Wife's Murder.* Jewish Exponent. Silverstein, Marilyn.

February 22, 1995. *Rabbi Given Leave From Synagogue. His Wife Was Slain Late Last Year. He is Seeking a Rest, Counseling and Time with His Family.* The Philadelphia Inquirer. Phillips, Nancy.

1994
December 30, 1994. *Focus on Rabbi 'Unfair' in Neulander Murder. Prosecutor Says Press 'Skewed' His Words.* Jewish Exponent. Silverstein, Marilyn.

December 23, 1994. *Reward Offered to Solve Slaying. The Killing of A Cherry Hill Rabbi's Wife was Carefully Planned, Said the Prosecutor. The Reward is $35,000.* The Philadelphia Inquirer. Jennings, John Way & Phillips, Nancy.

November 4, 1994. *Grief, Shock Follow Slaying of Cherry Hill Rabbi's Wife.* Jewish Exponent. Silverstein, Marilyn.

February 1, 1994. *The Healing Hand: Debra Warwick-Sabino Reaches Out Across Time and Terror To Hear the Stories of Pain and Abuse.* Sacramento Bee. Bojorquez, Jennifer.

1993
September 5, 1993. *Her Calling: Aid Clerics' Sexual Abuse Victims.* Sacramento Bee. Lindelof, Bill.

July 10, 1993. *Beth Israel Decides on an Interim Rabbi.* San Diego Tribune. Dolbee, Sandi.

June 19, 1993. *Jews Begin to Address Allegations of Sexual Misconduct by Rabbis.* New York Times National. Heiman, Andrea.

March 27, 1993. *Clergy Group Seeks Investigation After Rabbis Admit Having Affair.* Los Angeles Times.

1992

May 28, 1992. *Man Gets Life Sentence for Having Wife Slain.* Los Angeles Times.

1991

February 7, 1991. *Rabbi Loses Court Fight Against Dismissal.* The (London) Times. Gledhill, Ruth.

February 7, 1991. *Sacked Rabbi's Legal Action Fails.* London Independent.

1986

February 1986. *A Successful Commuter Marriage: They've Overcome Any Problems of Distance. Rabbi Jon Haddon and Dr. Charlotte Schwab.* Newington (CT) Town Crier. Zeldes, Edith.

Articles in Periodicals and Journals

CCAR Journal: A Reform Jewish Quarterly

Summer 1997: 053-061. *Sexual Harassment and Discrimination in the Rabbinate.* CCAR Journal: A Reform Jewish Quarterly. Liss, Janet B.

Summer/Fall 1995. *Teshuvah and Rabbinic Sexual Misconduct.* CCAR Journal. Arthur Gross- Schaefer.

Spring 1993. *A Stumbling Block Before the Blind: Sexual Exploitation in Pastoral Counseling.* CCAR Journal. Adler, Rachel.

Spring 1993. *Response (To Rachel Adler Article).* CCAR Journal. Salkin, Jeffrey.

Spring 1993. *Response (To Rachel Adler Article).* CCAR Journal. Spitzer, Julie.

Common Boundary

November/December 1996. *Soul Betrayal: Sexual Abuse by Spiritual Leaders Violates Trust, Devastates Lives, and Tears Communities Apart. No Denomination or Tradition is Immune.* Common Boundary. Simpkinson, Anne A.

Congregations

May/June 1993. *Clergy Sexual Misconduct: A Call for a Faithful,, not a Fearful, Response.* Congregations. Gross-Schaefer, Arthur & Singer, Jan.

Conservative Judaism

Summer, 1998: L (4): 59-66. *By the Power Vested in Me: Symbolic Exemplarhood and the Pulpit Rabbi.* Conservative Judaism. Bloom, Jack H.

Dulwich Centre Newsletter

1993 Nos. 3&4. *Common Errors in Treatment of Victims/Survivors of Sexual Misconduct by Professionals.* Minneapolis, Michigan. Dulwich Centre Newsletter. Schoener, Gary Richard.

Families in Society: The Journal of Contemporary Human Services

May 1992. *Religious Denominational Policies on Sexuality.* Families in Society: The Journal of Contemporary Human Services. 1992, v73n5. Bullis, Ronald K. & Harrigan, Marcia P.

Genesis

Spring 1989. *Abused Women Do Not Make Choices.* Genesis. Spiegel, Marcia Cohn.

Harvard Business Review

March-April 1981. *Sexual Harassment...Some See it...Some Won't.* Harvard Business Review. Collins, Eliza, G.C., and Blodgett, Timothy B.

Jerusalem Report

Oct. 31, 1996. *Sexual Harassment Calls to Reform.* Jerusalem Report. Halevi, Yossi Klein.

January 26, 1995. *A Blind Eye to Sexual Harassment.* Jerusalem Report. Hirschberg, Peter.

Jewish Currents

April, 1994. *Fighting Sexual Harassment.* Jewish Currents. Shire, Amy.

Journal Of Feminist Studies in Religion

Fall, 1996. 12:2 *Spirituality for Survival: Jewish Women Healing Themselves.* Journal of Feminist Studies in Religion. Spiegel, Marcia Cohn.

Journal of Religion and Health

1993. 32 (3) 1970208. *From Denial To Hope: A Systematic Response to Clergy Sexual Abuse.* Journal of Religion and Health. Vogelsang, John.

Lilith

Spring 1998. *A Paradoxical Legacy: Rabbi Shlomo Carlebach's Shadow Side.* Lilith. Blustain, Sarah.

December 24, 2000. *Sexual Abuse by Rabbis: A Letter to the New York Times.* http://www.lilithmag.com/features/000724a.shtml.

Schneider, Susan Weidman, Editor-in Chief, and Blustain, Sarah, Associate Editor.

Fall 2001. *Beyond Forgiveness: Women, Can We Emancipate Ourselves from a Model Meant for Men?* Lilith. Schnur, Susan.

Los Angeles Jewish Journal

October 18, 1996. *Rabbinic Misconduct: Sexual Exploitation by Some Spiritual Leaders Raises the Question, Are There Really Rules or is it An Old Boys' Network?* Los Angeles Jewish Journal. Cohen, Debra Nussbaum.

Majority Report

July 23-August 5, 1977. *Feminism and Therapy. Rape Victims: Handle With Care.* Majority Report. Javors, Irene and Schwab, Charlotte.

July 10-July 23, 1976. *The Making of Phobic Women.* Majority Report. Schwab, Charlotte and Javors, Irene

Moment

February, 1998. *Adultery: Revisiting the Seventh Commandment.* Moment. Gold, Michael.

October, 1993. *Survey Finds 70% of Women Rabbis Sexually Harassed.* Moment. Cowan, Jennifer.

April, 1990. *Rabbis Can Help By Speaking Out.* Moment. Greenberg, Yitzchak.

Neshama

Winter. 1994. 6:#4. *Old Symbols, New Rituals.* Neshama. Spiegel, Marcia Cohn. Also see her Bibliography at the end of the article.

The Reconstructionist

Spring, 1999. 63 (2) *Rabbi Sexual Misconduct: Crying Out for a Communal Response*. The Reconstructionist. Gross-Schaefer, Arthur.

Reform Judaism

Winter 1994. *Sexual Misconduct. How Vulnerable Are Synagogues?* Reform Judaism. Marder, Janet.

April 1994. 24/473. *Breaking the Silence: Rabbinic Sexual Misconduct.* Sh'ma Gross-Schaefer, Arthur.

Seminars, Workshops, and Symposia

PARR Symposium on Rabbi Boundary Violations. Dealing with Rabbis Who Have Committed Acts of Sexual Misconduct. February 1, 1997. Gross-Schaefer, Arthur.

PARR Symposium on Rabbi Boundary Violations. *Rabbi's Sexual Misconduct: Collegial Response and Methodology of Teshuvah and Communal Healing. Introduction.* February 1, 1994. Gross- Schaefer, Arthur.

PARR Symposium on Rabbi Boundary Violations. *Duty of Rabbi to Disclose Knowledge of Sexual Misconduct of a Colleague.* February 1, 1994. Lawson, Martin S.

PARR Symposium on Rabbi Boundary Violations. *Hearing the Voice of Survivors of Sexual Misconduct.* February 1, 1994. Fox, Karen L.

Tikkun

Jan/Feb, 1994. *Sexual Harassment and Jewish Education.* Tikkun. Ingwer, Carmela

Working Together

Winter 1997. *Rabbi Sexual Misconduct: Crying out for a Communal Response.* Working Together. Gross-Schaefer, Arthur.

Unpublished Papers

1998. *Rabbis and Sexual Misconduct: Maintaining Proper Sexual Boundaries in the Rabbinate.* Schwab, Charlotte. Lecture/seminar to Jewish Theological Seminary. New York.

November 13, 1996. *Assessment, Rehabilitation & Supervision of Clergy who Have Engaged in Sexual Boundary Violations.* Schoener, Gary Richard. Office of the House of Bishops, Episcopal Church. St. Paul, Minnesota.

April 1993. *Clergy Sexual Misconduct: The Need to React with Education Guidelines.* Gross-Schaefer, Arthur, & Singer, Jan.

2001. *Gender and Power.* Willerscheidt, Phyllis. With Kelly, Timoth; Lundin, John; and Peterson, Marilyn. Interfaith Sexual Trauma Institute

March, 1977. *A Training Model for Gynecologists and Psychiatrists: Rape Trauma Syndrome.* Charlotte Schwab. Mt. Sinai Hospital. New York.

US News & World Report

November 16, 1992. *The Unpardonable Sin.* US News & World Report. 1992, v113n19. Sheler, Jeffery L.

Videos

Chaya, Miriam and Montell, Judith. *Timbrels & Torahs: Celebrating Women's Wisdom.* 2000. (This must be ordered from: www.timbrelsandtorahs.com).

Kaplan, Carol and Kellman, Rich. *A House Divided.* (two parts; includes an interview with Dr. Charlotte Schwab). WGBH-Buffalo. 1999.

Charlotte Schwab

AFTERWORD

Kavannah is the Hebrew word for intention: in prayer, in relationships (in I/Thou), in marriage, in commitment, in any action or undertaking. My *kavannah*, my intention by writing this book is to help to bring about needed change in the rabbinate, to help to bring about a cessation of rabbis' sexual abuse of teen aged girls and women, and to help heal those who have been abused, including women victims/survivors of rabbis' sexual abuse, wives and ex-wives who have suffered through their rabbi/husbands' sexual abuse of other women, congregations, communities, Judaism.

In 1980, Florence Rush wrote a book to help dispel "The Best Kept Secret: Sexual Abuse of Children."[180] In the '90's Marcia Cohn Spiegel and others worked to dispel the secret of domestic violence in Jewish homes - mainly abuse of wives by their husbands. We have made a great deal of progress in those two spheres. Now, let us hope that this book will help dispel this "best kept secret" - sexual abuse of teen aged girls and women by rabbis.

I lost my naiveté and my trust, as well as my faith in Judaism, because of my rabbi/husband. I slowly gained back my ability to trust and to find people who are trustworthy and allow them into my life. I slowly gained back my trust in Judaism. I slowly found meaning from the suffering I endured with my rabbi/husband, found my purpose: to help other victims of rabbis' sexual abuse, and to write this book. I have found rabbis and other Jewish leaders to trust. Some of their names appear in this book. As Gary Rosenblatt wrote in the New York Jewish Week, February, 15, 2002,[181] "…. the most upsetting aspect (in both Catholic and Jewish cases, is) the failure of religious authorities to fulfill their sacred trust." In this article, Rosenblatt also quoted a writer who wrote about the cases of sexual misconduct in the Catholic church as saying that, "…. a couple of very high-level priests, including an archbishop, (told) me to back down, as a good Catholic.' I told them they misunderstood me; that I write about this

---

[180]Florence Rush. The Best Kept Secret: Sexual Abuse of Children. New York: McGraw-Hill Book Company. 1980.
[181]Gary Rosenblatt. "A Cautionary Tale From the Church." New York. Jewish Week. February 15, 2002.

not in spite of being Catholic, but because of it." I have had a few people tell me to 'back down,' not to write about rabbis' sexual abuse. I told them that I write about this because of being Jewish, because I hold Judaism as sacred.

The hardest part of researching and writing this book was reliving the experiences of abuse. Yet, it was also a catharsis. My parents, who died before I achieved many of my accomplishments, suffered through the oppression, the abuses of the Cossacks, the Nazis. I hope I have made my parents, who each came from a *shtetl* (my father from Mistatich, near Minsk, and my mother from Koslinich, near Kiev) to the freedom of the United States of America, proud of their daughter Shandele's work to end the oppression and the abuse of sexism, and particularly to end the abuse of rabbis' sexual misconduct.

Judaism holds that s/he who saves a single soul in Israel, it is as if s/he saves all Israel, saved the entire world. S/he who hurts one soul is as if s/he hurts all the world. Judaism needs to take the path of righteousness, of peace, of *shalom*. Hillel had it right: *"Marbeh tzedakah, marbeh shalom*: More righteousness more peace."

About the Author

Charlotte Rolnick Schwab, Ph.D., a Manhattan psychotherapist for twenty-five years, lecturer, seminar and workshop leader, specializes in helping women and men to communicate and negotiate effectively and to create healthy relationships, and counseling women in recovery from rabbis' sexual abuse, including wives and former wives of rabbis. She developed several trademarked programs including "The Schwab Model for Achieving Positive Self-Identity and Self-Defined Success"tm, "VECAM"tm, a communications training program, and "Gender Negotiations"tm. She is a former professor at Hunter College, City University of New York; Guest Faculty and Keynoter, Hebrew Union College; Lecturer, Seminar Leader: Jewish Theological Seminary, Union of American Congregations, Albert Einstein Medical College, American Psychological Association. Dr. Schwab now lives in Florida where she is a lecturer, mentor, and educator.

Printed in the United States
696100002B

9 781403 3380